THE LIFE OF
THOMAS LOVE PEACOCK

T. L. Peacock.
ætat 72.

THE LIFE OF THOMAS LOVE PEACOCK

BY

CARL VAN DOREN

NEW YORK / RUSSELL & RUSSELL

1966

FIRST PUBLISHED IN 1911
REISSUED, 1966, BY RUSSELL & RUSSELL
A DIVISION OF ATHENEUM HOUSE, INC.
BY ARRANGEMENT WITH THE ESTATE OF CARL VAN DOREN
L.C. CATALOG CARD NO: 65—18838

PRINTED IN THE UNITED STATES OF AMERICA

TO

MY FATHER AND MOTHER

With Reverence and Love

PREFACE

THERE has been no previous biography of Peacock. The principal source of information concerning him is the brief but admirable *Biographical Notice* prefixed by his granddaughter Miss Edith Nicolls (now Mrs. Charles Clarke) to the edition of Peacock's *Works* which appeared in 1875. Miss Nicolls depended for her facts, to a considerable extent, upon a collection of *Biographical Notes* made by Sir Henry Cole, of which only ten copies were privately printed. Dr. Richard Garnett furnished some additional material in his three articles on Peacock, in *The Encyclopædia Britannica* (1885), in the *Introduction* to his edition of *Headlong Hall* (1891), and in *The Dictionary of National Biography* (1895). In 1904 Dr. A. B. Young printed at Norwich his *Life and Novels of Thomas Love Peacock*, a dissertation presented at the University of Freiburg for the degree of Doctor of Philosophy, which contains the results of much useful research, but is marred by repeated inaccuracies.

While I am under obligations, which I am glad to acknowledge, to all these, I have tried to correct the errors of my predecessors where it has been possible. In no case have I accepted a statement at second hand when there was a chance to investigate the source. To the known facts I have been able to add more,

PREFACE

and at the risk of going into considerable detail, have attempted to give the biographical facts with minute accuracy.

My warm thanks are due Mrs. Clarke, who has generously placed at my disposal all the letters and other unpublished manuscripts in her possession, and has done in various other ways many things to assist me. To Mr. P. A. Daniel and to Mr. Alan S. Cole I am indebted for several kindly suggestions. Mr. William Foster, Secretary of the India Office, not only helped me to an examination of the Minutes of the Court of Directors, but most courteously put into my hands certain notes relating to Peacock's connection with the Company which he had already made.

The work was originally undertaken during the leisure afforded me by a fellowship in Columbia University, and was completed in London. By the officials of the Library of Columbia University, of the Bodleian, and of the British Museum, I have been accorded the most courteous treatment. It is a great pleasure to acknowledge the helpful advice of my former teachers, at present my colleagues, and always, I hope, my friends, Professor A. H. Thorndike, Professor Brander Matthews, and especially Professor W. P. Trent. In the preparation of the manuscript I have received great assistance from my friend Dr. F. H. Ristine.

CARL VAN DOREN.

COLUMBIA UNIVERSITY.

CONTENTS

PLATES

THE LIFE OF
THOMAS LOVE PEACOCK

CHAPTER I

BIRTH—EDUCATION

On December 8, 1825, Mrs. Sarah Peacock, then at her son's home in Stamford Street, Blackfriars, for some reason drew up an attestation which was preserved by her son and left by him to his granddaughter. "I hereby certify that my son Thomas Love Peacock was born on the eighteenth day of October in the year of Our Lord One Thousand Seven Hundred and Eighty Five, at a quarter past two in the morning, at Weymouth in Dorsetshire." Whatever is known of Peacock's ancestors is confined almost wholly to those on his mother's side of the family. The father, Samuel Peacock, was a London merchant who died in 1788, exactly when has not been discovered. Peacock is not an uncommon name, and there were families who bore it in Scotland, Yorkshire, Norfolk, Cheshire, Suffolk, and Lincolnshire, as well as in London. If the novelist himself knew anything of his paternal forebears, his habitual silence with regard to all family matters at least kept the information from any one else. The fact that Thomas was baptized at a Scotch kirk might lead one to suspect

THOMAS LOVE PEACOCK

that the father was one of those very Scots whom
his son delighted to ridicule, but there is no proof for
such a guess. The London directories for the latter
part of the eighteenth century, however, throw some
light on the subject. In Kent's Directory for 1778
there appears for the first time the entry, " Peacock
Samuel, Glass Warehouse, Holborn Bridge." Presumably, however, he had been in some kind of business at
least ten years, for his son possessed a scrap of parch-
ment, evidently a book cover, which bears the words,
" Day Book, 1768, Saml. Peacock." To judge from the
directory entries, there seems to have been a family of
Peacocks engaged in the glass business. An older firm,
Thomas Peacock, in Blackfriars, is mentioned as early
as 1766, and in 1783 a second Thomas Peacock ap-
peared as " Glassman and Potter " at 15 Borough.
The next year this second Thomas had united with
Samuel, as Samuel and Thomas Peacock, 46 Holborn
Bridge ; after Samuel Peacock's death, the firm be-
came George and Thomas Peacock, and continued
under the various names of Peacock and Roper, and
Peacock and Davidson, until the end of the century.
Sir Henry Cole's conjecture [1] that the novelist's father
belonged to the firm of Peacock and Pellatt in St.
Paul's Churchyard is thus shown to be without foun-
dation. That firm owes its inception to a later date.

What were the character and attainments of
Samuel Peacock we have no manner of knowing.
Perhaps the keen business ability which his son later
showed in his career at the India House may be taken
as in part a heritage. The merchant apparently left

[1] *Biographical Notes*, p. 1. This was followed by Miss Nicolls.

his widow a moderate fortune, for she and her son seem to have been in independent, though sometimes straitened, circumstances, till Peacock's appointment to the India service in 1819 gave them an assured income. In any case, the family connections of Mrs. Peacock would have been sufficient guarantee against actual necessity. Before her marriage she had been a Miss Sarah Love, born in 1754, eldest daughter of a master in the Royal Navy. Thomas Love was one of the Devon men who have contributed so much to the might of England on the sea. He had served on board H.M.S. *Prothée*, commanded by Charles Buckner, at Lord Rodney's defeat of the French under Count de Grasse in the West Indies, April 9 and 12, 1782. In the second engagement Thomas Love lost one of his legs, and was accordingly obliged to retire from the service to a quiet house in Chertsey, whither, on the death of his son-in-law, the widow and her three-year-old child came to live for a dozen years. The little which can now be known of Thomas Love is disguised under the veil of fiction. In *Melincourt* Peacock drew a slight but amusing character of his grandfather as Captain Hawltaught. The Captain, having been struck by the contemplative countenance of Sir Oran, whom he had found on the coast of Angola, succeeded in carrying off that true son of nature, by the undiscerning world called an ape, to be his companion on the frigate *Tornado*. After three years Captain Hawltaught, seriously wounded, was forced to retire to a village in the west of England, where he devoted his time to planting cabbages and watching the changes of the wind, supported by his prize-money and half-pay. There they lived in convivial felicity, unashamed. The Captain, damning all water-drinkers for hypocrites, had taught his companion the joys of wine ; Sir Oran had exhibited a natural bent for the arts by becoming a competent performer upon the French horn. So the two spent night after night, Sir Oran playing his horn, Captain Hawltaught roaring out old sea songs, and both drinking as merrily as if both were human. With due allowance for Peacock's inevitable caricaturing, it may be inferred that Thomas Love, like his reflection in Hawltaught, held to his fondness for the sea, his prejudices in favour of simple living, and his practice of sturdy potations and merry catches to the very day of his death. Certainly his grandson had all these characteristics in some degree or other ; they may have been partially due to the example set his youth. Certainly, also, there existed a most affectionate familiarity between the two. The boy learned to think of himself as belonging to a naval family—indeed several of his uncles and cousins were in the service—and he early acquired a marked fondness for ships and sailors which never left him. His old pilot, in the later years of Peacock's activities on behalf of steam navigation, always maintained that " Mr. Peacock was meant to be an admiral."

Peacock's mother, herself not a stranger to verse-writing,[1] was a woman of unusual ability. The date of her marriage to Samuel Peacock has not been ascertained. As the parish register at Chertsey, however, contains no record of it, presumably she had been married before her father's wound and

---

[1] See Cole, p. 2, for some verses by her.

consequent retirement. The fact that Thomas was an only child, and her early widowhood, naturally served to bring her and her son into the most tender intimacy. He passed many of his best years, he declared, with his mother, taking more pleasure in reading than in society. Nor was the companionship of the charming, spirited woman and her gifted son confined to his more impressionable years. As long as he lived his respect for her judgment led him to invite her criticism by reading her all his books before their publication; and after her death in 1833 he maintained he wrote nothing of value, as his heart was not in his work. That such intimate relations persisted after the beginning of his career as a novelist is good proof that Mrs. Peacock must have had rather unusual catholicity of taste. Her son's sardonic literary temper, unlikely to find many feminine sympathisers at any time, was not of the type approved for readers " of the female sex " during the days of George IV. One can scarcely imagine that the woman who enjoyed *Headlong Hall* and *Nightmare Abbey* had been educated wholly upon the principles inculcated by Mrs. Hannah More. It is a family tradition that Mrs. Peacock was an ardent reader of history, and that Gibbon always lay at the arm of her chair. Certainly she was no ordinary woman, nor did her encouragement of her son's work consist merely in expression of the pleasure which any mother might feel at signs of notable capacity in a child. Her direction of his reading in his boyhood was succeeded by a ready approval of his bent toward a life of study, unvaried by any profession which would have been a source of profit, although such a course evidently held them to a restricted mode of living for many years.

Born, as we have seen, at Weymouth, where it may be conjectured his mother had gone for the sake of her health, the child was taken very soon to London, and was baptized, according to a note his mother made some years later, by Dr. Hunter of the Scotch Kirk, London Wall, in the following December or January. The Scotch Kirk has disappeared from London Wall, and the register cannot be consulted to test the accuracy of Mrs. Peacock's memory. Of these first years in London nothing is known, not even Samuel Peacock's place of residence. His early death and Mrs. Peacock's removal to Chertsey took Thomas out of the environment of the city before he had become attached to it, and one need not be surprised that he grew up with a pronounced taste for the country and out-of-doors, which developed finally into a vigorous prejudice, as did most of his tastes, against the smoke and noise of London. At Chertsey he was almost wholly removed from urban influences. The village, twenty-two miles from London, on the south bank of the Thames, had as yet been little affected by the exodus of gentry and retired tradesmen from the city. In 1801 it had less than three thousand inhabitants, so that during Peacock's boyhood he lived in a country village, deriving what importance it had from its weekly market and four fairs a year.[1] The few anglers from the city who penetrated thither found the

---

[1] Allen, *Surrey and Sussex* (1830), ii. 49. [Unless it is otherwise stated, all references are to books published in London.]

curfew still a well-maintained institution.[1] If they climbed St. Anne's Hill, the slope of which begins just south-west of the village and reaches the summit about a mile to the westward, they looked down upon a straggling group of well-built houses, arranged chiefly along two streets at right angles to each other, and surrounded by a pleasant level plain, very low between the village and the Thames. The river, which here makes a splendid sweep just after passing under Chertsey Bridge, assisted the stage road in affording a means of transit to London, the smoke of which was distinctly visible from St. Anne's.

The details of Peacock's life during these early years at Chertsey are almost wholly lacking. His grandfather lived in a cottage called Gogmoor Hall, which may have owed its name to its location in the Gogmore Lane still to be found in Chertsey. The household consisted of Thomas and Mrs. Love, Mrs. Peacock, and the boy. He may very excusably have been spoiled, and doubtless was. His early and somewhat didactic precocity was probably due in part to his boyhood in a family of adults; perhaps, too, in his occasional petulant eccentricity one discerns the traces of a wilful childhood. If judgment is to be based upon his later writings, Master Thomas formed few acquaintances among the villagers of Chertsey or the farmers who came in to market on Wednesdays. At one house in the neighbourhood, however, we know he was a welcome visitor.

On the immediate outskirts of the village stood an old mansion called the Abbey House, from its location

---

[1] Manning and Bray, *Surrey* (1804–14), iii. 205.

near the site of the once powerful Chertsey Priory. Of the original Abbey almost nothing remained save a gateway, a part of an old wall, and " a sort of piscatorial panopticon, where all approved varieties of fresh-water fish had been classified, each in its own pond, and kept in good order, clean and fat, for the mortification of the flesh of the monastic brotherhood on fast days." [1] The Abbey House itself, built under Charles II., was occupied during Peacock's residence at Chertsey by a Mr. Roger Barwell, son to a former official of the India Company.[2] Mr. Barwell had a son—Peacock calls him Charles—who was Thomas's school-fellow at Englefield Green, and who became so devotedly attached to the boy from the village that he was never content unless their holidays were spent together. When an elderly man Peacock published his *Recollections of Childhood: The Abbey House*, in *Bentley's Miscellany*, and there he gives us practically all we know of his associates at Chertsey. As he remembered it in 1837, life at the Abbey House had taken on idyllic tints. There had reigned old-fashioned hospitality and country ease. The master of the house had not yet been awakened from a dignified retirement by the noise of England grown imperial, the ladies kept commendably at home, employed only in such household exercises as preserving and performance on the harpsichord. There the two boys played games, and got into scrapes and out of them. Charles, who was passionately fond of romances like *The Mysteries of Udolpho*, made tales

---

[1] *Calidore*, &c., ed. Garnett (1891), p. 25.
[2] Brayley, *Surrey* (1850), ii. 187–8.

of wonder and terror his familiars. The hard-headed
little doubting Thomas, although no more than seven
or eight, took small stock in spirits, and was only
amused when the grimmest passages were read to
him. One thinks of a later friendship of Peacock's,
when the unearthly spirit of Shelley found so congenial
this caustic analyst of mystery.

Peacock is said to have been a very handsome boy,
with dark eyes, a fine head, and splendid flaxen hair
which so attracted the attention of Queen Charlotte
that she once stopped her carriage to kiss him. By
that time he had doubtless already entered his first
and last school, at Englefield Green, where, by his
own account,[1] he spent about six and a half years,
leaving it before he was thirteen. The master, a
Mr. John Harris Wicks, he declares to have been no
great scholar, but to have had excellent assistants in
French and classics, and the happy faculty of inspir-
ing his pupils with a love of learning. Thomas, who
had already been taught by his mother to be fond
of reading, here continued his studies assiduously.
Mr. Wicks was much pleased by his pupil's progress
and praised him highly, indulging in the prophecy
customary to such cases, that he would one day
make his mark in the world. The juvenile pieces
of Peacock would not seem of themselves to have
warranted any extravagant enthusiasm over his
poetical powers, but a certain letter written when
he was about eleven years old, probably as a school
exercise, may be quoted as a good sign of his sober
precocity.

---

[1] See Miss Nicolls' *Biographical Notice* in the *Works*, i. xxvii.

THOMAS LOVE PEACOCK

"DEAR SIR,—The present alarming state of the
country points out the subject of a letter from me
to you. At this time, threatened by a powerful and
victorious enemy, and bending under a load of severe
exactions, I take up my pen to give you my sentiments.
Though I do not wish Mr. Pitt's removal from his
exalted station, yet I think he would have acted more
in conformity with the sentiments of the People had
he taxed every one according to their income. I think,
too, he was wrong to begin this war, but much more
to refuse peace when the French demanded it, since
which time we have suffered so many losses and now
vainly endeavour to extricate ourselves from a war
in which his imprudence involves us.

"The French, now inflamed by victory, in their
turn deny us peace ; not only that, but they are
making vast preparations to invade us. Does it not,
then, become each noble Briton to rise in defence of
his Country and show them that the British character
is still unchanged ? Shall we, like cowards, when the
existance [*sic*] of our country is at stake, when everything that is dear to us is devoted [*sic*], shrink back at
their approach and basely seek to preserve [ourselves ?]
by dastardly inactivity or concealment, leaving all
for which life is worth preserving, parents, wives,
sisters or children, to be cruelly slaughtered or their
honor violated by merciless Frenchmen ? Forbid
it, Heaven ! Let every one in whose veins English
blood flows bear for his motto, *Death before Dis-
honor !* In speaking to you, sir, I would be considered
as speaking to the people of England. Shall we, who
for ages have kept the world in awe, yield to a cowardly,

BIRTH—EDUCATION

vainglorious, pusillanimous nation? Shall Britain, once '*The terror and delight* of distant nations,'[1] yield to these hateful intruders, and thereby lose those laurels which our ancestors have gained with such danger and pains? No, my countrymen! Arm, bravely arm, in defence of your country, nor own yourselves what your posterity will shudder to think you—*Unworthy of English blood!*

"Were I to say more, my dear Sir, I should become enthusiastic in the cause of liberty, I should become impassioned with those sentiments which fire my breast when the dearest rights of humanity are at stake. Permit me therefore, my dear Sir, to conclude, hoping that what I have already said will be sufficient to inspire you with an active zeal for your country's welfare, and to make you rise, bravely rise, in defence of your liberty, your religion, and your laws.— I am, &c.,   T. L. P."[2]

With a smile for the boyish rhetoric, one may acknowledge that the piece indicates a very commendable thoughtfulness in a child of eleven, and is as devoid of humour as a humorist, serious, could make it. Epistolary philippics, however, did not occupy all his time during these years at school. A merry letter in verse addressed to his mother, and an epitaph on a school friend, Hamlet Wade, who died in 1795,

[1] Here is inserted the word " Thomson," apparently to indicate the source of the quotation. It may be found in *The Seasons*, near the end of *Summer*.

[2] Brit. Mus. *Addit. MSS.*, 36815, fol. 12–13. As there is practically no punctuation in the original (apparently a copy in his mother's hand), I have altered it to accord with the present practice. The letter was printed by Cole, pp. 5–6.

as well as another rhymed communication to a cousin in Madrid, have been preserved, and were all printed by Cole. They are not extraordinary. Peacock did no more than to show himself by his work at Wicks' school to be possessed of a keen intelligence, very quick and sympathetic, with an industry in the pursuit of agreeable knowledge well beyond the degree usually evinced by schoolboys. During these years he became well grounded in the rudiments of Greek, Latin, and French, and, what was more important, formed a taste for study which did not cease with the expiration of his life at school.

Of the games he played and the friendships he formed at Englefield Green no record has been kept. It is said that one of his friends there was Peter Auber. As Auber, however, was fifteen years his senior, the acquaintance could not have been a school friendship. Charles Barwell and Hamlet Wade have already been mentioned. Doubtless there were others, and the story runs in the family that he was a lad of great merriment, who was wont to keep one smaller boy in dread of a savage beast which Master Peacock declared he kept in his room; but even very early Peacock manifested a social self-sufficiency which always kept his circle of intimates small. When not reading, he spent most of his waking time in long, generally solitary, excursions through the surrounding country. The location of the school upon the borders of Windsor Forest may have created, certainly fostered, this taste. " I was early given to long walks and rural explorations," he later wrote, " and there was scarcely a spot of the Park or the Forest with which

I was not intimately acquainted. There were two very different scenes to which I was especially attached —Virginia Water, and a dell near Winkfield Plain." [1] To both these spots he was drawn, both as dreaming boy and later as melancholy man, by the unbroken solitude. But there was a hint of jealousy in his attachment to solitary places. When Virginia Water had become so popular a resort that it was no longer suitable to reveries, he lost the desire to visit it, feeling always that the new aspect of the place had nothing to compensate him for the disappointment his memory suffered. That lovely dingle which had an especial charm for him likewise surrendered its charm when it had been enclosed. The new popularity of Virginia Water, indeed, afforded enjoyment to many, whereas it had once been known to but few ; and the enclosure of various portions of the Park and of the vicinity near Windsor illustrated the scriptural maxim : "To him that hath much, much shall be given ; and from him that hath little shall be taken away even the little he hath." [2]   Yet not even the good of the majority or the consolation of seeing the truth of Scripture vindicated, could make him visit the Park in his later years. His fondness for wild and solitary places, early aroused and long persisted in, was a romantic attachment which sent him off to external nature, in search of a companion which would not disturb the dreams of his boyhood, and which, after he became a thoughtful youth, would never irritate or contradict one of his moods.

Just when Peacock's residence at Chertsey ceased

---

[1] *Calidore*, &c., p. 143.   [2] *Ibid.*, p. 147.

is uncertain, but by February 11, 1800, he was employed as clerk for a firm of merchants in Angel Court, Throgmorton Street. This appears upon the occasion of what seems his first printed work, and that in a periodical so ambitious as to deserve attention. A magazine for the young had been initiated at the beginning of the year 1800, the monthly numbers of which were called *The Monthly Preceptor*, but which, in bound volumes, assumed the title of *The Juvenile Library*. The title-page of the first volume will explain the modest scope of the undertaking : "*The Juvenile Library, including a Complete Course of Instruction on every useful Subject : particularly Natural and Experimental Philosophy, Moral Philosophy, Natural History, Botany, Ancient and Modern History, Biography, Geography and the Manners and Customs of Nations, Ancient and Modern Languages, English Law, Penmanship, Mathematics, and the Belles Lettres. With Prize Productions of Young Students ; and a Monthly Distribution of Prizes, value fifteen Guineas and upwards.*" It was hoped to carry out this Gargantuan programme in four or five volumes ; six seem to have been required. Here are stored up the early works of Leigh Hunt, De Quincey, W. J. Fox, George Ormerod, and Kirke White, as well as of " Master T. L. Peacock, *aged* 14," who, for the first number, February 1800, answered in verse the question, " Is History or Biography the more improving Study ? " His production was published, " not as a specimen of poetry particularly excellent, but as an extraordinary effort of genius in a boy of this age ; and as such the Proprietors have rewarded him with an *extra prize*, viz., an elementary book, value 5s."[1] Leigh Hunt had the fourth prize in the same contest. Peacock's poem contains forty-six lines of conventional heroic couplets in which, with unshaken solemnity, the young genius weighs the respective merits of Biography and "Hist'ry," and decided that, as Biography "follows one alone thro' life's uncertain ways," even though she can edify, she is less improving than "Hist'ry," whose "open, daring ray" is to Biography as the beaming sun to the humble-eyed morning star. Peacock's prize was, with an appropriateness which the editors of a Juvenile Library would easily have hit upon, a copy of "Elegant Extracts in Verse epitomised." In their attestation, Ludlow, Fraser & Co. certified that Peacock was in their employ, was only fourteen, and had received no assistance whatever.

The exact nature of his duties for this firm of merchants, and the length of his service, are not known. Apparently, however, he did not long remain a clerk, but soon exchanged the counting-house for the more congenial reading-room of the British Museum, which he made his school and favourite haunt for many years. There is no extant record, indeed, that he was admitted before April 14, 1823, when he received a reader's ticket on the recommendation of a Mr. Banks, but the superintendent of the reading-room is of the opinion that this may well have been a re-admission, to fulfil the requirements of the new regulations adopted in 1822. "I was early impressed," he says, "with the words of Harris [James Harris, author of *Hermes*]: 'To be competently skilled in ancient

---

[1] *Juvenile Library*, i. 54 *ff.*

learning is by no means a work of such insuperable pains. The very progress itself is attended with delight, and resembles a journey through some pleasant country, where, every mile we advance, new charms arise. It is certainly as easy to be a scholar as to be a gamester, or many other characters equally illiberal and low. The same application, the same quantity of habit, will fit us for one as completely as for the other.' Thus encouraged, I took to reading the best books, illustrated by the best critics; and amongst the latter I feel especially indebted to Heyne and Hermann." [1]

Peacock was as indefatigable and wide-ranging in his scholarly explorations as in his pedestrian tours, although he was not infallible as regards the minutiæ of learning. For instance, late in life he could translate " fluctibus educata " from the *Metamorphoses* of Apuleius by " the educated in the waves "; [2] it is obvious that he was very careless in regard to Greek accents; an easy paraphrase satisfied him in translation; frequent and particularly inaccurate misquotation may likewise be numbered among his scholarly offences. The bad translation was very possibly only a slip, and assuredly misquotation is venial enough. So far as Greek accents go, not a few besides Peacock have excused themselves as he did in that regard, [3] by quoting Martial :

> "Turpe est difficiles habere nugas
> Et stultus labor est ineptiarum."—(*Epig.* ii. 86).

lines which may be taken to indicate Peacock's general attitude toward meticulous accuracy. The trouble is,

---

[1] *Works*, i. xxvii.   [2] *Ibid.*, ii. 305.
[3] *Headlong Hall*, ed. Garnett (1891), p. 51 *n*.

however, that he exercised a certain wilfulness in his judgment as to what was worthy of scrupulously accurate treatment. He disliked Keats because " he could prove by a hundred quotations that the sleep of Endymion was eternal, whereas in the modern poem the Latmian shepherd is for ever capering up and down the earth and ocean like the German chaser of shadows." [1] Yet *The Misfortunes of Elphin* handles Welsh material with a freedom which does not differ very greatly from that which Keats allowed himself. Peacock, indeed, had a habit of judging poets and novelists by the rules of erudition. His utter demolition of Moore's *Epicurean* [2] on the ground that its pretensions to be an accurate picture of ancient life were ridiculously false, happened to be deserved in that particular instance, since the tale had little else to recommend it. Dr. Opimian's strictures upon Tennyson, [3] however, perhaps not far from Peacock's own opinion, seem pedantic, if they are to be taken, not as a sly laugh at the good doctor, but actually as a condemnation of *The Dream of Fair Women*, because Cleopatra is there represented as an enchantress of a swarthy complexion. If Peacock's mediæval novels were subjected to similar tests, modern research would be able to point out blunders in them as well. But no one could reasonably demand that *Maid Marian* follow its authorities with the timid fidelity of Becker's *Charikles* or Strutt's *Queenhoo Hall*. Rather than with professed philologists, Peacock is to be measured for the extent and accuracy of his learning with other

[1] R. Buchanan, *A Look around Literature* (1887), p. 175.
[2] *Westminster Review*, viii. 351–384.
[3] *Works*, ii. 408.

novelists or poets. Here he is on safer ground. Without the immense mediæval knowledge of Scott, or Thackeray's familiarity with the eighteenth century, he of course surpassed them both in classical scholarship, and was perhaps equalled in this respect among his contemporaries only by Landor and Coleridge. If Coleridge's reading was wider, it was less minute. Moreover, Peacock was exceptionally well read in Italian and French, and constantly informed as to the productions of his own generation, although often out of sympathy with it.

His reading was especially extensive in the few authors who were his favourites : Homer, Sophocles, Aristophanes, Nonnus, Cicero, Petronius, Virgil, Horace, Tacitus, Bojardo, Pulci, Ariosto, Rabelais, Voltaire, Samuel Butler, Wordsworth. Homer he quotes more frequently than any other poet. He long planned an edition of Sophocles, but never did more than project it. He revelled in the comedy of Aristophanes as " the most wonderful combination the world has ever seen of splendid imagery, exquisite versification, wit, humour, and moral and political satire." [1] Dickens, he said, was very comic, " but—not *so* comic as Aristophanes ! " [2] There is much in Peacock's own high spirits, sudden fancies, lyrical outbursts, tumbling humour, nipping sarcasm, and passionate Toryism to suggest on a smaller scale the merry muse of the Greek. The Aristophanic comedy in *Gryll Grange* is an indubitable example of literary influence. He had a distinct weakness for Nonnus, whose *Dionysiaca* he asserted was " the finest poem in the world after the

[1] *Fraser's*, lix. 368.   [2] Buchanan, p. 172.

Iliad," [1] and he used to take a malicious pleasure in
finding Oxford scholars who knew not the Panopolitan.
Cicero he read so much that he had committed nearly
all his more remarkable passages to memory ; [2] whatever was urbane and polished in philosophy made
a marked appeal to him. Horace, and then Virgil,
come next to Homer by the number of times they are
quoted in the novels. The sunny wisdom of the one
and the noble elegance of the other suited him better
than the intensity of Lucretius or Juvenal. That he
read Tacitus earnestly in his early life is attested by
his having taken a volume with him on a lonely
expedition into Wales in 1811, and by the symptoms
in his own style of a careful study of the " jolting
gravity " of the great historian. In his later life
Petronius succeeded to Tacitus, a change not un-
paralleled in Peacock's own temper. When *Gryll
Grange* was written, only Horace and Homer, if we
may judge by frequency of quotation, were so much
in the novelist's mind as the *Satyricon.* Among the
Italians, Dante suffered something the same fate in
Peacock's opinion as Lucretius and Juvenal. It was
the courtly Ariosto, the burlesquing Pulci, the
romantic Bojardo, that he preferred. The last-named
he esteemed especially, at first, it seems, only in the
rifaccimento of Berni, but still more after Panizzi had
made the original version of *Orlando Innamorato*
accessible (1830–31). All French literature contained
no name so dear to Peacock as Rabelais. Alcofribas
Nasier had a finger in the hilarious copiousness of
the second chapter of *Headlong Hall ;* the chess dance

[1] *Calidore*, &c., p. 20.   [2] Buchanan, p. 172.

in *Melincourt* is imitated boldly from a similar event at the court of Queen Quinte Essence ;[1] paraphrases from Rabelais are frequent in the novels. In a letter to Broughton in 1862,[2] Peacock testifies that he had just completed a reperusal of his arch-favourite. Strangely enough, he seems to have cared little for Montaigne. In Voltaire he took great delight as a modern satirist who united to a genuine moral purpose [3] a dexterity of wit not invariably associated with reformers. *Hudibras* was the mine from which Peacock repeatedly drew his mottos, and Wordsworth, much as Peacock ridiculed the Lake Poets, yet found few more appreciative readers than his very satirist, who quotes him again and again, and pays him a notable number of times the homage of misquotation.

Then there was, moreover, a great concourse of authors, without the pale of his especial affection, but still often read. He was fond of Athenæus and Livy. In his early youth he made translations of Guarini, and he had very early become acquainted with Petrarch, Tasso, Machiavelli, Alfieri, Metastasio. He was intimate with Rousseau, whose *Rêveries du Promeneur Solitaire* were probably not without their effect upon the solitary rambles of Peacock's youth. Chaucer's *Canterbury Tales* he was going through as old friends in 1862.[4] Shakespeare, of course, he quotes frequently—from *Hamlet* more than from any other play. He preferred Milton's prose to his poetry ;[5]

---

[1] Rabelais, v. 24–5.   [2] *Works*, i. xlvii.
[3] Peacock insisted upon this in an interesting comparison of Voltaire and Lucian. *Fraser's*, lix. 376.
[4] *Works*, i. xlvii.   [5] Buchanan, p. 173.

the dramatists of the Restoration shared his interest with the wits and poets of the age of Anne.[1] Most of his contemporaries, indeed, he was inclined to slash for the glory of the past, yet even there he commonly reserved his satire for pretension. Landor he thought a " frothy personage." [2] He called *Christabel* a " most beautiful little poem " [3] none the less honestly because of the exquisite parody of the composition of *Kubla Khan* in *Nightmare Abbey*. The delineation of Byron as Mr. Cypress in the same tale did not exclude the taste which made him say : " *Cain* is very fine ; *Sardanapalus* I think finer ; *Don Juan* is best of all. I have read nothing else in recent literature that I think good for anything." [4] Dickens he began to read late in life, but with the greatest pleasure. Although he was personally acquainted with Thackeray, we have no record of his opinion of his great contemporary in satire.

The mere enumeration of a man's reading is in part explanatory of his general tastes, when, as in the present case, he confines himself with notable pertinacity to the authors for whom he feels a distinct personal liking. Buchanan, in an account of Peacock as he appeared in his old age, confirms the impression which a glance at the list of Peacock's favourites will convey : " His sympathies, indeed, were less with the grand, the terrible, and the sublimely pathetic, than

[1] Buchanan, p. 173.
[2] *Thomas Love Peacock : Letters to Edward Hookham and Percy B. Shelley, with Fragments of Unpublished MSS.*, ed. Dr. Garnett (Boston, 1910), p. 89.
[3] *Westminster*, xii. 302.
[4] *Thomas Love Peacock : Letters*, &c., p. 94.

with the brilliant, the exquisite, and the delicately artistic." [1] To readers familiar with the authors of his choice, it will occur that another quality, that of a frankness which the nineteenth century in England did not countenance, is tolerably recurrent in much Peacock read. In this connection again an observation of Buchanan is apropos : " It must be admitted, moreover, that his mind was in itself a terrible ' thesaurus eroticus,' and there was to be found in it many a Petronian quibble and Catullian *double entendre* not to be discovered in Rambach." [2] Peacock, like Dr. Folliott, held that " even in these tight-laced days, the obscurity of a learned language allows a little pleasantry." [3] His classical and French models have perhaps to answer for an occasional approach to the thin ice of suggestion, but he never falls into grossness.

The belief of the priggish Mr. Falconer in *Gryll Grange* that Greek, Latin, Italian, French, and English, " comprise, with a few rare exceptions, all the best books in the world," [4] had Peacock's sympathy. In his old age he began the study of Spanish, to form a first-hand acquaintance with " the rare exceptions " in that language, particularly Cervantes ; in his youth he was for a time deeply under the influence of Ossian ; and *The Misfortunes of Elphin* was the fruit of tolerably serious studies in Welsh. But for the literature of Teutonic Europe, outside of England, he cared little. His early sentimental piece, *Fiolfar, King of Norway*, the juvenile drama, *The Circle of Loda*, and the char-

---

[1] Buchanan, p. 172. [2] *Ibid.*, p. 173.
[3] *Works*, ii. 220. [4] *Ibid.*, 299.

acter.of Odin in *The Philosophy of Melancholy* (book iv.),
depend for all the information necessary to writing
them—no excessive amount—upon Gibbon, Percy's
Mallet, and Cottle's *Edda*, which last Peacock very
properly said was " Cottle's Edda," not a " *Translation
of the Edda.*" [1] So far as German was concerned,
Peacock's knowledge was practically nothing. He had
no difficulty in agreeing with Porson's dictum, that
" Life is too short to learn German," a dictum cited
approvingly by Mr. Falconer, and explained by the
devotee of St. Catherine to mean, " not that it is
too difficult to be acquired within the ordinary space
of life, but that there is nothing in it to compensate
for the portion of life bestowed on its acquirement,
however little that may be." [2] The novels are full
of flings at German poetry and philosophy. Even
German scholarship, though he claimed that in
classical philology it was superior to English, did not
inspire in him any particular reverence. He could
quote with a chuckle Porson's rhymes (of course
inaccurately) :

> "The Germans in Greek
> Are sadly to seek ;
> Save only Hermann,
> And Hermann's a German." [3]

As long as he lived, he never outlived prejudices
formed when German literature was first making
itself heard in England, when the bilious spectres that
came with Kotzebue to the London stage repelled
the lover of classic order and graceful wit. His

---

[1] *Works*, i. 275 *n.*   [2] *Ibid.*, ii. 299.   [3] Buchanan, p. 179.

perversity inflicted upon him the extreme penalty of a life-long ignorance of Heine.

It was plainly an ardent student who joined to a tremendous appetite for poetry and philosophy a keen interest in such " philosophic philology " as occupied the pages of Horne Tooke's *Diversions of Purley*, James Harris's *Hermes*, and Lord Monboddo's *Origin and Progress of Language*. Monboddo's *Natural Metaphysics* and Sir William Drummond's *Academical Questions* were likewise particular favourites of Peacock. While in Wales he sent to London for mathematical instruments and Euclid ; he read with avidity Buffon's *Histoire Naturelle* and sundry less known histories, works on mythology, narratives of voyages and travels, topographical and archæological works. At the British Museum he accompanied his classical reading with a careful study of the remains of classic art, and acquired likewise a considerable familiarity with modern painting. It will later be seen that he became eventually a musical and operatic critic of at least such ability as to serve on *The Examiner* during its best days. Long before this he had been devoted in his attendance at Italian opera whenever visits or residence in London afforded him the opportunity.

Whether his mental curiosity would have been so untiring had he gone to one of the universities is a question which, being unanswerable, might afford endless discussion, if much general speculation on the relative merits of regular and irregular intellectual training had not already made anything but a brief specific comment superfluous. Peacock himself bestowed upon Oxford and Cambridge some of his most

pungent hits. He was never tired of praising col-
leges for their power to banish taste or to eradicate
a zeal for knowledge, and he had many a laugh at the
phrase " to finish an education." Academic circles,
by the testimony of his novels, are centres of idle
habits, of vain and fruitless verbal criticism, and of a
willingness, even an anxiety, to suppress free inquiry
in order to preserve intact the comfortable prejudices
which lie at the root of an old régime. Nor are his
censures wholly dramatic. In his review of Moore's
Letters and Journals of Lord Byron, is an angry digres-
sion concerning the little good the English universities
have done their most gifted sons.[1] He denied with
scorn that a college curriculum confers any disciplinary
benefit upon a student of real industry. Such men
as Milton, Locke, and Gibbon, he observed, disciplined
themselves to an extent which makes it impossible to
say that their hatred of the university arose from the
impatience of genius under restraint. To be sure,
similar censure would have come from Peacock with
slightly better grace if he had had any personal
experience with academic discipline ; and it will have
to be owned that his attitude toward the ordinary
process of making scholars has good precedent and
modern instance in the attitude of many other self-
made personages. The matter, however, is not a
question of giving the universities any of the defence
which they may or may not have needed at the
beginning of the century. It is only important to
note that Peacock seems to have been made for a
solitary scholar. One may doubt whether he would

----
[1] *Westminster*, xii. 284–88.

ever, during his youth, have submitted with grace to any discipline not self-imposed. To him the acquisition of knowledge was a passion which he gratified in a vein of the morose care often accompanying scholarship. It was a tolerably fitful emotion, and might have made him very impatient of any kind of academic rules whatever. Possibly enough, if he had once gone to a university he would have found the easy academic life of the day more engaging than he affected to believe it, and he might have had his social qualities developed so early as to spare us much of the metrical melancholy of his young manhood. But, after all, it would have been a genuine loss had he become a don and expended on academic tasks or the castigation of rival scholars the satirical powers which he directed instead at a whole generation.

CHAPTER II

EARLY POEMS

THE first five or six years of the new century Peacock continued to live in London—exactly where is not known—so much occupied with his books that only occasional long tramps into the country varied an outwardly uneventful existence. A few fragments of verse have been preserved from this period, and one poem, slightly longer than the others, probably attained the dignity of separate publication soon after its composition in 1804. In the edition of 1875 *The Monks of St. Mark* bears the date September 1804, and Mrs. Clarke remembers having seen a pamphlet containing it; but a careful search has failed to discover any trace of the poem until it appeared in the collected edition. This ballad has no particular merit save that it is interesting as a prophecy in several ways of the mature Peacock. The monks have met in the refectory for a grapple with Bacchus, heedless of the storm raging without. One brother spills a bowl of scalding punch in the lap of another, and during the uproar which follows most of them contrive to fall downstairs in the dark. It is only when they have returned to the real business of the night, and drunk themselves all under the table, that quiet once more reigns in the abbey. There is no sign here of the denial of the Comic Spirit so common in apprentices to poetry,

and almost invariable in Peacock's earlier attempts at
verse. The piece is not, indeed, exactly witty, consisting as it does chiefly of a series of boisterous physical
accidents, but Peacock always appreciated slips and
tumbles to a degree which marked his kinship with
Aristophanes and Rabelais. Occasional happy turns
of phrase and a cynical attitude toward the ascetic
spirit of the clergy are characteristic.

When *The Monks of St. Mark* was written, Peacock
had already under way the project of a volume of
poems which was announced as a new publication in
the *Edinburgh Review* for January 1806,[1] and first
reviewed by the *British Critic* the following month.[2]
Palmyra, the most considerable piece in *Palmyra and
Other Poems*, differs in few respects from the verses
which many dilettanti young gentlemen were writing
during the early years of the century. Peacock had
come across Robert Wood's *Ruins of Palmyra, otherwise
Tedmor, in the Desart* (1753), in the course of his
literary rambles, and had been moved, partly, one
hopes, by the magnificence of the folio, to sing the
glories of the fallen city. The poem is scarcely
joyous enough for a pæan, and a little too much so
for a convincing epitaph. Nor was it altogether
original in 1806 to grow meditative among the ruins
of forgotten grandeur. Volney gave his name to
extracts in the notes and his mood to the poem itself,
while frequent verbal reminiscences of Gray's *Elegy*
point to the influence of the so-called " Graveyard
School " of poetry. Years later Peacock commented
satirically on the same mood: " The sentimental

[1] vii. 508.   [2] xxvii. 186.

T. L. Peacock.

Ætat 18.

tourist (who, perching himself on an old wall, works himself up into a soliloquy of philosophical pathos on the vicissitudes of empire and the mutability of all sublunary things, interrupted only by an occasional peep at his watch, to ensure his not over-staying the minute at which his fowl, comfortably roasting at the nearest inn, has been promised to be ready), has, no doubt, many fine thoughts well worth recording in a dapper volume." [1] But it was by no means strange that the writer of these words should have been the author of *Palmyra* at twenty. Young poets immersed in the attempt to judge themselves by the study of days and men long gone by find often enough that the thought of time's inexorable passage arouses terror that the past is greedy, instead of a hope, which should be natural to them, that the future may prove benevolent. Joined to a powerful imagination, such a mood may produce a great poem, but Peacock happened not to be a great poet at twenty, and his irregular ode on *Tedmor in the Desart* will scarcely be read a second time by any but his biographer. Shelley, indeed, called the conclusion " the finest piece of poetry I ever read." [2] Whatever one may think of Shelley's critical acumen in 1812, it is only fair to him to explain that he had seen the second edition of *Palmyra*, which was entirely rewritten and very much improved from the version of six years earlier. Indeed the second version is practically a new poem, with only a hint from the juvenile effort. As this second edition, unjustly to Peacock, has never

[1] *Works*, ii. 154–5.
[2] *Letters*, ed. Ingpen (1909), p. 359.

been reprinted, the lines which won Shelley's praise may be quoted here :

"The flower, that drinks the morning dew,
    Far on the evening gale shall fly :
The bark, that glides o'er ocean blue,
    Dashed on the distant rocks shall lie :
The tower, that frowns in martial pride,
    Shall by the lightning-brand be riven :
The arch, that spans the summer tide,
    Shall down the wintry floods be driven :
The tomb, that guards the great one's name.
    Shall yield to time its sacred trust :
The laurel of imperial fame
    Shall wither in unwatered dust.
His mantle dark Oblivion flings
Around the monuments of kings,
Who once to conquest shouting myriads bore.
Fame's trumpet-blast, and victory's clarion shrill,
    Pass, like an echo of the hill,
That breathes one wild response, and then is heard no more.

But ne'er shall earthly time throw down
    The immortal pile that virtue rears :
Her golden throne, and starry crown,
    Decay not with revolving years :
For He, whose solemn voice controlled
    Necessity's mysterious sway,
And yon vast orbs from chaos rolled
    Along the elliptic paths of day,
Has fixed her empire, vast and high,
Where primogenial harmony
Unites, in ever-cloudless skies,
Affection's death-divided ties :
Where wisdom, with unwearying gaze,
The universal scheme surveys,
And truth, in central light enshrined,
Leads to its source sublime the indissoluble mind." [1]

[1] *Genius of the Thames*, &c., 2nd ed. (1812), pp. 116–118.

Palmyra is amply illustrated with notes, also revised in the second edition, from Gibbon, Volney, Isaiah, Ossian, but mostly from Wood's own explanatory matter. Besides *Palmyra*, which occupies only about one-third of the total contents, the volume of 1806 contained as a prefatory address *To the Reviewers*, a somewhat cleverly executed cento from Shakespeare, which seems to have mollified at least one reviewer's hard heart,[1] and twenty smaller pieces, of almost uniform unimportance. Of the longest, *Fiolfar, King of Norway*, it is perhaps sufficient to say that Fiolfar talks Ossian in anapestic couplets after the manner of Monk Lewis. Two of the poems are confessedly imitated from Ossian. There is a translation out of *Il Pastor Fido*, a paraphrase from Petronius, and one from Pindar. A tame attempt at Hebrew dialect competes in badness with four or five woeful ballads of which the sound sometimes suggests the " tragical mirth " of Pyramus and Thisbe, and the sense generally has the misfortune to confirm the suggestion.

To a period not far from the composition of *Fiolfar, King of Norway*, it seems best to assign the second of Peacock's recently published plays,[2] *The Circle of Loda*. The manuscript of this piece was preserved among his papers, a very careful copy in a boyish hand, written on paper made in 1801. Peacock himself would assuredly never have consented to the publication, nor has his editor done him any particular kindness in bringing it to light. It is

[1] *Critical Review*, series 3, vol. vii. p. 210.
[2] *Plays of Thomas Love Peacock*, ed. A. B. Young (1910).

bombastic, youthful, sentimental. Like *Fiolfar*, it deals with Scandinavian material, assumes the general tone of the narrative poem, and shows much the same immaturity of execution. Not impossibly, the drama may even have preceded the narrative poem, for the use made in both of the circle of Loda, a kind of Scandinavian temple, may indicate a case of borrowing not unlike that by which *Headlong Hall* took over details from the then unpublished comedies. It was *Fiolfar*, not the play, which was published, and, moreover, it was printed again in 1812. In any case, *The Circle of Loda* cannot have belonged to so late a period as to warrant the suggestion of its editor [1] that the strife between Mengala and Rindane for the love of Hidalvar refers to Shelley's marital difficulties. By 1814, when that sad chapter began, Peacock was out of the zone of sentimental heroics.

About the time of the publication of *Palmyra*, the young poet went back to Chertsey to live. His grandfather, Thomas Love, died December 10, 1805,[2] and Mrs. Love, thus left alone, probably desired the companionship of her daughter and grandson. A letter to Hookham, dated two years later, testifies that Peacock soon extended one of his walking tours much farther than he had hitherto gone, in an excursion to Scotland. " You went [he writes] over the same ground on which I wandered alone in the autumn of 1806. You visited Dalkeith. Is not the Esk a most delightful stream ? Did you see that enchanting spot where the North and South Esk unite ? . . . Did

---

[1] *Plays of Thomas Love Peacock*, p. x.
[2] *Gentleman's Magazine*, lxxv [2]. 1239.

you visit the banks of the sweet silver Teviot, and that most lovely of rivers, the undescribably fascinating Tweed ? . . . Did you sit by moonlight in the ruins of Melrose ? Did you stand at twilight in that romantic wood which overhangs the Teviot, on the site of Roxburgh Castle ? " [1] Nothing further is known of this Scottish tour, but from it probably dates Peacock's inveterate prejudice against the Scotch.

It could hardly have been long before the removal to Chertsey, if before at all, that Peacock made the acquaintance of Edward T. Hookham, to whom he wrote this letter, and with whom he was for many years on intimate terms. Hookham was the younger son of Thomas Hookham, a well-known bookseller in Old Bond Street. In quest of new books Peacock may well enough have met young Hookham at the " Literary Assembly " which his father had founded in 1794, and which long continued to be the resort of many people of varying degrees of learning and fashion. Edward Hookham, two years Peacock's junior, was interested in literature as well as business, and is said to have had leanings toward more liberal religious and political opinions than his generation approved. On the basis of common heresies the two young men formed a close friendship, but, to judge by the first of the few letters preserved from their correspondence, they knew each other only slightly so late as August 3, 1807. On that date Peacock wrote to Hookham, thanking him for past favours and

[1] Brit. Mus. *Addit. MSS.*, 36815, fol. 16. Dr. Garnett's text of the letters to Hookham in *Thomas Love Peacock : Letters, &c.*, is inaccurate. I quote from the original manuscripts.

acknowledging an offer which the publisher had just made, apparently to issue a new volume of verse. *The Genius of the Thames* had already been conceived, may, indeed, have already formed the subject of a discussion between them. "I shall avail myself of your generous offer [the letter ran], and put my little vessel again on the stocks. . . . I have some thought of arranging the poem in four divisions ; but of this hereafter. Perhaps I have undertaken more than I can perform, and shall be obliged at last to leave the work unfinished : however, as I have no better occupation, I will return to the 'idle trade' of writing verses." [1] It was three years later, however, before he completed the undertaking to which he was thus turning to escape the discomforts of idleness.

An event of the same summer might reasonably have been expected to lend a new impetus to verse-making. He fell deeply in love with a girl, a Miss Fanny Falkner, who lived in the neighbourhood of Chertsey, was successful in his suit, and became engaged at twenty-two to a sweetheart of eighteen. A summer's idyllic courtship followed, during which they met often at the ruins of Newark Abbey on the Wey, a few miles from the village. But the engagement was broken off by the officious interference of a relative, and the young lady, supposing herself deserted, hastily married another, only to die the next year. Peacock's grief at the loss of her love was made doubly cruel by the tragedy of her untimely death, so that even through the course of a very happy married life the memory of this first love remained bright. One need not

[1] Brit. Mus. *Addit. MSS.*, 36815, fol. 14.

sentimentalise the incident, as did Buchanan, to realise how deep an impression such an experience made upon him. Peacock was not a man of fierce passions; rather he was calm, restrained, sceptical; but he had a great fund of the tenderness which lies close to humour. A genuine sorrow rendered him much less free to play with emotion in the future than he had been in his early verses; in the presence of a genuine bereavement, he could see how puny was his feigning. *Remember Me* and *Al Mio Primiero Amore*, if not excellent, are at any rate without affectation, while in "I dug, beneath the cypress shade" he achieved one of his two or three best serious poems:

> "I dug, beneath the cypress shade,
>   What well might seem an elfin's grave;
> And every pledge in earth I laid,
>   That erst thy false affection gave.
>
> I pressed them down the sod beneath;
>   I placed one mossy stone above;
> And twined the rose's fading wreath
>   Around the sepulchre of love.
>
> Frail as thy love, the flowers were dead
>   Ere yet the evening sun was set:
> But years shall see the cypress spread,
>   Immutable as my regret." [1]

Thirty-five years later he wrote *Newark Abbey* in remembrance of the joyful August of 1807. Tennyson saw and admired the poem when it was published in

---

[1] This poem has not before been connected with the episode of his early love, though often quoted. It was found among his manuscripts, on paper bearing a water-mark of 1806, and first published in 1875. The date and the evident sincerity of the poem seem to point to the conclusion that he wrote it about 1807 or 1808.

Fraser's long afterwards, as must all who appreciate
the clear, simple expression of grief remembered still,
but with all bitterness lost in the sweetness of memory.
Even to the end of his life Peacock wore a locket
containing some of this girl's hair, a touch strongly
at variance with his public character as a ridiculer of
sentiment. He used frequently to visit the ruins of
Newark Abbey, and only a few days before his death
he told his granddaughter that he had been dreaming
of his youthful sweetheart, and that she had been
coming to him in his sleep for many weeks. He
allows himself in the novels a severity of scorn for
ill-matched or mercenary marriages which makes one
remember his own disappointment. Miss Touchandgo
of *Crotchet Castle* owes something to the character
of his first love.

His unfortunate love affair was in part responsible
for the new duties which he assumed in the fall of
1808. By the influence of his maternal uncles, both
in the navy, he was appointed secretary to Sir Home
Riggs Popham, then in command of the H.M.S.
Venerable, lying in the Downs, and spent the winter
in an occupation which he found very distasteful.
Too long bred to leisure and solitary habits, he discovered that the tradition of a sea-going ancestry was
not enough to make a sailor of him, nor could his
own preconceived affection for the sea stand the test
of nautical reality. In a letter to Hookham, November
28, he says :

" As to writing poetry, or doing anything else that
is rational in this floating Inferno, it is almost next to
a moral impossibility. I would give the world now

to be at home, and devote the whole winter to the composition of a comedy. I am most assuredly completely out [of] my element here. Why, then, do I stay ?—To please some of my friends, who advise me to do so, because there is a prospect of its conducing to advantage. England is the modern Carthage : the love of gold, ' the last corruption of man,' pervades the whole state, from the centre to the extremities. If any one be placed in a situation, attended with immediate or consequent profit, it is sufficient for the multitude to pronounce him well employed, and to raise a most vehement outcry against all who dare to dissent from them. It would be ridiculous to talk to them of degradation of mind, or contamination of morals." [1]

Peacock found some amusement, however, during the winter, for he wrote prologues for amateur dramatic performances given on board, and composed, even in that " floating Inferno," his *Stanzas Written at Sea*, first published in a note to *The Genius of the Thames*. The *Genius* itself occupied his attention considerably. He solaced himself, moreover, with the numerous books which Hookham sent him from time to time. " Have the goodness to send me," he says in a letter of February 10, " the fourth volume of Lewis's Romantic Tales, the Romance of the Forest, The Ring and the Well, Adelmorn the Outlaw, and something very elegantly *romantesque* in the poetical department, if you can find anything of that description which I have not yet seen. I have never read the Minstrelsy of the Scottish Border : if you can spare

[1] Brit. Mus. *Addit. MSS.*, 36815, fol. 16–17.

it conveniently, you may send that likewise." [1]   His letters abound with questions as to the doings in all departments of the republic of letters.   By March 13 he had finished the first draft of *The Genius of the Thames*, and was sending it to Hookham for the latter's consideration, and very soon after he followed his poem in person.   He walked from Deal to Ramsgate, thence around the North Foreland to Margate, and, after spending a day or two in visiting the cathedral and town of Canterbury, took coach for London, whither he had already sent his trunk and boxes in care of Hookham.

Once more in Chertsey, Peacock set steadfastly to work upon his poem.   Writing again to his friend in London, May 17, he says that the first part is all but finished, and that, in preparation for the second, he plans to follow the course of the river from Trewsbury Mead to Chertsey, a distance of one hundred and eighty miles.   Accordingly, a week or so later, after a Sunday spent with Hookham at the Wheatsheaf Inn, he took a Gloucestershire coach from Slough, and is next heard of at Farringdon, in Berkshire.   From Farringdon he walked by way of Shrivenham and Highworth to Cricklade, which he reached on June 1.   His exploration of the neighbourhood did not give him any very favourable idea of the place.   " Cricklade is the shabbiest place in England.   The church tower is fine, and the interior workmanship admirable :   the churchwardens have *beautified* it with whitewash.   Miscreants !   Several streams unite here :   the natives are not agreed which is the Thames :   they are the

---

[1] Brit. Mus. *Addit. MSS.*, 36815, fol. 18.

most perfect set of Vandals I ever met with." [1] A
longer account of his adventures at the source of the
river is contained in a letter he wrote from Oxford
on his return, and which is now for the first time
published entire.

"OXFORD, *June* 6, 1809.
" 10 P.M.

" MY DEAR EDWARD,—Having given you the space
of twenty-four hours to contemplate me in an attitude
of profound meditation over the source of the Thames,
I resume the thread of my narration.   Thames Head
is a flat spring, in a field about a mile from Tarlton,
lying close to the bank of the Thames and Severn
canal.   This spring in the summer months is totally
dry.   None of our picturesque tourists appear to have
asked themselves the question : How is it possible that
a river which is *perpetually flowing* can rise from a
source which is *sometimes dry ?*   The infant river in
Kemble Meadow is never totally dry, and to the
source by which the stream there is constantly supplied
can alone belong the honor of giving birth to the
Thames.   But this spring, Thames Head, would never
be totally dry, were it not for a monstrous piece of
machinery erected near it, for the purpose of throwing
up its water into the neighbouring canal.   The Thames
is almost as good a subject for a satire as a panegyric.
A satirist might exclaim : The rapacity of commerce,
not content with the immense advantages derived from
this river in a course of nearly 300 miles, erects a
ponderous engine over the very place of its nativity,
to suck up its unborn waters from the bosom of the

1 Brit. Mus. *Addit. MSS.*, 36815, fol. 26.

39

earth, and pump them into a navigable canal! It were to be wished, after all, that the crime of *water-sucking* were the worst that could be laid to the charge of commercial navigation : but we have only to advert to the conduct of the Spanish Christians in South America, of the English Christians in the East Indies, and of the Christians of all nations on the coast of Africa, to discover the deeper dye of its blood-sucking atrocities. A panegyrist, on the contrary, after expatiating on the benefits of commercial navigation, and of that great effort of human ingenuity, the Thames & Severn Canal, which ascends the hills, sinks into the vallies, and penetrates the bosom of the earth, to unite the two noblest rivers of this most wealthy, prosperous, happy, generous, loyal, patriotic, &c. &c. &c., kingdom of England, might say : And yet this splendid undertaking would be incomplete, through the failure of water in the summer months, did not this noble river, this beautiful emblem, and powerful instrument, of the commercial greatness of Britain, contribute to that greatness even at the instant of its birth, by supplying this magnificent chain of connection with the means of perpetual utility. I must again break off for the present, and will send you another letter, if possible, to-morrow.—Invariably yours,

"T. L. PEACOCK."

" *Thursday, June 8th.*—I am still in Oxford, having been persuaded to remain by a friend in Magdalen College. I shall set forward to-morrow, weather permitting, which at present is as unfavorable as possible. A little more rain will cause another inundation, and put an effectual bar to my proceedings. Favor me with a letter by return of post, if possible, directing to me at the Post Office, Pangbourn, Berkshire." [1]

Obviously the future satirist had been born. One wonders whether Peacock did not weigh seriously the relative advantages of satire and panegyric for his poem, and one must regret that, knowing satire, he still persisted in what was not, for him, the better part. His letters to Hookham from June to September indicate that, now again in Chertsey, he was frequently occupied with *The Genius of the Thames*, which he seemed to have difficulty in getting into satisfactory shape. Writing for some books, he says, " I want several of them for the purpose of manufacturing notes." [2] His poem was finished early the following year, and published in June or July. The first edition comprises about thirteen hundred lines of graceful verse, generally in octosyllabic couplets, making up two nearly equal parts, of which the first is devoted to praise of the river as a whole, and the second to a panoramic description of the scenery along its banks. To those familiar with the localities it describes, it has a mild charm, but of the few readers who are curious enough to begin it, even fewer will reach the end. *The Satirist* for August I attacked it in a savage and stupid review. [3] *The Anti-Jacobin* atoned for such critical obtuseness the next month by tendering whatever consolation a favourable notice in the

[1] Brit. Mus. *Addit. MSS.*, 36815, fol. 28-9.
[2] *Ibid.*, fol. 34.   [3] vii. 180-6.

THOMAS LOVE PEACOCK

Anti-Jacobin could afford. In " his chaste verses,"
the reviewer said, " there is none of that disgusting
affectation, none of that quaint frippery of speech,
none of that tawdry tinsel in which the poetasters of
the present day delight in arraying their gaudy Muses.
. . . the ideas and the sentiments are not fantasti-
cally refined, nor laboriously worked up ; but flow
naturally from the lips of genius . . . and there runs
throughout the whole a vein of pleasing melancholy,
an affecting pathos, that keeps alive the interest in the
heart, and disposes the mind to suitable and profitable
reflection." [1] Peacock's treatment of the Rosamund
episode is made the opportunity for a covert hit at the
very recent *Lady of the Lake :* " A *northern* bard,
with the aid of a dog and a boat, which might easily
have been introduced, and without the addition of
a single idea, would have spun out this simple story
to the length of a whole canto, if not to a still greater
length." [2] The review concludes with the assurance
that the author is " evidently a man of good religious
and moral principles." Shelley, acknowledging the
receipt of the second edition of the poem two years
later, praised the poetical quality displayed, though
obliged to regret that so much talent had been wasted
in the praise of commerce and the glories of the
British flag as instrumental to the progress of " liberty,
truth, and virtue." [3] After a hundred years, unread
miles of verse stretch out behind us to the day when
topographical poems were in the mode, and we need
neither refute the opinions of this piece, nor ascribe

[1] *Anti-Jacobin*, xxxvii. 82.   [2] *Ibid.*, p. 84.
[3] *Letters*, p. 359.

42

much of the Thames' renown to Peacock's poetic catalogue of its beauties. What significance the poem has is chiefly biographical. At twenty-five the witty sceptic, later so pregnant in denial, is still forcing himself to affirmation with an utter neglect of the strategic advantage of being always questioner of all things. Whereas later he laughed at Mr. Philpot, the lover of rivers (ΦΙΛοΠΟΤαμος : *Fluviorum amans*) in *Crotchet Castle*, here he himself is the partisan of a favourite stream ; the critic of the commercial spirit ascribes to " imperial commerce " the subliming of Britain's power ; he who would never speak of priests without laughter, laments the last of the Druids ; while the inveterate mocker of universities addresses Oxford :

> "Long, Oxford, may the nations see
> A second Athens rise in thee!
> Long may thy favoured sons explore
> The darkest paths of ancient lore!
> Long hear thy gifted bards prolong
> The voice of rapture breathing song!
> While future Lockes, with ken refined,
> Explore the labyrinth of mind;
> And Newtons pass, on wings sublime,
> The barriers of the solar clime,
>   To trace, in spheres afar,
> The mighty cause, the eternal ONE,
> Whose spirit glows in every sun,
>   And lives in every star." [1]

Considerable time was still to elapse before Peacock realised in what direction his real skill lay, and finally acknowledged his true character by the production of satire.

[1] Only in the first edition, pp. 83–4.

THOMAS LOVE PEACOCK

Not improbably he conceived the idea, while on his expedition to Thames Head, of a still longer journey in the same direction. Just after the beginning of the new year he found his way into the most mountainous district of North Wales, and took up his residence at Maentwrog in Merionethshire, " the land of all that is beautiful in nature, and all that is lovely in woman." " This is a delightful spot," he wrote Hookham, January 20, " enchanting even in the gloom of winter ; in summer it must be a terrestrial paradise. It is a beautiful narrow vale, several miles in length, extending in one direction to the sea, and totally embosomed in mountains, the sides of which are covered, in many parts, with large woods of oak. My sitting-room has a bow-window, looking out on a lovely river, which flows through the vale. In the vicinity are many deep glens, along which copious mountain streams, of inconceivable clearness, roar over rocky channels, and numerous waterfalls of the most romantic character." [1]

Here Peacock spent some months in a house called " The Lodge," near Tan-y-bwlch, delighted with the splendour of the mountains and the rural solitude. He corrected the proof for *The Genius of the Thames*, read assiduously in the large number of books which he had sent out to him along with his personal effects, and explored all the surrounding country. One good woman of the neighbourhood was impressed with a horror of his eccentricity : " Oh ! there Mr. Peacock lived," she told Shelley later, " in a cottage near

[1] Brit. Mus. *Addit. MSS.*, 36815, fol. 36.

Tan-y-bwlch, associating with no one, and hiding his head like a murderer ; but he was *worse than that*,—he was an atheist ! " [1]   One of the few people the wicked fellow saw was, strangely enough, Dr. Gryffydh, the parson at Maentwrog, whom Peacock irreverently characterised in a letter to Hookham as " a little dumpy, drunken, mountain goat," and later caricatured as the Vicar of Llanglasrhyd in *Calidore*. Two extracts from another letter to Hookham deserve quotation.

" I sit down with a resolution to write a very long letter, so put on your nightcap and compose yourself at full length on the sofa. When your letter arrived last week, announcing the departure of my *library* and *wardrobe*, I resolved to devote the whole interval to exploring the vicinity, and have been climbing about the rocks and mountains, by the rivers and the sea, with indefatigable zeal, carrying in my mind the heroic triad, that a poet should have an eye that can see nature, a heart that can feel nature, and a resolution that dares follow nature : in obedience to which latter injunction I have nearly broken my neck. Now, were I to attempt a description of all I have seen, and felt, and followed, I might fill seven sheets of foolscap, and still leave the cream of the tale unskimmed : I shall therefore content myself with promising, when you come here in August (which may no evil genius prohibit !) to show you scenes of such exquisite beauty and of such overpowering sublimity, as, once beheld, can never be forgotten.

" The other day I prevailed on my new acquaint-

---

[1] Shelley, *Letters*, p. 368.

ance, Dr. Gryffydh, to accompany me at midnight
to the *black cataract*, a favorite haunt of mine,
about 2½ miles from hence. Mr. Lloyd, whom
I believe I have mentioned to you more than
once, volunteered to be of the party; and at 20
minutes past 11, lighted by the full-orbed moon, we
sallied forth, to the no small astonishment of mine
host, who protested he never expected to see us all
again. The effect was truly magnificent. The water
descends from a mountainous glen down a winding
rock, and then precipitates itself, in one sheet of
foam, over its black base, into a capacious bason, the
sides of which are all but perpendicular, and covered
with hanging oak and hazel. Evans, in the Cambrian
Itinerary, describes it as an abode of damp and horror,
and adds that the whole cataract cannot be seen in
one view, as the sides are too steep and slippery to
admit of clambering up, and the top of the upper
fall is invisible from below. Mr. Evans seems to have
labored under a small degree of alarm, which prevented accurate investigation, for I have repeatedly
climbed this *unattemptable* rock and obtained this
impossible view; as he or any one else might do with
very little difficulty; though Dr. Gryffydh, the other
night, trusting to a rotten branch, had a fall of
15 feet perpendicular, and but for an intervening
hazel, would infallibly have been hurled to the bottom.
But a similar mistake is not likely to occur in daylight." [1]

"There is more truth than poetry in the remark
of Wordsworth that ' as high as we have mounted in

[1] Brit. Mus. *Addit. MSS.*, 36815, fol. 40.

delight, in our dejection do we sink as low.' You saw this exemplified in me last summer, when I was sometimes skipping about the room, singing, and playing all sorts of ridiculous antics, at others doling out staves of sorrow, and meditating on daggers and laurel water. Such is the disposition of all votaries of the muses, and, in some measure, of all metaphysicians : for the sensitive and the studious are generally prone to melancholy, and the melancholy are usually subject to intervals of boisterous mirth. Poor Cowper was a lamentable instance, and Tasso, and Collins, and Chatterton—a list that might be prolonged almost *ad infinitum*. I do not mean to say that the effects of this morbid disposition are always so fatally exemplified as in the four I have mentioned, of whom three were driven to insanity, and one to suicide. Cratinus, Democritus, Horace, and others, have opined that a certain degree of *noncomposity* is essential to the poetical character, and I am inclined to think that there is considerable justice in the observation." [1]

These remarks on melancholy may have been occasioned in part by another acquaintance Peacock had already made. It will throw some light upon his attentions to Dr. Gryffydh to mention that the clergyman had a daughter, Jane, whom her father's friend, with pardonable superlatives, called " the most innocent, the most amiable, the most beautiful girl in existence." Miss Gryffydh pleased her admirer " by talking of Scipio and Hannibal, and the Emperor Otho " (Peacock planned a tragedy on Otho), as

[1] Brit. Mus. *Addit. MSS.*, 36815, fol., 41.

well as by her personal charms, so that he became more than interested. He did not, however, permit himself any declaration of his love—indeed, he seems to have fought against it. "It is now a month since I saw her," he wrote to Hookham, "and Richard is himself again."[1] That was June 12, and as the letters to Hookham later than August 18 have not been preserved, there is no way of knowing how far "the Carnarvonshire nymph" occupied Peacock's mind during the rest of the year. It is not even certain how long he remained in Wales, but at any rate he saw Miss Gryffydh again the following April, either at the end of a very long Welsh residence, or on the occasion of another visit, and took regretful leave of her before setting out on his walk homewards through South Wales. For eight years he did not see her again, even though he visited Wales once more two years later. That he did not forget her, the sequel clearly indicates, but he evidently felt that his fortunes did not justify him in seeking her in marriage, and he did not allow his ardour to force him into any employment which would have mended them. If his calm endurance of the hope deferred for almost a decade meets with the disapproval of that world which gives its suffrage to lovers, at any rate the unusual manner in which he proved his constancy after so long was sufficient to make Miss Gryffydh forgive the silent delay.

On his return to England Peacock walked first to Dolgelly, and the next day continued his journey on foot "through a succession of most sublime scenery

[1] Brit. Mus. *Addit. MSS.*, 36815, fol. 42.

to the pretty little lake, Tal-y-llyn, where is a small public house, kept by a most original character, who in the triple capacity of publican, schoolmaster, and guide to Cadair Idris, manages to keep the particles of his carcase in contact. I ascended the mountain with him, seated myself in the Giant's Chair, and 'looked from my throne of clouds o'er half the world.' The view from the summit of this mountain baffles description. It is the very sublimity of Nature's wildest magnificence. Beneath, the whole extent of Cardigan Bay; to the right, the immense chain of the Snowdonian mountains, partly smiling in sunshine, partly muffled in flying storm; to the left, the wide expanse of the southern principality, with all its mountain summits below us." [1] From Cadair Idris Peacock went to Machynlleth, from which a letter to Hookham says that he plans to proceed to Towyn, and Aberystwyth, and Hafod. " I have a clean shirt with me, and Luarch,[2] and Tacitus. I am in high health and spirits. On the top of Cadair Idris I felt how happy a man may be with a little money and a sane intellect, and reflected with astonishment and pity on the madness of the multitude." [3]

The remainder of the year saw the composition of *The Philosophy of Melancholy*, which may have been begun even before Peacock's departure from Wales. Announced in the *British Critic* for February, 1812,[4]

[1] *Thomas Love Peacock : Letters*, &c., pp. 43–4.
[2] This should be Luath, the name of the dog which accompanied him on many of his rambles.
[3] *Thomas Love Peacock : Letters*, &c., p. 44.
[4] xxxix. 211.

and in the *Monthly Magazine* as a new publication
for March,[1] it had already appeared in a handsome
quarto with Hookham's imprint by April, when
it was treated to an extended review in the *Anti-
Jacobin*.[2] The poem is considerably shorter than
The Genius of the Thames, but thick paper, wide
margins, large type, a formidable array of notes,
and the price of eighteen shillings, helped make
up a very satisfactory volume. It has never been
reprinted.

The title is something of a misnomer, for, although
the poem aims to justify solitary and meditative
habits by arguing in favour of the mental temper
which causes them, it does not educe a " philosophy "
of anything ; the title might better have been *The
Praise of Melancholy*. Like some other encomiums,
this one ascribes to its subject a good many qualities
which do not belong to it by any definition save the
author's. To Peacock, melancholy is not, as to Burton,
a disease, to be cured by various " rectifications,"
such as wholesome diet, " mirth and cheerful company," as well as by simples, but the thoughtful mood
to which the spirits of men are sobered at the con-
templation of perpetual flux and eternal accident.
This " philosophical melancholy " includes the sources
of virtue, and courage, and genius ; it is synonymous,
moreover, with the quality which the eighteenth
century called sensibility. Whoever takes pleasure
in external nature, especially mountain scenery,
in the ruined magnificence of the past, in painting,
music, poetry, art, romance, owes his enjoyment

[1] xxxiii. 272.   [2] xli. 337.

to the spirit of melancholy.   True, there is Comedy,
but—

> " Can the fantastic jest, the antic mirth,
>   The laugh, that charms the grosser sons of earth,
>   A joy so true, so softly sweet, bestow,
>   As genius gathers from the springs of woe?"[1]

Love, charity, and filial affection can be genuinely felt
only by the philosophically melancholy.   And finally,
it is only in this spirit that the mind can rise supreme to
calamity, and ascend to the elevation from which it can
be seen that apparent discord is only apparent, and that
the universe is really in the hands of an " all-perfect
wisdom which arranges the whole in harmony."

Criticism need not point out the confused sense
in which melancholy is used, nor the literary insin-
cerity evident in the greater part of the poem.   It is
sufficient to note that Peacock was little nearer to the
point of self-knowledge at the outset of 1812 than he
had been in his earlier poems.   More sincere, however,
and also better poetry, are the passages in which he
refers to his recent sojourn in Wales, and, as *The
Philosophy of Melancholy* is not now easily accessible,
they may be quoted as specimens of the poem.

> "Oh beauteous Meirion! Cambria's mountain-pride!
> Still memory sees thy eddying waters glide,
> As when, embowered in sweet Festiniog's vale,
> I shunned the storms that man's close haunts assail,
> Lulled by the ceaseless dash of confluent streams
> In fairy-fancies and Arcadian dreams.
> O'er the blue deep thy mossy castles frown :
> Thy mighty cataracts burst and thunder down:

---

[1] *Philosophy of Melancholy*, p. 26.

The rock-set ash, with tortuous branches grey,
Veils the deep glen, and drinks the flying spray;
And druid oaks extend their solemn shades
O'er the fair forms of Britain's loveliest maids.
　　Thee, melancholy! oft I hailed alone,
On Moëlwyn's heights, and Idris' stormy throne,
While mists and clouds, contracted or unfurled,
Now closed from view, now half-revealed the world.
　　By the wild glens, where struggling Cynfael raves,
On swift Velenrhyd breaks his echoing waves,
Sublime the task, in autumn's humid day,
To watch the impetuous torrents force their way,
High-swoln by rains, and chafing with the breeze,
Hurling the loosened stones, the uprooted trees,
With meteor-swiftness rushing from the steep,
To roll the mountain-havoc to the deep.
　　More wildly sweet, nor less sublime, the scene,
When winter smiled in cloudless skies serene,
When winds were still, and ice enchained the soil,
O'er its white bed to see the cataract toil.
The sheeted foam, the falling stream beneath,
Clothed the high rocks with frost-work's wildest wreath.
Round their steep sides the arrested ooze had made
A vast, fantastic, crystal colonnade:
The scattering vapor, frozen ere it fell,
With mimic diamonds spangled all the dell,
Decked the grey woods with many a pendent gem,
And gave the oak its wintry diadem " [1]

Another passage, if it reached the eyes of Miss Jane
Gryffydh, may have betrayed the unspoken secret of
a year before. In the midst of an address to mutual
love, the poet says :

---

[1] Pp. 14–16. Peacock refers to this same frozen cataract in a letter
to Hookham : " The sublime magnificence of the waterfalls in the frost—
when the old overhanging oaks are spangled with icicles, the rocks
sheeted with frozen foam, formed by the flying spray, and the water,
that oozes from their sides, congealed into innumerable pillars of crystal."
Feb. 26, 18.0.　Brit. Mus. *Addit. MSS.*, 36815, fol. 38.

EARLY POEMS

"If e'er in woodland shade, by Cynfael's urn,
  Thy altar saw my votive incense burn,
  May thy propitious star, thy deathless flower,
  Illume my path, and twine my rustic bower.
      May that fair form, ah! now too far remote!
  Whose glossy locks on ocean-breezes float;
  That tender voice, whose rapture-breathing thrill,
  Unheard so long, in fancy vibrates still;
  That Parian hand, that draws, with artless fire,
  The soul of music from her mountain-lyre;
  Led by thy planet from the billowy shore,
  Resume these groves, and never leave them more.
      Then let the torrent rage, the meteor fly,
  The storm-cloud blacken in December's sky!
  Love's syren voice, and music's answering shell,
  Shall cheer the simple genius of our cell:
  The plaintive ministrel's legendary strain
  One added charm of softest power shall gain,
  When she, whose heart thy purest fount supplies,
  Bids thy own songs, oh, melancholy! rise "[1]

In the same volume is included a "mythological ode" called *The Spirit of Fire*, in which that spirit finds a voice and utters a panegyric of itself to Mahomet at a time when he is subverting a fane of the Magi. The ode is Pindaric at least to the extent of being regular.

[1] Pp. 42–43.

CHAPTER III

SHELLEY—COMEDIES

THE year 1812 may be held to mark the close of Peacock's earlier poetic period. He ventured again upon two poems of a more or less elaborate type, but one was soon laid aside unfinished, and the other betrays few signs of the faults of his first volumes. It seems almost as if the pestilent gloom of these juvenile pieces had not been able to survive the attempt to formulate its principles in *The Philosophy of Melancholy*. The spirit of satire, overcome by panegyric in the struggle for *The Genius of the Thames*, grew gradually stronger, and finally Peacock himself was obliged to own it as a characteristic quality which he could not neglect in the pursuit of literary ambitions. At the same time his feeling for comedy developed rapidly and displaced the predilection for things tragic which seems to belong by right and practice to the formative stages of comic writers. Some may find it strange that this last development was parallel with his friendship for a man who had almost no comic sense himself, and whom no one would think likely to arouse it in others.

The circumstances and place of Peacock's first meeting with Shelley are not absolutely certain. On August 18, 1812, Shelley, then with his first wife at

Lynmouth in Devonshire, wrote to Hookham in acknowledgment of a parcel which he had received the night before from the publisher. It had contained a copy of the recent *Philosophy of Melancholy* and of the still more recent second edition of *The Genius of the Thames*. Shelley was full of admiration for the genius and learning displayed in the latter volume— *The Philosophy of Melancholy* he had not yet had time to read—and only regretted, he said, " that my powers are so circumscribed as to prevent me from becoming extensively useful to your friend." [1] This remark makes it seem that Hookham had recommended Peacock to the notice of the ardent young reformer, heir to a baronetcy, as a worthy man of letters who had received quite inadequate recognition. Apparently the poets were not yet personally acquainted, but met soon after. The place of meeting has ordinarily been given as Nant Gwillt, near Rhayadr in Radnorshire, where Shelley stayed during April, May, and part of June. But there is no record to indicate that Peacock was in Wales at all during 1812, and, moreover, he declares specifically [2] that he visited Nant Gwillt at a subsequent date for the sake of seeing the spot which he had doubtless heard Shelley praise. Peacock says that he " saw Shelley for the first time in 1812, just before he went to Tanyrallt." [3] As Shelley went twice to Tanyrallt that year, once directly from Lynmouth, and again after his visit to London to raise funds for the embankment scheme of Madocks, Peacock's remark might still leave a

[1] *Letters*, p. 359.   [2] *Memoirs of Shelley* (1909), p. 26.
[3] *Ibid.*, p. 28.

55

difficulty, if it were not clear that he thought [1] Shelley had come first from Lynmouth to London. There can be no reasonable doubt, then, that Hookham introduced the two men some time during Shelley's visit to London in October and the early part of November.

The acquaintance did not become intimate at once. Peacock's superior age and learning, his keen intellect, many-sided interests, and genuine hatred of intolerance, however, could not fail to impress the generous Shelley, much as the latter may have missed in Peacock the true revolutionary fire. Writing to Hogg, though a year later, Shelley said of his new friend : " He is a very mild, agreeable man, and a good scholar. His enthusiasm is not very ardent, nor his views very comprehensive ; but he is neither super-stitious, ill-tempered, dogmatical, or proud." [2] It is likely that when Shelley sent to Clio Rickman on December 24 for books he included in the list Mon-boddo's *Origin and Progress of Language*, Sir William Drummond's *Essay on a Punic Inscription*, and Horne Tooke's *Diversions of Purley*, solely on Peacock's recommendation. All these books were favourites of the latter, while Shelley would scarcely have turned to them, even with his curiosity, had they not been suggested to him. Peacock had already sent Shelley some verses in which he censured the Welsh, much to Shelley's pleasure, as it appears from a letter to Hookham on December 3. The reference seems to be to the *Farewell to Meirion*, which has not yet had any

---

[1] *Memoirs of Shelley*, p. 26.
[2] *Letters*, p. 415.

date whatever assigned to it, but which probably
indicates the mood in which Peacock had left Wales
the year before.

> "Meirion, farewell! thy sylvan shades,
> Thy mossy rocks and bright cascades,
> Thy tangled glens and dingles wild,
> Might well detain the Muses' child.
> But can the son of science find,
> In thy fair realm, one kindred mind,
> One soul sublime, by feeling taught,
> To wake the genuine pulse of thought,
> One heart by nature formed to prove
> True friendship and unvarying love?
> No—Bacchus reels through all thy fields,
> Her brand fanatic frenzy wields,
> And ignorance with falsehood dwells,
> And folly shakes her jingling bells.
> Meirion, farewell—and ne'er again
> My steps shall press thy mountain reign,
> Nor long on thee my memory rest
> (Fair as thou art—unloved, unblest)
> And ne'er may parting stranger's hand
> Wave a fond blessing on thy land,
> Long as disgusted virtue flies
> From folly, drunkenness, and lies,
> Long as insulted science shuns
> The steps of thy degraded sons,
> Long as the northern tempest roars
> Round their inhospitable doors."

These verses, with their strange forgetfulness of
the presence of Jane Gryffydh in the land thus anathe-
matised and their splenetic resolution of exile from
the beauties of Meirion, did not hinder another trip to
Wales on the part of Peacock in the summer of 1813.
During the preceding winter or spring he had varied his
classical studies with the composition of *Sir Hornbook ;*

or, *Childe Launcelot's Expedition*, which he called *a Grammatico-Allegorical Ballad*, and which is a kind of grammatical pellet in the sugar-coating of a nursery rhyme. It had considerable popularity for nearly half a century.[1] The summer found him again roving, but of his second Welsh expedition nothing is known save that he visited the neighbourhood of Tanyrallt, where he heard people discuss the mysterious assault upon Shelley, and that he did not see Miss Gryffydh. Probably on his journey to Wales, though it may have been the following year, he visited in Leicestershire with an old friend, a Mrs. Simpson, formerly Mrs. Ebenezer Roebuck, whose son, J. A. Roebuck, at that time but a boy, later gave an account of Peacock as he then appeared.

"Whilst in Gumley, Leicestershire, we had a visitor, a friend of my mother's—who in after years was the cause of a mighty effect upon my whole life. This was Thomas Love Peacock, who excited my curiosity by his conversation. He was at the time studying Greek, was reading some Greek dramatist and a commentator, and excited the wonder of the farmers who came into the house by reading, as they said, two books at once. He used to sit on a chair on one side of the fire, at a sort of shelf, which drew out of the wall, which shelf held his books, and in the evening his light. Every day after breakfast he folded about a dozen paper boats, which he told me he was accustomed to sail or set afloat in any piece of water

---

[1] See *Bibliography*. The book seems not to have appeared until 1814. It was reviewed in the *British Critic*, new series, i. 543 (May 1814).

which he found in his walk—which walk he began as soon as his boats were made, and continued till our dinner, which was about five o'clock, P.M. These long solitary walks, his paper boats, his books, and the fact that he was a poet, made him a sort of mysterious being to the country people, who certainly were afraid of him." [1]

It is barely possible that Peacock's habit of being caustic and mystifying in his dealing with the farmers may have worked quite as much upon their fears as the harmless practice of sailing boats, or of reading books, or even as much as his reputation for possession by a poetical demon.

The events of the next few years of his life are known mostly because of his association with Shelley. On Peacock's return from Wales in the late summer or autumn of 1813, he found that Shelley, whom he had seen once or twice that spring, had taken the house called " High Elms " at Bracknell, and he went thither for a visit on Shelley's invitation. " At Bracknell, Shelley was surrounded by a numerous society, all in a great measure of his own opinions in relation to religion and politics, and the larger portion of them in relation to vegetable diet. But they wore their rue with a difference. Every one of them, adopting some of the articles of the faith of their general church, had each nevertheless some predominant crotchet of his or her own, which left a number of open questions for earnest and not always temperate discussion. I was sometimes irreverent enough to laugh at the fervour with which

[1] Roebuck, *Autobiography* (1897), p. 8.

opinions utterly unconducive to any practical result were battled for as matters of the highest importance to the well-being of mankind; Harriet Shelley was always ready to laugh with me, and we thereby both lost caste with some of the more hot-headed of the party."[1] The Newtons and Boinvilles, indeed, were not the sort of people to appeal very strongly to Peacock, nor yet, on the other hand, to take pleasure in the amused scepticism with which he honoured their flights. They were annoyed at his common sense, piqued by his failure to sympathise with them, and jealous of the friendship which Shelley felt for him. A mere cold scholar, Mrs. Newton thought him, without taste or feeling. She was sure that Shelley, " whose warm nature craves sympathy," would sooner or later discover Peacock's shortcomings and relinquish the new acquaintance for his more rapturous friends. But the " two or three sentimental young butchers, an eminently philosophical tinker, and several very unsophisticated medical practitioners" who made up, according to Hogg, the coterie at Bracknell, were disappointed in the hope that the intimacy would speedily cease. When the Shelleys set out for Edinburgh about the beginning of October, Peacock made one of the party. They proceeded by the way of Warwick, the Lakes, Keswick, and probably Matlock, to the Scottish capital, where they remained until nearly Christmas. As this journey was undertaken in secret, we know little of the details of the stay, save that the two men studied together, and that under Peacock's direction, in a mental atmosphere

[1] *Memoirs of Shelley*, pp. 29–30.

the antipodes of that of the affected circle at Bracknell, the young poet busied himself with the restrained and wholesome art of Greece which had so great an influence upon his later work. Peacock was a better guide in such matters than might appear from his previous poems. They had represented but a literary fashion, and were only in small degree illustrative of his real character. In reading or discussion he was not, in 1813, much the junior of the author of *Nightmare Abbey*.

Toward the end of the year the Shelleys returned to take a house at Windsor, while it is to be conjectured that Peacock, who may or may not have returned with them, went to live at Chertsey. For Peacock the winter passed uneventfully. His granddaughter is of the opinion that he was translating novels from the French for Hookham, and in all likelihood one or another of his comedies received his attention during the same time. A letter to the *Morning Chronicle*, dated April 8, points out a parallel between the speech of Phædra's nurse in the *Hippolytus* of Euripides and Hamlet's soliloquy. To this same winter or spring may likewise be ascribed the composition of the fragment of *Ahrimanes* which has been preserved in manuscript with an elaborate prose outline for its continuation. The limits to the date of its composition seem tolerably certain. Shelley quoted the motto from it near the end of June,[1] a fact which probably indicates that the poem itself was then more or less advanced, while its inception, as the subject attests, could not have antedated the

---

[1] *Memoirs of Shelley*, p. 48.

visit which Peacock paid to Bracknell the preceding year. *Ahrimanes* is an attempt to poetize, with twelve cantos in the Spenserian measure, the zodiacal system which was so amusing a crotchet of Mr. Newton, Shelley's friend at Bracknell. Peacock did not get much beyond a single canto, but the very undertaking shows from how thin a soil these early poems of his sprang. He was still willing to begin an elaborate poem on an astrological subject, in which he could not have had the slightest tincture of belief, and at which, indeed, he later laughed heartily in his sketch of the character of Mr. Newton.[1] It is testimony to his growing maturity, however, that there is less bathos and poetical tip-toeing in the fragment than in *The Philosophy of Melancholy*. In addition, the book of the strife between Oromazes and Ahrimanes for the possession of the world has yet another great superiority to its predecessor—it remained unfinished and unpublished.[2] To all appearances, Peacock soon wearied of his plan and threw it aside, perhaps because he found more congenial occupation in writing his first satire.

The British Critic for March 1814 announced in the " Monthly List of Publications " *Sir Proteus, a satirical Ballad. By P. M. O'Donovan, Esq.*[3] In this ballad, consisting of six parts and an *envoi*,

---

[1] *Memoirs of Shelley*, pp. 30–32.

[2] It was edited for the *Modern Language Review* (vol. iv. No. 2) from the holograph in the British Museum (*Addit. MSS.*, 36816, fol. 1 *ff.*), by Dr. Young. This version is highly inaccurate, but most of the worst errors were pointed out by Mr. Brett-Smith, in the same journal vol. iv., No. 4). The fragment is also included in Dr. Garnett's *Thomas Love Peacock : Letters*, &c.

[3] New series, i. 335.

Peacock attacked pretty much the whole world of contemporary letters, paying special attention to Southey, Coleridge, Wordsworth, Montgomery, Sir John Carr, Scott, and the reviews. The piece has a heavily sarcastic dedication to Lord Byron, without any of the easy aloofness which may free ironic personalities from the appearance of bad taste. Lord Byron himself only laughed off the matter with a brusque quotation from Dr. Johnson, " Are we alive after all this censure ? " [1] It must be owned that P. M. O'Donovan, Esq., put into his notes, by far the most important part of the satire, a Juvenalian indignation which little in the objects of his wrath called for. It was much as if he had renounced all indulgence in the department of literary foible himself, and now intended to reform the rest of the poetical world with the zeal of a converted offender. In so serious a business he kept the poem quite barren of the quality of easy badinage which might have been a prophecy of *Headlong Hall*.

Some time in June Shelley sent for Peacock to come up to London, where the satirist found his young friend in fearful perturbation over the conflict between his old feelings for Harriet and his newly conceived love for Mary Godwin. This is not the place to discuss Shelley's marital difficulties ; too many pens have done that already. It is enough to say that Peacock took Harriet's part with stout resolution, utterly refused then or later to believe that there had ever been any mutual compact to their separation, and was " content to rest the explanation of his [Shelley's]

[1] Byron, *Letters and Journals*, ed. Prothero (1898–1901), iii. 89–90.

conduct on the ground on which he rested it himself
—that he had found in another the intellectual
qualities which constituted his ideality of the partner
of his life." [1] Peacock's championship of Harriet
very probably kept Shelley from making him a con-
fidant as he might have done under other circumstances, but there is no just ground for denying that
Peacock, keen observer and sensible judge that he
was, has a right to be heard before Harriet Shelley
suffers condemnation from her husband's ardent
vindicators. When the eloping lovers were at Troyes
on their continental tour, Shelley wrote to his wife
that he had left directions for her support with
Peacock, who, though he was "expensive, incon-
siderate, and cold," [2] would not forget his obligation and would render her any needful assistance.
Peacock did so, and on Shelley's return was almost
the sole friend who resumed friendship at once on
the old footing. Even Hogg was not reconciled for
several weeks, but Peacock, during this anger of
Hogg's, and later, when Hogg had resumed the old
intercourse, was a frequent caller in the evening and
often walked out with Shelley during the day.
Apparently Peacock and his mother removed to
London some time between the early part of September,
when he witnessed the driving of the deer into Windsor
Park,[3] and the end of October, when Shelley was
obliged to take refuge from his creditors at Peacock's
apartments in the Southampton Buildings, Chancery

[1] *Memoirs of Shelley*, p. 65.
[2] *Letters*, p. 427.
[3] See *The Last Day of Windsor Forest*, in *Calidore*, &c., pp. 151–53.

Lane. Very early in the new year Shelley had an opportunity to do a similar service in return for the protection given him, for it appears from Mary Shelley's diary [1] that in January 1815 Peacock was actually arrested for debt and had to appeal for help to his friend. To judge from Shelley's previous unkind reference to the interest which would keep Peacock warm on Harriet's behalf,[2] there had already been assistance, or promise of assistance, given, and certainly after Shelley came to terms with his father, he increased the debt of Peacock's gratitude by making him an annuity of one hundred pounds.[3]

When Shelley took a house at Bishopsgate in August 1815, Peacock had already returned from London to Marlow, and, the distance between the two villages being short, frequently walked over to spend a few days with his friend. He acted as Shelley's guide to many places in the neighbourhood, and accompanied the Shelleys and Charles Clairmont when, at the end of the summer, they set out to row as far as possible toward the source of the Thames. Starting from Old Windsor, they ascended the river by easy stages to Lechlade, " and as much higher as there was water to float our skiff. It was a dry season, and we did not get much beyond Inglesham Weir, which was not then, as now, an immovable structure, but the wreck of a movable weir, which had been subservient to the navigation, when the river had been, as it had long ceased to be, navigable to Cricklade. A solitary sluice was hanging by a

---

[1] Mrs. Marshall, *Mary Wollstonecraft Shelley* (1889), i. 104–5.
[2] *Letters*, p. 427.
[3] Dowden, *Shelley* (1886), ii. 114.

chain, swinging in the wind and creaking dismally. Our voyage terminated at a spot where the cattle stood entirely across the stream, with the water scarcely covering their hoofs." [1] On the way up they had conceived the scheme of going through the Thames and Severn Canal and then proceeding to the head of the Severn. Shelley, with characteristic enthusiasm, even proposed that they extend their journey beyond North Wales, to Durham and the Lakes, upon the Tweed, out to the Forth, and even to the falls of the Clyde; but as the Severn Canal could not be passed for less than £20, his fine project fell through, and they turned back to Old Windsor, which they reached after an absence of about ten days. Years later the guests of Ebenezer MacCrotchet, Esq., of Crotchet Castle, did not consider such an obstacle of moment, being rich and fictitious, and so carried out in the novel the very journey which their real prototypes had planned. The voyage in *Crotchet Castle* owes its general outlines and many of its details to the trip of 1815. It was at Oxford on the way up that the earlier expedition halted to visit the scene of Shelley's discomfiture at the hands of orthodoxy, and that Peacock offered the valuable prescription, " Three mutton chops, well peppered," [2] which relieved Shelley of the ills his vegetable regimen had brought on.

Charles Clairmont wrote an account of the voyage for his sister, one paragraph of which says : " Peacock was here when I came ; with him I was a good deal

[1] *Memoirs of Shelley*, p. 54.
[2] *Ibid.*, p. 55.

pleased from the first ; I am so still, and should have been more so if Shelley had not prejudiced me.   He seems an idly-inclined man ; indeed, he is professedly so in the summer ; he owns he cannot apply himself to study, and thinks it more beneficial to him, as a human being, entirely to devote himself to the beauties of the season while they last ; he was only happy while out from morning till night.   I readily joined him in his daily excursions.   Peacock is perfectly acquainted with this part of the country ; he has lived here the chief part of his life." [1]   Just how Shelley had prejudiced Clairmont against Peacock is not clear ; probably it was by something he had said during a fit of petulance at Peacock's mocking laughter and apparent coldness toward projects for universal and immediate reform.

Headlong Hall must have been begun very soon after the return from Lechlade, but no hint of it occurs till its announcement at the end of the year. After a summer of out-of-door pleasures, Peacock now retired to his winter studies, very often carried on at Bishopsgate, whither he walked frequently from Marlow.   Hogg used often to walk down from London.   " This winter was, as Mr. Hogg expressed it, a mere Atticism.   Our studies were exclusively Greek." [2]   It was Peacock who furnished Shelley with the title for his *Alastor ; or, The Spirit of Solitude*, and later he was always amused to see how frequently the lack of Greek scholarship led people to think Alastor the name of the hero, instead of recognising

[1] Dowden, i. 528.
[2] *Memoirs of Shelley*, p. 55.

the true significance of the word. During Shelley's tour on the Continent in the summer of 1816, Peacock acted for him in certain financial arrangements with Harriet [1] and in looking out for a house which the Shelleys might occupy on their return. He seems to have been engaged on some kind of " historical labours," to judge by a letter from Shelley,[2] but beyond this almost nothing is known of his life or work. *Melincourt*, however, had been begun before the end of September. By that time the travellers were back in Marlow. " At the end of August, 1816 [really not until September 8], they returned to England, and Shelley passed the first fortnight with me at Marlow. July and August, 1816, had been months of perpetual rain. The first fortnight of September was a period of unbroken sunshine. The neighbourhood of Marlow abounds with beautiful walks ; the river scenery is also fine. We took every day a long excursion, either on foot or on the water." [3] After a residence of several weeks at Bath, Shelley visited Peacock again early in December, and when a little later the sad news of Harriet's suicide reached them, Peacock was one of those who were consulted, and who strongly urged an immediate legalising of the union with Mary Godwin.

A letter from Shelley on December 8 had promised to introduce Peacock to Leigh Hunt ; and early in April Peacock probably met Godwin for the first time, when that indignant moralist finally agreed to forgive his son-in-law and visited him at Marlow.

[1] Dowden, ii. 64.   [2] *Letters*, p. 504.
[3] *Memoirs of Shelley*, p. 60.

Shelley, Godwin, and Peacock went to Bisham Wood and on the river to Medmenham Abbey. The following summer beheld many long walks throughout the surrounding country, on which they "saw everything worth seeing within a radius of sixteen miles. This comprehended, among other notable places, Windsor Castle and Forest, Virginia Water, and the spots which were consecrated by the memories of Cromwell, Hampden, and Milton, in the Chiltern district of Buckinghamshire. We had also many pleasant excursions, rowing and sailing on the river, between Henley and Maidenhead."[1] A feature of these walking tours was dinner at the various inns in the neighbourhood. Peacock maintained that the infallible sign of a well-kept inn was the state of its mustard-pot and *cabinet*, and he and the humorous Hogg, who was frequently of the party, would oftentimes astonish an innkeeper by walking into the house, demanding without explanation to see those prophetic objects, and then leaving or staying as their condition decided. As this was done without a smile, it probably caused occasional astonishment. Their journeys often reached as far as to London, thirty-two miles away, which they reached by going across "fields, lanes, woods, and heaths," to Uxbridge, and then by the high road into the city. There they generally remained two nights, frequently spent at the theatre, and returned on the third day. It was during the Marlow residence that Peacock attempted to overcome Shelley's prejudice against the theatre. He took him to *The School for Scandal*,

---

[1] *Memoirs of Shelley*; p. 62.

which so displeased Shelley that he never went to another comedy, to Dean Milman's *Fazio*, which he enjoyed, and to Italian opera, of which he became an assiduous frequenter. Leigh Hunt and his wife came to visit the Shelleys several times during this summer. The late Dr. Furnivall used to tell that his father, Shelley's physician, once came upon Peacock, Hunt, and Shelley in an ardent discussion concerning the merits and general desirability of suicide, of which Peacock claimed to be particularly enamoured. They had just decided that suicide was one of the necessities of life, when the unpersuaded man of physic, to test their sincerity in this new article of faith, offered them enough poison to gratify their taste for mortality. Thereupon they all grew sceptical with convenient speed. Mrs. Shelley and Mrs. Hunt sometimes accompanied the shorter expeditions, but they perhaps found Peacock's sarcastic temper less pleasing than did their husbands. A letter from Mrs. Shelley seems to indicate that she never quite forgave the champion of her predecessor in Shelley's affection. "Peacock dines here every day, *uninvited*, to drink his bottle. I have not seen him ; he morally disgusts me ; and Marianne [Mrs. Hunt] says that he is very ill-tempered." [1]

Toward the end of the year Peacock was engaged on poetical work of his own, but he probably found time to serve on the "literary committee" which assisted in the revision of *Laon and Cythna*, and to help the Shelleys in the study of Italian, when, shortly after the beginning of 1818, they began preparations

[1] Dowden, ii. 141.

for going to Italy. Gossip had it at the time [1] that Shelley was leaving because of the systematic plundering he had suffered from his impecunious dependents, especially from that resolute philosopher, William Godwin, who used to grow so violent in his entreaties for money that Shelley was accustomed to send for Peacock to protect him from annoyance. It would be pleasant to know how this was accomplished, but as Peacock was quite able to take care of himself, doubtless the satirist did not come off badly in his encounters with the panegyrist of reason. During the brief stay of Shelley's party in London just before their departure, Peacock, who had now begun to be called "Il Pavone" in Jane Clairmont's diary,[2] was a frequent guest in the evenings, along with Hunt, Keats, Godwin, Novello, and Charles and Mary Lamb. He saw his friend last on the evening of March 10, when, having come in from the first performance in England of an opera of Rossini, *Il Barbiere di Siviglia*, he took supper with the family, and then said the farewell which proved final.

Although Shelley kept constantly in communication with his friend during the few years which remained to him, the parting in March 1818 closed a chapter in Peacock's life. Within a few months he had produced his caricature of Shelley in *Nightmare Abbey*, and only a little later was transformed into an East India official whose idle days were over. Their friendship had been a reasonably close one, but it was not productive of any of the great changes

[1] Miss Mitford, *Letters*, 2nd series (1872), i. 51.
[2] Dowden, ii. 179.

sometimes elicited by ardent friendships between men of letters. The minute student is able to point out a few insignificant references to *Melincourt*, Shelley's favourite among the novels, in *Œdipus Tyrannus* and *Peter Bell*,[1] and it is held that *Alastor* and *The Revolt of Islam* are under some vague obligations to *Ahrimanes*. By descent into the infinitesimal, he may note that the word " hupaithric," for which the New English Dictionary gives no example but Shelley's use of it in *The Revolt of Islam*, becomes anglicised in the second line of *Rhododaphne* to " hypæthric," of which the wide drag-net of the great word-hoard seems to have encountered no example at all. The poem on Otho which Shelley projected and begun in 1817 may not unnaturally have owed its origin to Peacock, among whose manuscripts [2] has been preserved a carefully written title-page and a list of *dramatis personæ* for *Otho, a Tragedy*—an undertaking which never went beyond the plan. But these are the merest fragments of an influence, and practically negligible. Nor did the style of either man take on the colour of that of

---

[1] When Shelley speaks of the " name which orthodoxy loves, Court Journal or legitimate Review," in *Œdipus Tyrannus* (*Poetical Works*, ed. Forman, 1882, ii. 341), it is possible that he alludes to the *Legitimate Review* of *Melincourt*. The outcry of critical desire, "Oh that mine enemy had written a book ! " with which Part VI. of *Peter Bell* begins, had already been uttered by Mr. Feathernest in *Melincourt* (*Works*, i. 174). Moreover, stanzas 13, 15, and 16 of the same Part VI. are probably reminiscent of Peacock. Speaking of Kant's writings, Shelley says, " A friend too spoke in their dispraise,—He never read them," an allusion that may well be to Peacock. (See the note to *Melincourt* (*Works*, i. 242), for additional light on these stanzas.) The punning name "P. Verbovale," in stanza 16, is explained by an eminently Peacockian etymology ; while in the same note with the whimsical etymologising is a reference to "*pure anticipated cognition*," one of the phrases which Peacock ridicules again and again.

[2] Brit. Mus. *Addit. MSS.*, 36816, fol. 198.

his friend, although *Rhododaphne* is a clearer, brighter poem than any of the long pieces which Peacock wrote before 1812. Whatever obligation Shelley owed his friend was for much ironic criticism and a new interest in sounder literary models than those which had attracted his youth. That uncritical adulation, with which the Bracknell coterie had tried to spoil him, was by no means forthcoming from the " Laughing Philosopher " and invincible Grecian, sceptical of progress, who contested with common sense the wild enthusiasm of Shelley, explained away mystery with reasons, and laid ghosts with a jest. It is true that in the upper reaches of poetry Peacock could not be companion to his friend. What Shelley required, however, was never stimulus to his poetical rapture, but restraint to his extravagant theories. There can be no more doubt that Peacock helped in this regard, although, of course, he must not be given credit for the natural influence of a rapidly maturing taste and judgment in Shelley himself during the years 1813 to 1816, than that Peacock's direction in the classical studies of the same years was contributory to the introduction into Shelley's work of newer and higher tendencies. Upon Peacock, on the other hand, the friendship did not fail to have its effect as well. He had the experience, common in men who associate with younger friends, of recognising in Shelley some of the identical extravagances of opinion by which he himself had been possessed but a few years before. Now, it is only a step from the discovery that one was foolish in the past to the search for folly in one's present self, and Peacock would be prompt in suppressing signs of a mood which he might have coddled at twenty-one, but which he now branded as affectation and unwisdom since he had viewed its counterpart in another. Thereon followed naturally the ridicule of all similar pretensions, and the final willingness to allow the germ of satire, long dormant, opportunity for growth. Such a psychological development, by no means uncommon, is of course much longer and more complex than a curt enumeration of its successive degrees may seem to indicate. But it is a comprehensible one, and it is to all appearances the one which Peacock experienced in his relations with Shelley. That Shelley was a great poet, and that his *furor poeticus* was no folly, is a contention, however true, quite beside the point. The point is, that Peacock recognised in its external manifestations sundry traits which he accordingly discarded from himself, and with them discarded practically all that had impelled him to his early poems. What was left him was a satirical bent, and to that he gave good play in the novels which constitute his claim to literary attention. This contemporary progress of Shelley from *Queen Mab* to *Alastor* and of Peacock from *The Philosophy of Melancholy* to *Headlong Hall*, is an interesting example of the interaction of two strong personalities, where, instead of an attraction of qualities, there occurs a mental repulsion which brings out strongly the genuine character of each and casts aside the less important characteristics which they had in common.

The two comedies from Peacock's pen which, after lying in manuscript for nearly a century, have been recently published by Dr. Young, almost certainly belong to the five or six years preceding the appearance of *Headlong Hall*. The fact that a preliminary sketch for one of the songs in *The Dilettanti* has been preserved on paper made in 1807,[1] serves to fix the earliest limit for the date of that play, while Peacock's remark to Hookham on November 28, 1808, that he " would give the world to be at home, and devote the whole winter to the composition of a comedy," may have been in the spirit of prophecy as regards this very piece. There is, however, no account in the letters to Hookham of any dramatic undertaking, and so it seems best to take Tactic's plan for going with his bride to a farm in the mountains of Wales as testimony that *The Dilettanti* was written after Peacock's first Welsh expedition in 1810. There can be no doubt that the second comedy, *The Three Doctors*, belongs to a date after 1810, for its scene is laid, with realistic detail, at the seat of a Welsh squire in Merioneth.[2] As *Headlong Hall* borrows freely from *The Three Doctors*, and in a less degree from *The Dilettanti*, the posterior limit is obvious. Of these two, *The Dilettanti* seems the earlier. There is a general air of immaturity in its likeness to contemporary farces, which has been more or less outgrown in *The Three Doctors*, although even here the later Peacock appears only in patches. Rapid, somewhat boisterous action, and moderately clever dialogue, constitute the chief virtues of the two pieces. But the learning, witty allusions, ironic satire, and occasional

---

[1] Brit. Mus. *Addit. MSS.*, 36816, fol. 47.

[2] A writer in *The United States Magazine and Democratic Review* (New York) for June 1845, declared that Squire Headlong was studied from an actual person in Wales (xvi. 581).

lyrical outbreaks of *Headlong Hall and Maid Marian* are not present. Moreover, Peacock loses immensely from his incapacity to indulge in the sardonic comment which is the soul of his later work. Whether he realised these shortcomings himself, there is no telling; more than likely his comedies remained in the kindly obscurity of manuscript, where they might very well have been left, because he could find no manager to produce them. At any rate, when he later hit upon the novel form, he had no hesitation in plundering himself for material. Thus Mr. Chromatic, the fiddler of *Headlong Hall*, owes his name to the fiddler of *The Dilettanti;* Humphrey Hippy, Esq., in *Melincourt*, is under a similar obligation to Squire Hippy in *The Three Doctors;* Marmaduke Milestone of the same farce not only lends his name to *Headlong Hall*, but is taken over body, soul, and occupation, even to several speeches; Sir Peter Paxarett, deceased, of *The Three Doctors* bequeaths a tender and convivial memory to the song, " In his last binn SIR PETER lies," in *Headlong Hall*, and contributes also a name, perhaps a son, in the person of Sir Telegraph Paxarett, who adorns one of the pages of *Melincourt* [1] with a song which he slyly quotes from the unpublished comedy; Sir Patrick O'Prism of *Headlong Hall* displays a similar commendable, but unexpected and unconfessed, knowledge of manuscript sources by quoting from his compatriot, the gallant O'Fir of *The Three Doctors;* [2] and last, not least, *The Three Doctors* has the incident of a tumble into the water which Peacockian comedy seems never able to dispense with. The

[1] *Works*, i. 94. [2] *Ibid.*, i. 48, and *Plays*, p. 152.

songs in the farces are generally inferior to the later ones.

It was probably as the result of some acquaintance formed while trying to get his plays produced that Peacock was asked to write the Prologue and Epilogue for John Tobin's posthumous piece, *The Faro Table ; or, The Guardians*, which, under the second title, was brought out for the first time at Drury Lane, November 5, 1816. The play ran several nights,[1] but was not a success, and was soon withdrawn. In the printed version of the same year, Peacock's Prologue was mistakenly given as by E. Peacock, Esq., but his Epilogue, spoken by Harley in the character of Hint, was omitted, and another, partly by Tobin, took its place.

[1] *European Magazine,* lxx. 454.

CHAPTER IV

"HEADLONG HALL"—"MELINCOURT"

PEACOCK's first novel was written some time during 1815 and advertised as having been published in December of that year,[1] but the title-page of the first edition, in accordance with a not uncommon practice, bears the date 1816. Nothing is known as to the details of composition except that, obviously, *Headlong Hall* was attempted after *The Three Doctors* had failed of a hearing, and some of the material of the play was taken over to serve in the tale. The partial identity of Mr. Escot and Mr. Foster, moreover, with Peacock and Shelley respectively, probably points to an origin for the story in the duels of opinion which the two friends had fought in their walks of the preceding summer and fall. But *Headlong Hall* is neither a comedy padded with stage directions and extended asides to the proportions of a novel nor the bare record of a series of conversations. It is the first appearance of the true Peacock, almost fully matured, and with a worthy score of crotchets on his crown. In the main he does not follow a native tradition in fiction as much as he does his French models, the *contes* of the eighteenth century; but it is well to remember that such novels as George Walker's very clever, though

[1] *British Critic*, new series, iv. 675.

forgotten *Vagabond* (1799), and Isaac Disraeli's *Vaurien* (1797) and *Flim-Flams* (1805), had earlier shown almost the same influence in the embodiment of opinion in fiction, and that they, too, had satirised living Englishmen. Peacock's specific indebtedness to any predecessor is slight. Professor Saintsbury has already pointed out [1] that Miss Cranium, "the beautiful Cephalis," clearly owes her name to "la belle Cephalide" of Marmontel's *Marriages samnites, anecdote ancienne*, and the reader interested in analogues may remember, when Mr. Escot, ardent vegetarian that he is, helps himself liberally to slices of beef, that he has an amusing prototype in the virtuous Ariste of *Le Philosophe soi-disant*, who likewise varied his avowed herbivorous principles with occasional carnivorous practice. The term philosopher, as applied to Mr. Escot, Mr. Foster, and Mr. Jenkison, is a direct translation of *philosophe* as used in French revolutionary fiction, while the reverend Dr. Gaster, his name amusingly taken from the Greek Γαστήρ, stomach (*Venter, et præterea nihil*, Peacock's charitable explanation has it), and who was "of course neither a philosopher nor a man of taste," owes his existence less to the amenities of English theological controversy than to the sorry rôle played by the ecclesiastic in French satirical literature from the mediæval fabliaux to the romances of the Revolution. In a fashion less direct, *Headlong Hall* constantly reminds one of French comic writings by a clearness of conception and a certain witty elegance not characteristically English.

---

[1] *Maid Marian*, &c., ed. Saintsbury (1895), p. viii.

It mocks with equal delight the stupidity of the orthodox and the headstrong folly of heretics ; it is satisfied
to affirm nothing, yet to judge all things ; its standard
is the common sense which laughs at extreme notions
as untenable by a sane philosophy, and at passionate
belief as likely to be subversive of the comfort of well-
bred society. *Headlong Hall* exceeds the majority of
its French models in freedom from any genuine
polemic attempt. Years later Peacock expressed himself as much gratified when one of his readers, who
was also an acquaintance, was unable to find out which
characters in the novels represented the author's own
opinions.[1] His characters, indeed, for all they lack
in verisimilitude, are not avowedly mere types, sufficiently identified by the names Philosopher, Geometer,
Prince, or Savant, who live in the land of Nowhere
and undertake wonderful journeys in the neighbourhood in quest of enlightenment. Peacock's philosophers and worthy Welshmen pretend to humanity in
externals. At the same time, his ideals of comic
writing did not render him at all scrupulous in
furnishing them out completely in that regard. Aristophanes, Petronius, Rabelais, Swift, and Voltaire, all
his masters, belong, he said,[2] to the class of comic
writers who deliberately make implied or embodied
opinions the main matter of the fiction, while the
characters are kept subordinate. It was to a natural
bent toward actuality that Peacock owed the com-
promise he effected in his fiction between his favourite,
the type which neglects character for opinion, and

[1] *Calidore*, p. 18.   [2] *London Review*, ii. 70.

the type which does the reverse. He bridged the gap by allowing each principal personage of his little comedy a fixed system of belief which may be defended against all comers for the sake of the witty dialogue which is the staple of the book, but which need not be acted upon. Each character thus possesses a mild share of normal human characteristics, intellectually dominated by an opinion or prejudice which constitutes rather a crotchet than a conviction. This intellectual crotchet is an invariable trait of Peacockian character.

Headlong Hall, perhaps more than any of the later novels, is a battle-ground of opinion from first to last. Sentiment is lacking, and the only genuine emotion, Mr. Escot's love for the beautiful Cephalis, does not modify his disputing habit. The scene, like that of *The Three Doctors*, is laid at the home of a Welsh squire, in this case, Harry Headlong, who in some strange fashion has formed an ambition to be thought a philosopher and man of taste, and has consequently acquired several friends of varying degrees of taste and philosophy. These he assembles for a protracted symposium in the vale of Llanberris in Carnarvonshire, where they, like Homeric heroes, pass their days and nights in alternate eating and talking, to the delight of the hospitable squire. Mr. Foster, the perfectibilian, and Mr. Escot, the deteriorationist, generally stand in the forefront of the argument, while Mr. Jenkison, the statu-quo-ite, himself assured that the world requires no remaking, is always ready to serve as the buffer between them, and the Reverend

Dr. Gaster, lover of delicate living, as befits a shepherd of souls, hovers constantly near to preserve the sacred grounds of orthodoxy from trespass. These four illuminati come together from London to Headlong Hall, and there meet a number of pleasing guests, among whom is a certain Mr. Cranium, a devout phrenologist, toward whose daughter it very soon appears that Mr. Escot has conceived a tender passion. Mr. Cranium, however, aggrieved by Mr. Escot's obtuse lack of reverence for phrenology, has refused his consent. Then there are a number of minor characters, Mr. Marmaduke Milestone, the landscape gardener, Mr. Gall and Mr. Treacle, two poetical critics, Mr. Nightshade and Mr. MacLaurel, two critical poets, Mr. Cornelius Chromatic, a violinist with two charming daughters, Tenorina and Graziosa, Sir Patrick O'Prism, a dilettante painter, Miss Philomela Poppyseed, a compounder of novels chiefly in the female tongue, and Mr. Panscope, who has taken all the sciences for his province, and understands them all equally well. During several days, discussion rages about such fruitful topics as the blessings of civilisation, the excellence of primitive man, landscape gardening, vegetarianism, the principles of the picturesque, the disposition of literary people, periodical criticism, human disinterestedness, phrenology, alcoholic potation, child labour, the introduction of machinery, the right of might, physical deterioration, dancing, formal society, the relations of music and poetry, and the advantages of matrimony. As the result of a passage-at-arms between Mr. Escot and

Mr. Panscope, the latter decides to direct the full battery of his charms, his learning, and his ten thousand virtues (ten thousand pounds a year), against the heart of the beautiful Cephalis, in the hope, apparently, of confirming the deteriorationist in his belief that every step in this world is toward a worse position. Mr. Escot, however, little sanguine as he may be concerning universal progress, believes there is one possible change for the better in his particular case, and finally manages to overcome the wrath of Mr. Cranium by giving him a skull confidently asserted to be that of the great Cadwallader. The parental objection removed, Mr. Escot quickly ousts his rival and proceeds with the beautiful Cephalis to the altar, delighted at the success of his love, but still staunch in his general contention that, though there may be now and then a "slight oscillation of good in the instance of a solitary individual," the deterioration of the civilised world is assured. In this new step he is followed by Squire Headlong and Miss Tenorina, Mr. Foster and Miss Caprioletta Headlong, and Sir Patrick and Miss Graziosa, who have hastened to conclusions and venture upon matrimony with a degree of humorous haste which might persuade a cynical spectator to expect that they would all shortly become converts to Mr. Escot.

This amusing *dénoûment*, however, is quite of a piece with the rest of the novel, and not out of keeping with a plot built up of the farcical elements of irresponsible comedy. It may be taken as the general model for all of Peacock's later novels of contemporary life. The people who appear in it are externally life-like ; they speak the speech, more or less, of men and women, and some of them stick in the memory. Yet the action of the piece is nearly independent of those who play it. It is almost as if some enterprising manager of marionettes had substituted real men for his wooden mannikins, but still continued to produce the traditional, and somewhat unvaried, pantomimic classics of his repertory without consideration of the new actors. In *Headlong Hall* the wires which manipulate the show are the creeds attached by Peacock to the different performers.

> " All philosophers who find
> Some favourite system to their mind,
> In every point to make it fit,
> Will force all nature to submit,"

runs the motto. " And you know his system," asserts Mr. Cranium, " is of all things the dearest to every man of liberal thinking and a philosophical tendency." [1] It is hardly to be wondered at that among a whole houseful of philosophical guests, each enamoured of a system and devoted to its propagation, there should arise enough discussion to obscure almost all but the argumentative qualities of the guests. And when disquisition waxes so hot, the soundest man is likely to preach faiths which he leaves to the practice of others. Dr. Gaster rejoices that the antediluvian patriarchs knew not the use of the grape, and tosses off a bumper of Burgundy. Mr. Escot, notably, allows his polemic pessimism to suffer contradiction

[1] *Works*, i. 72.

from his actions. While exalting the pure and peaceful manners of Homer's Lotophagi and the frugivorous Hindoo, he grapples with a magnificent round of beef. It is he, although he denies the existence of disinterestedness, who pulls the obdurate Mr. Cranium out of the lake, just after Mr. Cranium has promised his daughter to Mr. Panscope. The same valiant champion of the wild man of the woods inveighs against the dancing of civilised communities, and prefers to it the dances of the American Indian—so long, that is, as the beautiful Cephalis has another partner—but the minute the set is ended, off he flies to reclaim the lady, " and probably felt at least as happy among the chandeliers and silk stockings, at which he had just been railing, as he would have been in an American forest, making one in an Indian ring, by the light of a blazing fire, even though his hand had been locked in that of the most beautiful *squaw* that ever listened to the roar of Niagara." [1] The very foundation of the Peacockian crotchet is the obvious fact that extreme notions may have very little effect upon the people who hold them, no matter how stoutly. It is just here that the attitude of the author of *Headlong Hall* toward the discordant opinions which fill his pages, makes itself evident. He is radical in his gibes at the universities and at dogmatic theology or politics, but he has nevertheless a kind of portable orthodoxy of his own—the orthodoxy of satire. Whoever ridicules must do it by an indication of the discrepancy between the object of his comment and

[1] *Works*, i. 62.

a standard to which he and his auditors assume in common that the ridiculed object should conform. There may be satirists whose orthodoxy consists of a complete acceptance of things as they are, and who ridicule, by comparison with the present, both the out-grown past and the half-grown future. Others will censure the present for divergence from the noble past, or for its failure to attain to the possibility of a gorgeous future. But still a third class mocks alike the present, past, and future, in the name of the canons of common sense which all three offend. To this third class Peacock belongs. Such a satirist need not ally himself either with Liberal or Conservative ; he is free from the necessity of institutional attachment ; the orthodoxy to which he holds is synonymous with reason. His philosophy of life includes him in that class of individuals, difficult to define and too often maligned by the assumption of their name on the part of persons unworthy to bear it—sensible men. Peacock was keen enough to perceive how slow stupidity can make the world's progress to better things, if there are better things, and could yet appreciate the admirable social qualities of stupidity. He could admire the devotion that shoulders a lost cause without expecting that the solid work of the world will ever be done by fanatics. He elected the rational wisdom of the middle ground, the wisdom that leads to practice, and justified it by an appeal to reason and the sense of the majority of sensible men. Each sensible man has the germ of a satirist in him ; with Peacock it was a well-developed quality, very quick to note deviation from the bounds of reasonableness, and equally capable of turning it to laughter. Nearly all foibles, indeed some of his own, served him as legitimate ground for mirth. This catholic mockery of his may lead many readers into the error of thinking that he had no principles of his own at all, because he seems to laugh at nearly every deed or thought of a foolish worldful of mortals. It may be pretty safely assumed that any satirist who holds the world up to measurement by the standard of reason will continue to find matter to ridicule for some years yet, and will, likewise, long be deemed a merely negative force by the extensive body of readers to whom the satiric denial of most approved opinions seems an absolute denial of all bases of faith and practice whatever. Peacock, indeed, delighted in whimsy and intellectual caprice so much that he often admits ridicule which is, soberly speaking, unjust. But the methods and aims of comic satire are not those of solemn justice, and Peacock must be judged on different grounds. To his private opinions, indeed, he clung with peculiar tenacity, but the testimony of his novels alone must not be trusted in the search for the truth concerning them.

Readers in 1816 perhaps found it easy to recognise satirical allusions to topics and personages of recent notoriety which we have now forgotten. Thus, one should remember that the ironical portrait of Mr. Cranium has reference to the contemporary craze over phrenology which had led *The Edinburgh Review*, in June 1815, to devote its full powers to a refutation of the *Physiognomical System of Drs. Gall and Spurz-*

heim, those two noted quacks whose international renown indicates the extent to which their doctrines had become known. Mr. Marmaduke Milestone is plainly intended for a caricature of Humphrey Repton, the landscape gardener, whom Payne Knight, in his poem *The Landscape*, had attacked for his habit of formalising scenery.[1] The name Milestone, although here taken from *The Three Doctors*, was originally given because of an altercation between Repton and Knight over the latter's charge that Repton had suggested placing the family arms on neighbouring milestones for the sake of giving greatness of character to an estate.[2] Peacock's sympathies are all with Knight, the champion of nature and simplicity. The allusions to the unnamed review which had sent its two reviewers to Headlong Hall are slight, and scarcely warrant our certain identification of it with any review of the period, although it was taken by one contemporary[3] at least to be the *Edinburgh*. The selection of an opinion from the pages of that periodical[4] for ridicule lends colour to the supposition, and it must be owned that the epithet " critical Napoleon " might quite as well apply to Jeffrey as to Gifford, whom Dr. Garnett suggested.[5] Neither here nor elsewhere, however, should one be too literal in explaining " who " Peacock's characters are. His own confession that

[1] *The Landscape* (1794), pp. 10–11, and 2nd edition (1795), pp. ii.–v.
[2] Repton, *Sketches and Hints on Landscape Gardening* (1794), p. 51. See also *Works*, i. 10.
[3] *Critical Review*, series 5, iii. 70.
[4] *Works*, i. 15. See *Edinburgh Review*, vii. 310.
[5] *Headlong Hall* (1891), p. 68 *n.*

"the opinions and public characters" of actual individuals were shadowed in *Melincourt*,[1] can only be taken to mean that in that book, as in the others, he had accepted hints for the persons of his story from men or women so well known at the time that caricatures of them would add piquancy to the novel. He felt free to exercise the privilege of the cartoonist, and to produce his likeness by the exaggeration of a salient feature. Although Mr. Nightshade may be Southey, it seems impossible to identify MacLaurel or Treacle, whose names merely complement those of Nightshade and Gall, Mr. Chromatic, Sir Patrick O'Prism, or Miss Poppyseed. As to Mr. Panscope, "the chemical, botanical, geological, astronomical, mathematical, metaphysical, meteorological, anatomical, physiological, galvanistical, musical, pictorial, bibliographical, critical philosopher," who is heir-apparent to ten thousand a year, and can fiddle, flirt, and warble a fashionable ditty, he illustrates very well, if he really stands for Coleridge, the liberties which Peacock could take with a character. Mr. Panscope and his supposed original suffered from the same encyclopædic learning and contemporary charges of wilful obscurity. There all resemblance ceases.

In the case of the three philosophers, Mr. Foster, Mr. Escot, and Mr. Jenkison, on whose names Peacock exercised his choicest gifts in humorous etymology,[2] there is a somewhat better chance to study Peacock's method of caricature. It is natural at the outset to

---

[1] *Works*, i. 78.　　　　[2] *Ibid.*, i. 3.

suspect that Mr. Foster, whose zealous defence of the theory of progress is his principal characteristic, must have been in part suggested to Peacock by the similar habit in Shelley ; and it is equally natural to suspect further that Mr. Escot, the pessimist, may very reasonably represent Peacock himself, or rather, the character which Peacock would assume in the presence of such a Shelley as Mr. Foster. It has not apparently been noted that the arguments for vegetable diet in *Headlong Hall* are drawn in part from Shelley's long *Vindication* in the notes to *Queen Mab.*[1] This is one indisputable sign that the fictitious philosophers were indebted to the real ones ; it is not to the point that Mr. Escot, instead of Mr. Foster, champions vegetarianism. What Peacock took was merely the original situation, the intellectual contention of two men, one an earnest disciple of Condorcet through Godwin, and the other driven to a pessimistic opposite pole by the accident of association with an optimist. This scheme once hit upon, it was natural enough that each disputant of the novel should be made to assume opinions appropriate to his character and business in the story, or even to take on characteristics opposed to those of his prototype for the purpose of disguising his identity. For instance, Mr. Foster is older than Mr. Escot, is very dark in complexion, urges an animal diet, and sees in mechanical progress a sign of the approaching millennium. Not one of these features was true of Shelley. Mr. Escot, though good Peacock in the matter of doubts concerning pro-

---

[1] *Works*, i. 7-9. Compare Shelley, *Poetical Works*, iv. 520-24.

gress, fondness for wild scenery, and dislike for literary people and periodical criticism, eschews both flesh and wine, and seeks to convert the world to his spare diet. These are two adequate examples of the way Peacock handles real personages in his fiction. He seizes upon some obvious peculiarity in his original, some crotchet, abnormality, or affectation, and, like a skilful cartoonist, exaggerates that single feature into the identifying feature of his fictitious character. Any other traits which the person may have are determined solely by reference to their being in keeping with the first. The result may be, in the strict sense, an unjust likeness, but it will be easily recognised. Peacock converted the duet of argument into the safer trio by adding Mr. Jenkison as a kind of stationary pivot upon which the extremes might whirl. The statu-quo-ite thus increases the humour of the situation without the necessity of having any character or opinions whatever.

Headlong Hall was popular enough on its first appearance to warrant a second edition near the end of August,[1] but contemporary reviewers gave it scant notice. *The Critical Review* honoured Peacock with the title of laughing philosopher [2] which he bore among his friends to the end of his days, and the notice in *The Eclectic Review* for April was reprinted three months later in *The Analectic Review* in Phila-delphia.[3] The moderate encouragement which he may have derived from their perfunctory remarks,

---

[1] *Critical Review* (Aug. 1816), series 5, iv. 213.
[2] *Ibid.*, iii. 69.   [3] *Analectic Review, Phil.*, viii. 55.

however, probably influenced him less than the
stimulus of a second edition to proceed with a new
novel on the same general lines. " Tell Peacock to
make his book ' funny,' " [1] wrote Jane Clairmont to
Shelley, then Peacock's guest at Marlow, the following
September. On December 8 Shelley spoke of Peacock
to Leigh Hunt in a letter which has already been mentioned. " Peacock is the author of ' Headlong Hall,'—
he expresses himself much pleased by your approbation—indeed, it is an approbation which many would
be happy to acquire ! He is now writing ' Melincourt '
in the same style, but, as I judge, far superior to
' Headlong Hall.' He is an amiable man of great
learning, considerable taste, an enemy to every shape
of tyranny and superstitious imposture. I am now
on the point of taking the lease of a house among
these woody hills, these sweet green fields, and this
delightful river—where, if I should ever have the happiness of seeing you, I will introduce you to Peacock." [2]
The new book must by that time have been nearly
completed, for it was in the press by February,[3] and
appeared either the same month [4] or very soon after-
ward. Its length—it appeared in three volumes—doubtless deterred some readers, but no such obstacle could
deter the zeal of a criticulus in *The British Critic*.
That periodical, of which Peacock had earlier remarked
that it proceeded " on the enlightened principle that
nothing can possibly be good coming from a heretic,
or a republican," [5] spied the " cloven foot of infi-

---

[1] Dowden, *Shelley*, ii. 45.   [2] *Letters*, p. 531.
[3] *European Magazine*, lxxi. 172.   [4] *Monthly Magazine*, xliii. 162.
[5] *Works*, iii. 125.

delity," as it said, and set about the castigation of the heretic.[1] *Headlong Hall* had not been deemed worthy of notice, but *Melincourt*, although, of course, such "miserable trash" could do no harm, had made use of Monboddo's doctrines, laughed at the sacred cloth of the clergy, and mocked Gifford, Southey, and Wordsworth in the characters of Vamp, Feathernest, and Derrydown, to such an extent that no thwacking could be too severe for its perpetrator. All of this is especially blameworthy when coming from an anonymous author, continues the reviewer. "Who the latter may be, we know not, as he has wisely chosen to conceal his name. Were he a poor man writing for bread, we might pity him ; were he a young man, discharging the scum of an enthusiastic brain, we might pardon him. We suspect him to be neither. From a certain dictatorial slang observable throughout, we imagine that he has been accustomed to lay down the law to a circle of dependents ; from his citations we know him to be sonorous, rather than a solid scholar ; from his ludicrous perversions of Holy Writ, we should suppose he was an adept in blasphemy. He has chosen the form of a novel, to disguise his venom, and to vent his bitterness with the more effect : but never was poison more innocent, nor malice more impotent. It wants but the name of the author to consign it to hopeless and fearless oblivion." [2] The review concluded by the acute guess that the culprit was Sir William Drummond of

---

[1] *British Critic*, new series, viii. 430.
[2] *Ibid.*, p. 441.

the *Academical Questions*, of whose previous existence
in the literary world the reviewer is plainly ignorant,
unaware that nearly fifty pages in *The British Critic*
had been devoted to the refutation of Sir William's
book a dozen years before. The guess of *The British
Critic* became the positive ascription of *The Portfolio*
in Philadelphia, which pilfered from the English
review quite unabashedly.[1] The book was promptly
reprinted, doubtless piratically, in America, and translated into French. Shelley much preferred it to
Headlong Hall, because of its greater seriousness;[2]
Lord Byron, whom Shelley speaks of as having shared
his own admiration,[3] seems to have been under the
mistaken notion that Sir Oran Haut-ton in some way
referred to his bear.

In *The Monthly Magazine* for June 1817,[4] *Melincourt* is said to have had already two imitations in
Six Weeks at Long's and *Three Weeks at Fladong's*.
These two productions, the earlier and better of which
has been ascribed to Eaton Stannard Barrett,[5] show
indeed some likeness to *Melincourt*. *Six Weeks at
Long's* has a character, Lord Leander, who is very
evidently meant for Byron, a Mr. Little, meant for
Thomas Moore, and a Mr. Perrywinkle, the atheist,
who believes with Monboddo that apes are akin to
men, and has brought up one in the country. The
general scheme of the work is much the same as that of
Melincourt, and the execution on the whole is clever.

[1] *Portfolio*, Phil., series 4, v. 321.
[2] *Letters*, p. 831.   [3] *Ibid.*, p. 897.
[4] xliii. 453.   [5] *Notes and Queries*, 1st series, viii. 423.

The fact that it was reviewed, however, as early as March 1817,[1] while the first review of *Melincourt* seems to have been that in *The Literary Gazette* for March 22, seems to preclude the idea of imitation. The resemblances must have been only accidental. *Three Weeks at Fladong's*, an inferior piece, seems from its title and general features to have been an imitation rather of *Six Weeks at Long's* than of *Melincourt*. It too has a character representing Byron, a certain Lord Stanza. In any case, the two novels throw light upon contemporary taste, even if they do not, as *The Monthly Magazine* thought, attest to Peacock's popularity.

More than any other of Peacock's novels, *Melincourt* has lost force and appeal with the passage of time, for the reason that the objects of its satire were in many cases of ephemeral interest. Rotten boroughs, the irresponsible issue of paper money, slavery in the West Indies, Malthusian principles of population, the night of German transcendentalism, the humanity of our simian kin, do not to-day press upon our attention very imperatively, and the subjects of really perennial significance, unjust division of property, the responsibility of the rich, fashionable extravagance, theological obtuseness, ideals in husbands and wives, truth to convictions, fail to come in for comment pungent enough to enliven the whole mass. For all Anthelia Melincourt is an excellent young woman, cultured, intelligent, full of virtues, her most resolute admirer must admit her conversation smacks of the treatise.

---

[1] *Monthly Review*, lxxxii. 330.

THOMAS LOVE PEACOCK

Mr. Forester and Mr. Fax grow more than boresome
with their interminable disputes, especially Mr.
Forester, who adds to the offence of being a solemn
replica of Mr. Escot through three volumes, the habit
of being a prig. All the debates in *Headlong Hall* had
been satirically conceived. In *Melincourt* Peacock
tries to atone for the purely negative tendency of the
earlier book by the advocacy of some constructive
schemes. He loses just so far as he attempts it.
Perhaps the influence of Shelley, perhaps his own
failure to perceive how much his real power lay in
mockery, had led him astray. Mr. Forester is made
to abstain from sugar for the sake of expressing his
disappoval of the West Indian slavery which produced
it, just as Peacock himself had actually done. But
whereas in Mr. Escot any such scheme would have
been laughed at as Quixotic, here it has the author's
evident approval, and gets preached by Mr. Forester
to a length that makes it quite impossible to admire
his self-restraint. Peacock seems not yet to have been
willing to pay the cynic's penalty by laughing at what
he secretly admired, sustained by the consciousness
that in the cynic branch of comedy all things are
folly, in a sense, and fit for nothing so much as laughter.
Accordingly the book lacks that easy freedom from
partisanship which makes the absence of any apparent
conviction the mocker's virtue. A further objection
to *Melincourt* is its length. If the peripatetic homi-
lists, Mr. Fax and Mr. Forester, could have been
made more laconic, the proportions of the novel need
not have exceeded those of *Headlong Hall*. The

number of incidents in the two is nearly the same; but *Melincourt* is three times as long, and the padding of debate must be blamed for the tale's comparative unpopularity.

In the midst of many tongues, it is pleasant to note one personage who never imperils his gravity by a single utterance, Sir Óran Haut-ton, an orang-outang from Angola who has been brought into the fashionable world in London, there to find himself completely at home. Mr. Forester, his patron, contends that he really thinks Sir Oran a member of the human family, whom he wishes to see established among his brothers with the gift of speech. Sir Oran was conceived primarily to reduce to an absurdity Monboddo's doctrine, held quite independently of Rousseau, that the ape had been unjustly degraded by the zoologists to a rank below man. Peacock takes the opportunity to point out many unflattering similarities and still more unflattering contrasts between Sir Oran and his associates. The principal episode, the dumb baronet's election to Parliament, constitutes by far the best portion of the whole book. Sir Oran's inability to learn to speak keeps him from occupying so prominent a place as he might, but he is really the hero after all. His sound moral qualities, his great usefulness as a rescuer of distressed maidens, and his hearty good fellowship leave little to be desired except his more frequent appearance on the stage of action. It would be difficult to find in fiction another hero of equal reticence. So far as probability goes, an unimportant matter in the Peacockian comedy, Sir

Oran does not suffer by comparison with any of the
gentlemen about him.

One feels in turning from *Headlong Hall* to *Melincourt* that some of the satirical pungency of the first
has been lost. It is also evident, and it becomes
increasingly so as one goes through the series of novels,
that invention was not Peacock's strong point. There
are several obvious repetitions. The Reverend Mr.
Grovelgrub is but a second and despicable Dr. Gaster ;
this second reverend gentleman and Lord Anophel
Achthar fall from the high rock on which Sir Oran
had placed them, much as Mr. Cranium had fallen
into the lake, and very much, likewise, as Dr. Gryffydh
had actually fallen on the midnight expedition which
he had made with Peacock to the Black Cataract half-
a-dozen years before. The machinery of the fable is
almost identical with that of *Headlong Hall*. Anthelia
lives alone at Melincourt, as Squire Headlong had
done at Headlong Hall ; when she is about to be
invaded by an army of suitors, instead of the houseful of philosophers who visit Squire Headlong, she
sends for an unmarried relative, Mr. Hippy, quite as
Headlong had sent for his sister, Caprioletta. *Melincourt*, however, is prolonged by the eighteenth-century
episode of Desmond, by the journey to Onevote, and
the melodramatic abduction of Anthelia, which
cannot, however, put a period to her lover's
argumentative habit, but merely allows Mr. Fax
and Mr. Forester to walk aimlessly and talk eagerly
on the quest of the beloved object of Mr. Forester's
passion.

There would be no complaint on the ground of
excessive length, however, if only the whole of the
book were as good as the account of the election in
the two chapters, " The City of Novote " and " The
Borough of Onevote." As " the ancient and honourable borough of Onevote was situated almost at the
extremity of the kingdom," [1] from Melincourt in
Westmoreland, the satire is probably aimed at the
condition of affairs in Cornwall, where Gatton and
Old Sarum were not much better off in fact than
Peacock makes out. Even though some time has
elapsed since rotten boroughs and virtual representation were deemed such venerable features of the British
constitution, and there are no more cities of Novote,
with fifty thousand inhabitants and no representative,
while a borough of Onevote has its " free, fat, and
dependent burgess," Mr. Christopher Corporate, who
returns two members to Parliament, the satirical
portrait has lost little of its original colours. The
speech in which Simon Sarcastic, Esq., Sir Oran's
fellow-candidate, flatters his plural constituent, con-
soles the unrepresented citizens from Novote, and
then lays down the lofty philosophy of virtual representation, is too characteristic not to be quoted
in part :

" The duty of a representative of the people,
whether actual or virtual, is simply *to tax*. Now this
important branch of public business is much more
easily and expeditiously transacted by the means of
virtual, than it possibly could be by that of actual

[1] *Works*, i. 183.

99

representation. For when the minister draws up his scheme of ways and means, he will do it with much more celerity and confidence, when he knows that the propitious countenance of virtual representation will never cease to smile upon him as long as he continues in place, than if he had to encounter the doubtful aspect of actual representation, which might, perhaps, look black on some of his favourite projects, thereby greatly impeding the distribution of secret service money at home, and placing foreign legitimacy in a very awkward predicament. The carriage of the state would then be like a chariot in the forest, turning to the left for a troublesome thorn, and to the right for a sturdy oak; whereas it now rolls forward like the car of Juggernaut over the plain, crushing whatever offers to impede its way.

" The constitution says that no man shall be taxed but by his own consent : a very plausible theory, gentlemen, but not reducible to practice. Who will apply a lancet to his own arm, and bleed himself ? Very few, you acknowledge. Who then, *à fortiori*, would apply a lancet to his own pocket, and draw off what is dearer to him than his blood—his money ? Fewer still, of course : I humbly opine, none. What then remains but to appoint a royal college of state surgeons, who may operate on the patient according to their views of his case ? Taxation is political phlebotomy : the Honourable House is, figuratively speaking, a royal college of state surgeons. A good surgeon must have firm nerves and a steady hand ; and, perhaps, the less feeling the better. Now, it is manifest, that, as all feeling is founded on sympathy, the fewer constituents a representative has, the less must be his sympathy with the public, and the less, of course as is desirable, his feeling for his patient— the people. Who, therefore, with so much *sang froid*, can phlebotomise the nation, as the representative of half an elector ? " [1]

Sarcastic, who in his youth had been " troubled with the *passion for reforming the world*," but who has been long since reformed to the easier programme of laughing at invulnerable folly and custom, is a more direct mouthpiece than Peacock usually allows himself.

A writer in *The North American Review* for September 1817 identified Derrydown with Scott, Feathernest with Southey, Vamp with Gifford, Mystic with Coleridge, and Paperstamp with Wordsworth. Making due allowance for caricature, these may be taken to be the actual personages Peacock had in mind. But the attempt at greater seriousness in *Melincourt* led to a display of spleen in the portraits of contemporaries which seriously disfigures one or two chapters. Derrydown, the young man who had found all learning vanity, and had been saved from despair by the discovery of Percy's *Reliques*, and now spends his time in " posting about the country, for the purpose, as he expressed it, of studying together poetry and peasantry, unsophisticated character and the truth of things," [2] stands for Scott, of course, only in a vague way. Feathernest, the despicable parasite, who had " burned

[1] *Works*, i. 198–9.   [2] *Ibid.*, i. 118.

his old ' Odes to Truth and Liberty,' and had published a volume of Panegyrical Addresses ' to all the crowned heads in Europe,' with the motto ' Whatever is at court is right,' " [1] has, I take it, nothing particular in common with Southey except that he too is the target for virulent abuse on the charge of apostasy. Vamp, the editor of the *Legitimate Review*, is pretty plainly Gifford, and here gets some return for the systematic abuse which he dealt about so freely. There is less excuse, however, for the acrid arraignment of Wordsworth as Peter Paul Paperstamp, Esq., of Mainchance Villa, who is " chiefly remarkable for an affected infantine lisp in his speech, and for always wearing waistcoats of a duffel gray," [2] and who has a large finger in the public purse. Moley Mystic, Esq., of Cimmerian Lodge, plainly enough aims to be a portrait of Coleridge, but the caricature is a mere daub, which owes its chief interest to its being a prophecy of the admirable sketch of the same figure in *Nightmare Abbey*. Then there are several minor figures. Captain Hawltaught has already been identified with Thomas Love. The " learned mythologist, who has long laboured to rebuild the fallen temple of Jupiter,' [3] is Thomas Taylor, the Platonist. Mr. Fax, " the champion of cold reason, the indefatigable explorer of the cold clear springs of knowledge, the bearer of the torch of dispassionate truth," [4] is clearly, from his emphasis on over-population, Malthus. Canning's versatile partisanships and his editorship of *The Anti-*

[1] *Works*, i. 117. [2] *Ibid.*, p. 227.
[3] *Ibid.*, p. 109. [4] *Ibid.*, p. 113.

Jacobin account for the name Mr. Anyside Antijack. The chapter on Mainchance Villa, where Mr. Fax and Mr. Forester pause for fifteen pages of conversation during the heat of their search for Anthelia, and where Antijack, Paperstamp, Vamp, Killthedead, and Feathernest unite in a chorus of praise for things as they are, bases its satire upon an article on parliamentary reform in the *Quarterly* for October 1816. Specific references are given in Peacock's notes. Finally, Mr. Killthedead from Frogmarsh Hall, " a great compounder of narcotics, under the denomination of BATTLES," who, whenever he hear of a deadly field,

> "He fought the BATTLE o'er again,
> And twice he slew the slain,"[1]

stands for Peacock's kinsman by marriage, John Wilson Croker. Various originals have been wrongly suggested, but the name Frogmarsh would be sufficient to point to Croker, even if Peacock himself, by a reference in *Sir Proteus*, did not establish the identity.

> "Here Cr–k–er fights his battles o'er,
> And doubly kills the slain"[2]

Croker's once popular *Battles of Talavera* (1809) explains the allusion.

Mr. P. A. Daniel has kindly helped me to find a contemporary allusion to *Melincourt* which has not been noted. In Ackermann's *Repository* for March 1, 1822, is a burlesque poem by one P. W., which contains some pertinent lines.

---

[1] *Works*, i. 227.   [2] *Ibid.*, iii. 139.

THOMAS LOVE PEACOCK

"The author of a novel lately written,
      Entitled 'Melincourt,'
      ('Tis very sweet and short),
Seems indeed by some wondrous madness bitten,
      Thinking it good
      To take his hero from the wood :
And though I own there's nothing treasonable
In making ouran-outangs reasonable,
      I really do not think he should
      Go quite the length that he has done,
      Whether for satire or for fun,
      To make this creature an M.P.
As if mankind no wiser were than he.
      However, those who've read it
      Must give the author credit
      For skill and ingenuity,
Although it have this monstrous incongruity.

In Leadenhall he gives a close attendance,
      Where, if I not mistake
      He now contrives to make
A very comfortable *India*-pendence :
      But be it known,
Or good or bad, this pun is not my own."[1]

Without comment upon the goodness or badness of the pun, it is sufficient merely to note that this hit belongs to a date five years subsequent to *Melincourt's* appearance, when Peacock was a public and official figure. During that five years he had increased notably his title to prominence.

[1] Ackermann's *Repository*, xiii. 133.

CHAPTER V

"RHODODAPHNE"—"CALIDORE"—"NIGHTMARE ABBEY"

WHILE Shelley was completing *Laon and Cythna* at Marlow, Peacock too had ventured upon a new and last long poem. The first mention of it is in a letter from Shelley to Hogg near the end of 1817. " Peacock has finished his poem, which is a story of classical mystery and magic—the transfused essence of Lucian, Petronius, and Apuleius. I have not yet heard it all, but in a few days he will send it to the press." [1] By January [2] its publication was under way, and it appeared simultaneously the next month [3] with *The Revolt of Islam*. Shelley, who had recently reviewed Godwin's *Mandeville*, did the same for *Rhododaphne*, but the review, found among Leigh Hunt's papers, was not printed until 1879, when Mr. H. B. Forman's pious care brought it to the light. " This it is to be a scholar ; this it is to have read Homer and Sophocles and Plato," [4] Shelley exclaims. " We are transported to the banks of the Peneus and linger under the crags of Tempe, and see the water lilies floating on the stream. We sit with Plato by old Illissus under the sacred Plane tree among the sweet scent of flowering sallows ; and above there is the nightingale of Sophocles in the ivy of the pine, who is watching the sunset so

---

[1] *Letters*, p. 995.
[2] *British Critic*, new series, ix. 112.
[3] *Blackwood's*, ii. 588.
[4] *Prose Works* (1880), iii. 19.

that it may dare to sing; it is the radiant evening of a burning day, and the smooth hollow whirlpools of the river are overflowing with the aërial gold of the level sunlight." [1]   Shelley confidently predicted " extraordinary success " [2] for the poem which he describes with such eloquence; Byron sent word to Peacock that he should be willing to father the " Grecian Enchantress " himself; [3] Poe, never light of praise, called it " brimful of music," [4] and Medwin rendered it a degree of commendation which would have been more flattering but for the fact that he spoke of it as " Rhododendron." [5]   A certain lady in Paris had told him, Medwin declares, that she read the poem several times a year, and every time with increased pleasure. Finally, an unknown admirer in 1840 dramatised *Rhododaphne*, and had a friend write to Peacock a letter, which is still preserved, asking for the requisite permission before taking steps to bring it upon the stage !

All these glances of affection seem a little wan after many years; tastes are capricious and poetical fashions change. Peacock's " Maid of Greece " undoubtedly belongs to the increasing body of verse which continues to be reprinted, discussed occasionally, and sometimes read. Yet the passages of exquisite charm which it contains can scarcely win for it more than largely qualified applause. It nowhere compels with power or enchants with beauty. Peacock's capa-

---

[1] *Prose Works* (1880), iii. 17–18.   [2] *Letters*, p. 596.
[3] *North British Review*, new series, vi. 92.
[4] See his *Marginalia*.   [5] *Life of Shelley* (1847), i. 308–9.

city as poet lay in the direction of brief, unpremeditated snatches of song which sprang from him naturally into glees or catches, but which took on an air of stiffness when he set himself seriously to poetry. His poetic constitution was bound up too closely with a scholarly temper and a sardonic restraint ever to admit the divine madness which overcomes cold prudence. When he deprived himself voluntarily of his best characteristic, humour, he could be moved only by a strong personal emotion, such as that which produced *The Cypress Shade* or his epitaph for his daughter Margaret, to poetry well above mediocrity. At the same time, *Rhododaphne* marks a genuine advance upon the long poems of his earlier period. That same ironical aloofness which was his limitation preserved him now from the faults of artificiality and overstrain which had hurt his poetry before. His test of ridicule had proved useful to himself as well as to Shelley. It cannot fail to be observed, too, how much more of a Greek quality this poem has, even leaving quite out of account the matter of the narrative, than the early poems had exhibited. There are passages which recall, in delicate clarity of outline, the marbles in the British Museum among which Peacock's youth had been spent :

> " He bore a simple wild-flower wreath :
> Narcissus, and the sweet-briar rose ;
> Vervain, and flexile thyme, that breathe
> Rich fragrance ; modest heath, that glows
> With purple bells ; the amaranth bright,
> That no decay nor fading knows ; " [1]

[1] *Works*, iii. 161.

and, equally clear, but with movement added to the silent poise of these lines, is the account of the chase in Canto VII. :—

> " And oft they rouse with clamorous chase
> The forest, urging wide and far
> Through glades and dells the sylvan war.
> Satyrs and fauns would start around,
> And through their ferny dingles bound,
> To see that nymph, all life and grace
> And radiance, like the huntress-queen,
> With sandaled feet and vest of green,
> In her soft fingers grasp the spear,
> Hang on the track of flying deer,
> Shout to the dogs as fast they sweep
> Tumultuous down the woodland steep,
> And hurl along the tainted air,
> The javelin from her streaming hair." [1]

Few of Peacock's undertakings show so many signs of his romantic affinities. This is a tale of Thessalian magic, full of portents and wonders, yet nowhere is there a hint of the mocking laughter with which he was accustomed to greet the marvels of his romantic contemporaries. The scenes of the poem are laid in the remote and lovely valleys of ancient Greece ; its chief matter is the romantic love of Anthemion for Calliroë. Only the beauty and antique charm of its subject find place in the story. In a story of Greek life Peacock would scarcely have ventured upon satire ; there he unconsciously acknowledged the genuine core of romance which he possessed. The modern world he could hold up to ridicule with complete freedom. He did it by the right of Attic nurture, in the spirit

---

[1] *Works*, iii. pp. 207–8.

of a Greek mocking barbarians. But the Attic curl disappeared from his lips whenever he left London for Arcadia. As he grew older, this feeling hardened into a terrible prejudice against the new world which has superseded the gods and bards of Greece. When he wrote *Rhododaphne*, however, it was still a romantic longing for the exquisite world of the imagined past.

> " Great Pan is dead :
> The life, the intellectual soul
> Of vale, and grove, and stream, has fled
> For ever with the creed sublime
> That nursed the Muse of earlier time." [1]

For some reason or other, *Rhododaphne* was published anonymously, but there could have been little doubt as to its authorship. One or two reviewers hinted in a knowing way that they were in the secret. *The Literary Gazette* was more explicit. " This poem is from the pen of Mr. Peacock, known to the world, if not generally by name, at least pretty generally as the author of ' The Genius of the Thames,' ' Headlong Hall,' and ' Melincourt.' " [2] In America, however, where the book was immediately reprinted by Matthew Carey at Philadelphia, gossip ascribed it to Richard Dabney, the Virginia poet, and a Richmond journal put the ascription into print.[3] Dabney himself denied it, and at his death in 1825 charged his sister to refute the claim. Carey, appealed to, owned that *Rhododaphne* was an English production, but the letter was not made public, and the report still circulated.

---

[1] *Works*, iii. 173.   [2] ii. 114–5.
[3] *Evangelical and Literary Magazine*, Jan. 1819.

THOMAS LOVE PEACOCK

During the troublous times through which *The Southern Literary Messenger* passed just after the death of its founder, Thomas W. White, in 1843, his friend James Heath reprinted *Rhododaphne* in the magazine for June and July. A controversy over the authorship immediately arose,[1] and Dabney was proved not to have been responsible for it. The name of the real author was nowhere mentioned, and although it of course became subsequently known, *Rhododaphne* has been held to be Dabney's in very recent years.

During the years 1816 to 1818 Peacock was busied with several literary schemes which proved abortive. He projected a poem with nympholepsy for its subject, to which Shelley refers in a letter of August 16, 1818. Among Peacock's manuscripts has been preserved a prose abstract [2] which tells how a youth of Bacchus' train, the son of a king, falls deeply in love with a beautiful nymph and, failing to win her, runs mad with love till the nymph breaks her vow of maidenhood out of pity for the terrible effects of his disease. The bacchanals, deserted by the youth, slay him at the instigation of the angry Diana, and the nymph, with Ovidian facility, dissolves into a fountain of tears. It is interesting to notice Peacock's method of working, how he carefully prepared a prose version of his poem and made notes for details from various authors, particularly Nonnus, before he ever set his pen to actual composition. His work on this piece, however, was delayed, and finally given up altogether on the

---

[1] *Southern Literary Messenger*, ix. 390–1 ; 557–8 ; 638–9.
[2] Brit. Mus. *Addit. MSS.*, 36815, fol. 120–2.

appearance in 1821 of Horace Smith's *Amarynthus the Nympholept*. It would obviously have been a second *Rhododaphne*. A greater loss to readers of Peacock was his failure to complete a semi-mythological novel which he began during this period, but did not carry much beyond four chapters. The fragment *Calidore* has been printed in full only within the past few months in Dr. Garnett's *Thomas Love Peacock*. Peacock's manuscripts show that perhaps his earliest attempt at prose fiction had been made about 1811 or 1812 with a tale called *Satyrane ; or, The Stranger in England*.[1] Of this a very brief fragment only remains, in which a shipload of missionaries bound for Australia are wrecked on an island and all but one are drowned. That one, advancing inland, has just been met with a "scene that made him groan in spirit and showed that he was in the dominion of Satan," when the narrative disappointingly ends. But it is quite evident that the earlier piece was absorbed into *Calidore*, for King Arthur and his court, who have taken refuge on a solitary island with the banished gods of Greece, are invaded by just such a chosen vessel as the missionary of *Satyrane*. Moreover, Calidore is once or twice called Satyrane in the manuscript, instead of by the name he later received, and thus the identity is established almost beyond doubt. Why Peacock did not complete his story, it is difficult to say. It is not, so far as it goes, inferior to his completed novels, and one might think he would have found especially congenial the opportunity to satirise modern life by the

---

[1] Brit. Mus. *Addit. MSS.*, 36815, fol. 118.

scheme of sending into England a youth who had been nurtured among gods and heroes, with no less a person than Merlin for his tutor. There is matter of biographical interest in his character of Ellen Ap-Nanny, the Welsh girl with whom Calidore falls in love during his search for a wife and a philosopher, very much as Peacock himself had done with Jane Gryffydh, Ellen's prototype. It is not entirely fanciful to see in Calidore a projection of his creator, who had lived more in the company of Pan, Bacchus, Arthur, and Merlin, than in that of the English and Welsh of the story. The account of life on the island has particular spirit, but, whatever was his reason, Peacock made no use of *Calidore* except to borrow the unusual locution, " jeremitaylorically pathetic," for *Nightmare Abbey*, to transfer his description of Miss Ap-Nanny, Ellen's elder sister, to Miss Lemma Crotchet, and to utilise the situation of Merlin and Arthur on a desert island in *The Round Table ; or, King Arthur's Feast*, a nursery rhyme very much of the order of *Sir Hornbook*, but with English history for its content instead of grammar. As the paper on which *Calidore* is written bears the watermark 1816, and as *Nightmare Abbey* appeared in 1818, the date of *Calidore* is thus fixed with tolerable accuracy.

More is known of the composition of *Nightmare Abbey*. It had probably been begun when Shelley left England in March, for he refers to it in a letter from Milan, April 20. Some six weeks later Peacock himself wrote to Shelley : " I have almost finished ' Nightmare Abbey.' I think it necessary to ' make

a stand' against the 'encroachments' of black bile.
The fourth canto of 'Childe Harold' is really too
bad.   I cannot consent to be *auditor tantum* of this
systematical 'poisoning' of the 'mind' of the 'reading
public.' "¹   The book had already been announced as
in press,² and on June 14 Peacock wrote that it was
completed.   "I hope that you have given the enemy
no quarter," Shelley replied.   "Remember, it is a
sacred war." ³   Some unexplained delay, however, put
off publication till November,⁴ and Scythrop's prototype, who had suggested the passage from *Every Man
in His Humour*, which, with some omissions, serves as
the second motto, did not receive a copy until June
of the following year.   Then, however, he was delighted
with it, none the less, apparently, because he and
Mrs. Shelley both recognised the caricature.   "I
think Scythrop," he wrote, "a character admirably
conceived and executed;   and I know not how to
praise sufficiently the lightness, chastity, and strength
of the language of the whole.   It perhaps exceeds all
your works in this.   The catastrophe is excellent.   I
suppose the moral is contained in what Falstaff says—
'For God's sake, talk like a man of this world,' and
yet, looking deeper into it, is not the misdirected
enthusiasm of Scythrop what J. C. calls the 'salt of
the earth' ? " ⁵

The query of Shelley, of course, indicates the
difference between his position and Peacock's.   "I
thought I had fully explained to you the object of

---

¹ *Thomas Love Peacock : Letters*, &c., p. 64.
² *Blackwood's* (April), iii. 101.   ³ *Letters*, p. 607.
⁴ *Blackwood's*, iv. 243.   ⁵ *Letters*, p. 694.

Nightmare Abbey," Peacock wrote, " which was merely
to bring to a sort of philosophical focus a few of the
morbidities of modern literature, and to let in a little
daylight on its atrabilarious complexion." [1] The novel
does not aim to look deeper into any matter than was
requisite to point out ridiculous traits in such a reformer as Scythrop. The attempt has been taken too
seriously. The resemblance of the hero to Peacock's
friend is not the most notable feature of the novel.
The tale is a brilliant achievement, bright, piercing,
wholesome. As a work of art it deserves to be considered quite apart from any relation it may have to
the person who happens to serve as model for its chief
character. There are affectations always with us
which afford perennial ground for the satire which
mocks the folly of too much weeping at the world.
The world is not to be wept at or laughed over, but
to be understood. It will always contain its quota
of young Scythrops, full of noble, if uninformed,
aspirations, who take hurt at the inertia which opposes
their schemes for remaking the universe nearer to
some fine heart's-desire. No plan of education seems
able to prevent their coming to grief when they are
jerked from their dreams. Yet wiser men lose some
of their normal obligation to pity or sympathy when
it is resisted by affectation on the part of the Scythrops.
They need then no longer hold back from laughter.
Mirth has saved many a soul from the gloom of
twenty-one. Peacock himself would have profited had
there been some one to laugh away the blue devils of

[1] *Thomas Love Peacock : Letters, &c.,* p. 77.

his youth. Now that he was grown older, he perceived it with especial clearness when he saw his own extravagances multiplied in Shelley. And Shelley was not the sole object of laughter. Peacock held Byron one of the worst offenders against a rational view of life ; he blamed the whole literary tendency of the generation. Like Mr. Hilary in the novel, who stands for Peacock's point of view on more than one occasion, he could not see what good was going to result from " all this mystifying and blue-devilling of society." The solid wisdom of antiquity had been cheerful, and Shakespeare and Socrates " the most festive of companions." The wisest, then, are those who look serenely at both good and evil with the eyes of serene understanding, and who extract comedy from the perception of faults that would be tragic to the ignorant.

It will probably be objected that Peacock fails to make due allowance for the superb genius which Shelley and Byron actually possessed. The objection has no real validity, so far as *Nightmare Abbey* is concerned, though it may be justly enough urged against the catholicity of Peacock's private taste. But Peacock's private taste is not here the question. Such an objection may be urged equally well against the whole body of satire. The mockery of this book aims only at specific follies. To censure a folly with a smile does not constitute a stern accusation against the foolish one. Satire is one-sided by the very laws of its nature, as are all correctives. Perhaps there is more or less justice in the dictum that the limitation of the man is the excellence of the satirist. Perhaps, too, merry humorists like Peacock, who are not impelled by a solemn didactic purpose, do not feel the pressure of the world's evil as do grimmer souls. One must never forget, however, that in *Nightmare Abbey* the concern is with the affectation of grief, not real misery ; with the pretence of talent, not with genius itself. Peacock had expressed, in the words of Anthelia Melincourt and Mr. Forester, a firm belief that if the world is indeed to be made a more habitable place, it must be through the disinterested ardour of enthusiasts. That did not bind him to think no wrong-headed reformers ridiculous. He had a full artistic right to laugh at the objects of his ridicule, provided only he did not step out of the bounds of harmless laughter, as he had done in *Melincourt*, where, under cover of ridicule directed at the absurdities of Wordsworth and Southey, he had aspersed their moral characters.

Scythrop (Σκυθρωπος, of a sad or angry countenance) Glowry is undoubtedly the principal personage of the book. The son of an " atrabilarious " gentleman in Lincolnshire, Scythrop runs through a hurried course of education at school, at the university, and in a boyish love affair which disappoints him. He thereupon solaces himself with wine and plans for reforming the world, put forth in the shape of a treatise called *Philosophical Gas ; or, A Project for a General Illumination of the Human Mind.* He manages promptly to fall in love again, this time with a girl who does not reject him, and the two are about to be made happy, when a more romantic and intellectual woman, Stella, her name assumed for the time being from Goethe's

drama, wins him from his earlier love. Then ensues great perturbation in Scythrop's mind, which
finally results in his loss of both the girls, who marry
rival suitors with Peacockian precipitation. His reforming zeal, his visions and impracticable dreams, his
hesitation between the two women, were undoubtedly
meant to identify him with Shelley. Peacock himself
tacitly acknowledges as much.[1] Certain attempts
which have been made to defend Shelley against the
injustice of the caricature, amusing as they are, merely
indicate how far Peacock's spirit of comedy is misun-
derstood. The rules of caricature are not those of
photography. Ironical mirth must be accepted in
the mood of laughter, and not refuted with solemn
reasons. One may pay Shelley all the homage due
his real character and genius without taking any less
pleasure in laughing at his undoubted follies. Few
men loved him more than the very friend who thus
transformed him into a comic personage by a distortion
of some of his traits. It is testimony to the firmness
of their friendship that Scythrop never came between
them for an instant. Shelley, little gifted with laughter
as he was, apparently had sufficient sense of humour not
to be irritated by *Nightmare Abbey*, merely remarking,
as we have seen, that there was something to be said
on both sides. Peacock, however, had relieved himself from the necessity of saying anything on the other
side by omitting the higher qualities of Shelley and
changing about pretty much at will the traits which
complete the character. Thus Scythrop is an only

---

[1] *Memoirs of Shelley*, p. 93.

child, motherless, who completes his work at the university to the satisfaction of the master and fellows of his college ; he has been taught to drink deep by academic discipline ; he retires to take up a melancholy and recluse existence after his first love affair. More important variations are, that Scythrop's misanthropy is not relieved by the charity which his original possessed, nor is it anywhere indicated that his follies were only the effervescence of a splendid intellectual force. Peacock was satisfied with a degree of verisimilitude sufficient to give satiric point, and in no way had the intention or desire to present a just portrait of any living man.

In one respect, however, there can be no denial that he was treading on dangerous ground. That is in the matter of Scythrop's plural affection. Some ingenuity has recently been expended in the attempt to prove that this refers really to the Miss Hitchener episode of Shelley's youth,[1] and not to his desertion of his first wife for Mary Godwin. It must be remembered that only about a year and a half before Peacock wrote *Nightmare Abbey*, Harriet Shelley had committed suicide under peculiarly tragic circumstances. Peacock had been very fond of her, and he knew that Shelley experienced the deepest distress in remembering her. Yet here is a caricature of which one of the most emphatic traits is the same instability in love which had brought upon Shelley his greatest reproach. One wonders whether the fact that Shelley knew nothing of the book's contents before he left

[1] *Mod. Lang. Notes* (Baltimore), vol. xxv., No. 2, pp. 41–5.

England, and that he was not enlightened until he received a copy nearly a year after it had been completed, may not have been partly because the author wished a little longer time to elapse, so that the poet might have increased reason for regarding Scythrop as the picture of a self long outgrown. The Shelley that was caricatured was of course the Shelley of the days of German romance and of the Dublin pamphlet, *Proposal for an Association of Philanthropists.* Perhaps Shelley in 1819, looking back upon that period of his life, may have connected Stella with Miss Hitchener, with whom she has in common the highly significant feature of a dark complexion ! If he did, the fact is quite beside the point. So far as he took Marionetta and Stella to be real women at all, he could not have helped the recollection that he had grown cold in his love for the woman who was presented, in many respects to the life, in the character of Marionetta, and that his change of heart had been for both of them a tragedy. Perhaps he took the matter more seriously than one is led to suspect from his generous praise of *Nightmare Abbey.* His reticence concerning his first wife was very great. However this may be, it appears that by June 1819, the lapse of five years since he had eloped with Mary Godwin enabled him to look back upon the whole event and its consequences as a chapter which, however tragic it might have been to the actors, could be viewed from an angle which presented comic features. In him it reveals either an unsuspected sense of humour, or magnanimity, or coldness. In Peacock it displays either very sound judgment as to how Shelley would take the caricature, or else a willingness to exercise his gift of laughter in an affair which must suggest the memory of bitter regret.

Of the other characters who are partly studied from life, Mr. Flosky is the most elaborate, and a great advance upon the Mr. Mystic of *Melincourt*. Lover of shadows and mystery, he had renounced his early faith in the French Revolution, and had taken refuge in the "central opacity of Kantian metaphysics." " I pity the man who can see the connection of his own ideas," says Mr. Flosky. " Still more do I pity him, the connection of whose ideas any other person can see." [1] A corollary of his love of obscurity is his love of whatever is old. He scorns contemporary literature—although he owns that he and Mr. Sackbut, Southey, have raised up some of the best modern goblins—on account of its horrors and depraved search after novelty. He himself is all for mystery, in literature as in logic. " Mystery is the very keystone of all that is beautiful in poetry, all that is sacred in faith, and all that is recondite in transcendental psychology. I am writing a ballad which is all mystery ; it is ' such stuff as dreams are made of,' and is, indeed, stuff made of a dream ; for last night I fell asleep as usual over my book, and had a vision of pure reason. I composed five hundred lines in my sleep ; so that, having had a dream of a ballad, I am now officiating as my own Peter Quince, and making a ballad of my dream, and it shall be called Bottom's Dream, because

---

[1] *Works*, i. 331.

it has no bottom." [1] It would be hard to produce
a more delightful parody of Coleridge's account of
the composition of *Kubla Khan*. Best of all is Mr.
Flosky's remark, founded upon a witty remark which
Coleridge is said [2] actually to have made in reply to a
lady's question : " I can safely say, I have seen too
many ghosts myself to believe in their external existence." [3] If one comes down to the question of
reality, Mr. Flosky has quite as little in common with
Coleridge as Scythrop has with Shelley, but he never
ceases to be amusing. Most laughable, too, is the
Manichæan millennarian, Mr. Toobad, who goes about
constantly asserting that " the devil is come among
you having great wrath," and evinces a positive genius
for introducing his slogan at every turn. His Ahri-
manic philosophy seems to make him out a study from
the zodiac-loving Mr. Newton of Bracknell, whose
system had once run the narrow risk of being buried
beneath Peacock's poetic exposition, but survived to
be rendered reasonably immortal in his satire. The
Hon. Mr. Listless was a caricature of Sir Lumley
Skeffington, a dandy and social arbiter of the time, who,
as well as Peacock, had been consulted on the question
whether Shelley should be married to Mary Godwin
at once after Harriet's death. As Mr. Listless, he is
represented in that last degree of exhaustion which
Peacock affected to consider the idea of refined elegance.
The original Sir Lumley was by no means so lacka-
daisical a creature. The name given to Mr. Sackbut

[1] *Works*, i. 344.
[2] C. R. Leslie, *Autobiographical Recollections* (1860), i. 47–8.
[3] *Works*, i. 365.

alludes to Southey's annual perquisite of a butt of
sack as laureate. The novel *Devilman* which comes
by post from London is an anagram for Godwin's
Mandeville. Mr. Cypress appears only for a single
chapter, but during his brief stay he indulges in quite
enough lamentation over blasted hopes—paraphrased
from the fourth canto of *Childe Harold*—to make
clear his identity with Byron. His song, " There is a
fever of the spirit," is all the more admirable a parody
because it parodies the Byronic spirit, and not any
specific poem. Peacock could never have written it
but for his own sympathy with romantic melancholy,
of which his earlier poems had been such evidence.
Byron, it is interesting to know, was delighted with the
caricature, and gave Shelley a rosebud, still preserved,
to be taken to Peacock with his love. Cypress's song
meets with prompt reply in the admirable *Seamen
Three* of Mr. Hilary and the Rev. Mr. Larynx. Peacock's drinking songs have been deservedly popular.
Critics of such diverse temper and ideals as Thackeray [1]
and Professor Saintsbury [2] agree upon a common
superlative in their praise. *Headlong Hall* had contained two songs, " A heeltap ! a heeltap ! " and the
Headlong chorus, which can hold up their heads,
though a little robustious, among the best of the
anacreontic sort, and of Mr. Chromatic's " In his last
binn SIR PETER lies," it is interesting to note that

> " He never made a brow look dark,
> Nor caused a tear but when he died,"

---

[1] *North British Review*, new series, vi. 89.
[2] *Headlong Hall*, &c., ed. Saintsbury (1896), p. xv.

recalls the touching lines from one of the most touching of songs, *Le Roi d'Yvetot*,

> " Ce n'est que lorsqu'il expira
> Que le peuple, qui l'enterra
> Pleura."

Melincourt has only one jovial snatch, but that is *The Ghosts*, which must surely be ranked with *Seamen Three* of *Nightmare Abbey*, and " If I drink water while this doth last " of *Crotchet Castle*, as one of the three finest convivial pieces Peacock wrote. They all have a fine abandon, just this side tipsy jollity, and add to it generally a touch of the vinous sentiment which makes the fortune of such attempts. The more serious songs of the early novels are not, as a rule, remarkable, although *The Sun-dial* in *Melincourt* constitutes an exception.

Lovers of literary influence may be tempted to see in the title of *Nightmare Abbey* a reminiscence of *Northanger Abbey*, which had appeared with *Persuasion* at the very beginning of 1818. As a matter of fact, there seems to be no ground for connecting them, unless it be the suspicion itself. They are both, however, anti-romances of a delightful effectiveness, and they have in common a principal character who suffers from an exaggerated appetite for romantic fiction. But Catharine Morland's career is a hit at the Gothic romances which had filled with pleasant horror the green days of the romantic movement, while the historian of Scythrop has his eye chiefly upon the tumult of reforming zeal in the wake of the French Revolution, and upon the romantic melancholy practised and prescribed by Lord Byron. Jane Austen's

123

criticism is directed chiefly at a false literary fashion ; Peacock, more acquainted and more concerned with ideas, aims at the opinions which gave rise to the prevailing mode. *Northanger Abbey*, partly by consequence, excels as a reflex of contemporary manners ; it falls short of *Nightmare Abbey* in ironic point and fancy. In the latter regards, Peacock surpassed his own previous efforts. The shortest of his novels suffers from none of the diffuseness of *Melincourt*, nor does it accomplish its laconism by means of the over-bluntness which had occasionally been noticeable in *Headlong Hall*. Its phrases are more neatly turned than those of the earlier novels, and its style clearer and more pungent. To all appearances, Peacock's conscious stand against the same black bile of which he had been the singer in *The Philosophy of Melancholy*, had met with the reward of a tolerable freedom from spleen in his dealings with the faults he now censured, having outgrown them. The savage assault on Burke and Southey, however, which lurks in a note,[1] can scarcely be thought anything but senseless.

Nightmare Abbey seems to have appeared in America in 1819,[2] and perhaps not long afterwards was translated into French as *L'Abbaye de Cochemar*. The translation, however, did not find a publisher, and was still in the possession of Dr. Garnett in 1891.[3] Contemporary critics generally neglected it. *The Literary Gazette* ascribed it to Peacock,[4] but took no

---

[1] *Works*, i. 350–1.
[2] *North American Review*, ix. 215.
[3] *Nightmare Abbey*, ed. Garnett (1891), p. 12.
[4] ii. 787–8.

notice of its satirical treatment of living persons. Miss Mitford, who called it "the pleasantest of all Mr. Peacock's works," [1] recognised the caricatures of Byron and Coleridge, but not, seemingly, of Shelley. In 1818 Shelley's character was so little a matter of public repute that it is not surprising that very few readers marked the likeness. The vast growth of interest in Shelley, however, has had its effect upon *Nightmare Abbey*, so that, to judge by the number of editions, it has shared with the tale generally printed with it, *Headlong Hall*, the honour of being the most popular of all the novels, although *Maid Marian* has perhaps enjoyed a greater popularity than either during the last two decades.

[1] Miss Mitford, *Letters*, 2nd series, i. 41.

CHAPTER VI

INDIA HOUSE—MARRIAGE—THE FOUR AGES OF POETRY—PAPER MONEY LYRICS

FROM various fragments of evidence that remain, it is possible to throw a little light upon the Peacock of 1818, before he settled into official harness. Physically, he was strong and active, somewhat above the middle height, with a great mass of very fair hair, and bright blue eyes. He was good at swimming, walking, and rowing, and seemed quite unable to remain under a roof or to engage in any very arduous intellectual effort when pleasant weather called him out of doors. During the summer he lived in the open air from sunrise till dark ; when winter set in he descended to work again. It was his custom to rise very early in the morning, a habit which he kept up to the end of his days, and to read from about five till his breakfast at eight, always with great attention, but with frequent digressions and change of subject. Whenever he was engaged in composition, the forenoon was generally devoted to it ; his afternoons he customarily gave to exercise. In the evenings again he read, or spent the time with some of his few intimate friends. Peacock, by 1818, had largely outgrown the melancholy, based on philosophical principles, to which he had clung in his youth, and as the champion

of cheerfulness in *Nightmare Abbey* had said farewell
to the sentimental loneliness of a few years before ;
but he was by no means so converted by mirth to
social habits as to become fond of society in the
ordinary sense of the term. During his walks or boat-
ing trips he ordinarily dispensed with companions
unless they were recommended by unusual qualities
of congeniality or silence. On the only known occasion
on which he ever went to a ball, he is said to have
sat comfortably in a corner, where he commented on
his fellow-guests, declaring they should all have the
degrees D.D. (Deuced Dunce) or F.R.S. (Fellow
Remarkably Stupid), until he put a period to his own
raillery by falling asleep. When he was aroused, he
exclaimed quite unconcernedly, with a punning allusion to a then popular satire, " Oh, I made myself *The
Peacock at Home*."

In spite of the fact that he affected great sus-
ceptibility, and once laughingly gave his cousin Harriet
Love permission to write " The Thousand and One
Loves of Thomas Love Peacock," he was really very
much a man's man. He could be courteous to women,
and was ; his devotion to his mother never flagged.
But his favourite garb was the easy undress of a
bachelor evening, where learning, frequently recondite,
wit, often Rabelaisian, and wine, always Madeira,
might have equal share in the entertainment. Walter
Coulson, " The Admirable Coulson," whom Peacock
had probably first met at Marlow in October 1817,
Hogg, and Horace Smith were particular friends. He
met Keats, certainly as early as February 11, 1818,

when they were both present at a party given by Leigh Hunt,[1] but did not care much for him. "If I should live to the age of Methusalem, and have uninterrupted literary leisure, I should not find time to read Keats's *Hyperion*,"[2] he wrote Shelley. Keats, in his turn, mentions Peacock in a letter to Haydon, March 21, 1818, as having "damned satire," apparently by the badness of his satirical writings. Another incident, given as authentic, but so long buried in the columns of *Fraser's Magazine* that no one seems to have discovered it, may here be quoted in full, even at the risk of admitting a rather pointless anecdote, because anecdotes of Peacock are too scarce to be neglected.

"Some years ago it entered the imagination of Hunt and Keats, and some others of that coterie, to crown themselves with laurel, and take off their cravats. This was the janty [*sic*] thing and quite poetical. While the coroneted and uncravated company were sitting thus one day, 'with their singing robes about them,' Peacock came in. 'Do,' said a lady, who officiated as coronet manufacturer, 'do, dear Mr. Peacock, let me weave you a chaplet, and put it on your head; then you will sit as poets altogether.'

"'No, ma'am,' said Peacock, wiping his head, 'no, ma'am; you may make a fool of your own husband, but there is no need of your making a fool of me.'"[3]

---

[1] Dowden, *Shelley*, ii. 183.
[2] *Thomas Love Peacock : Letters*, &c., pp. 89-90.
[3] *Fraser's*, iv. 19.

THE FOUR AGES OF POETRY

Peacock was later intimate with Barry Cornwall, though he disliked his poetry, and seems to have known Hazlitt and Novello slightly. From Barry Cornwall's words,[1] it appears that Peacock may have met Charles Lamb at a supper given by Leigh Hunt, but not even Mr. E. V. Lucas has been able to throw any light upon the relations of the two humorists. He is doubtless right in conjecturing that Lamb held aloof by reason of his antipathy to Shelley. A very interesting friendship, but one concerning which almost no facts are known, was that with Thomas Taylor, the Platonist, who, in the character of " the learned mythologist " of *Melincourt*, hailed Sir Oran Haut-ton as Pan, and addressed to him an Orphic invocation. Taylor and Peacock had much in common. The older man was devoted to Greek with a lifelong passion, he was a foe to Greek accents, he thought Oxford dons " haughty and superficial." He praised the greater freedom of intelligence, the liberal scepticism, and the calm virtue of the ancients. He had early been fired with a desire to render into English all the extant philosophy of Greece, and in the process of carrying out his plan, had become so much a pagan that he hated roundly the new cult which had dispossessed the Olympian divinities. Gossip had it that he offered sacrifices to Jupiter in his house at Walworth, that he desired to establish a pantheon in London, and even that, during the French Revolution, he had led a procession of priests, himself at their head as Archflamen, to perform the rites of lustration before

[1] B. W. Proctor, *Autobiographical Fragment* (1877), p. 196.

the Exchange and receive the sleeping city into the dominions of the king of gods and men. Disraeli had ridiculed Taylor in the character of the Platonist in *Vaurien*, but Peacock seems to have been restrained by his friendship, or by secret sympathy, from merriment at Taylor's eccentricity. Peacock himself—" Greeky-Peeky," Taylor always called him—might have had, but for a strong sense of humour and great reticence, a reputation nearly the same as that of the modern Pletho. Years later a young acquaintance wrote of Peacock : " I think my good old friend, if he had worshipped anything, would have been inclined to worship Jupiter, as it was said that Taylor did." [1] This pagan bias caused Peacock to be suspected in Marlow of dangerous principles, as a man " who keeps everybody from going to church." [2]

For a time after Shelley left for Italy, Peacock's movements can be traced in some detail by reference to his letters to his friend—of which, however, not all have been preserved—and to a diary which Peacock kept from July 7 to September 26, 1818.[3] On the first date he and his mother moved into a new house in Marlow, and the next week was spent in getting to rights. July 19 he wrote to Shelley an account of the change :

" I have changed my habitation, having been literally besieged out of the other by horses and children. I purpose to remain in the one I am now in

---

[1] Sir M. E. Grant Duff, *Notes from a Diary*, 1851–1872 (1897), i. 41.
[2] *Thomas Love Peacock : Letters*, &c., p. 83.
[3] Brit. Mus. *Addit. MSS.*, 36815, fol. 2–9.

till death, fortune, or my landlord turns me out. It is cheap, and exceedingly comfortable. It is the one which Major Kelly lived in when you were here, facing the Coiting Place, in West Street. The weather continues dry and sultry. I have been very late on the river for several evenings, under the beams of the summer moon, and the air has been as warm as the shade by day, and so still that the tops of the poplars have stood, black in the moonlight, as motionless as spires of stone. If the summer of last year had been like this, you would not, I think, be now in Italy; but who could have foreseen it? Do not think I wish to play the tempter. If you return to England, I would most earnestly advise you to stay the winter in a milder climate. Still I do [Dr. Garnett's text erroneously inserts " not "] speculate on your return within two years as a strong probability, and I think where you are likely to take up your abode. Were I to choose the spot, I would fix you on one of the hills that border this valley. The Hunts would plant you at Paddington.[1] Your own taste, and Mary's, would perhaps point to the Forest. If ever you speculate on these points among yourselves, I should be glad to understand the view you take of them. It is pleasant to plant cuttings of futurity, if only one in ten takes root. But I deem it a moral impossibility that an Englishman who is not encrusted either with natural apathy or superinduced Giaourism, can live many years among such animals as the modern Italians.

---

[1] This sentence, omitted in Dr. Garnett's text, is supplied from an earlier quotation. See *Headlong Hall* (1891), p. 23.

" No number of ' Cobbett ' has been published for three weeks ; it is said he is coming home. Brougham has lost the Westmoreland election by a small difference of number. The Cumberland Poets, by their own conduct on this occasion, have put the finishing stroke to their own disgrace. I am persuaded there is nothing in the way of dirty work that these men are not abject enough to do, if the blessed Lord (Lonsdale) commanded it, or any other blessed member of the holy and almighty seat-selling aristocracy to which they have sold themselves, body and soul. I hope to have another letter from you soon. I shall be glad to hear that you have received the box. There is nothing new under the political sun, except that the forgery of Bank notes increases in a compound ratio of progression, and that the silver disappears rapidly, both symptoms of inextricable disarrangement in the machinery of the omnipotent paper-mill." [1]

Peacock's diary for the next two months contains little of importance. Nearly all of the afternoons, and many of the forenoons and evenings, he spent on the river, generally alone, but sometimes in the company of Hogg or of his mother. An occasional guest to dinner, tea at his uncle's, attendance at the Marlow Pony Races on July 22, and the Egham Races on August 25, and a little practical gardening are noted, but for the most part the journal is merely a record of his reading : Jarvis' *Don Quixote*, Gifford's *Juvenal*, Stanley's *History of Philosophy*, Nonnus, Buffon, Bacon's *Novum Organum* and *Essays*, Statius, Burke's *Letter*

[1] *Thomas Love Peacock : Letters,* &c., pp. 72–4.

to a Noble Lord, Bayle's *Dictionary*, Pindar, with Heyne's commentary, *The Merry Wives of Windsor*, Hume's *Essays*, *The Wealth of Nations*, and various English poets, Burns, Wordsworth, and Cowper among them. Writing to Shelley on August 30, he comments on his own doings :

"I am also scheming a Novel[1] which I shall write in the winter, and which will keep me during the whole of that season at home, in despite of Ambrogetti and Miss Milanie. I do not find this brilliant summer very favourable to intellectual exertion. The mere pleasure of existence in the open air is too absorbing for the energies of active thought, and too attractive for that resolute perseverance in sedentary study to which I find the long and dreary winter so propitious. To one who has never been out of England, the effect of this season is like removal to a new world. It is the climate of Italy transmitted to us by special favour of the gods ; and I cannot help thinking that our incipient restoration of true piety has propitiated the deities, and especially *hoc sublime candens quod vocamus omnes Jovem*. You have done well in translating the " Symposium," and I hope you will succeed in attracting attention to Plato, for he certainly wants patronage in these days, when philosophy sleeps and classical literature seems destined to participate in its repose.

"I passed a day or two with St. Croix and his bride this last week. I went to the races. I met on the course a great number of my old acquaintance by

[1] *Maid Marian.*

the reading portion of whom I was asked a multitude of questions concerning *Frankenstein* and its author. It seems to be universally known and read. The criticism of the " Quarterly," though unfriendly, contained many admissions of its merit, and must, on the whole, have done it service. It seems the discovery ships have failed in their object, and are returning *re conclamata*.

" I have lately read the *Thebais* of Statius, which, though too ornate and inflated, contains many fine passages, and is certainly well worth reading. I read *Nonnus* occasionally. The twelfth book, which contains the ' Metamorphosis of Ampelus,' is very beautiful, and concludes with an animated picture of the dance of the inebriated Satyrs when Bacchus made his first wine-press, by digging a hole in a rock, and horn (afterwards sacred in consequence) was used instead of cups.

" For the most part, my division of time is this : I devote the forenoon to writing ; the afternoon to the river, the woods, and classical poetry ; the evening to philosophy—at present, the *Novum Organum* and the *Histoire Naturelle*, which is a treasury of inexhaustible delight. My reading is, as usual at this season, somewhat desultory. I open to myself many vistas in the great forest of mind, and reconnoitre the tracts of territory which in the winter I propose to acquire." [1]

His forenoon, theoretically devoted to writing, could not have been very busy. A few letters to

---

[1] *Thomas Love Peacock : Letters*, &c., pp. 74–6.

THE FOUR AGES OF POETRY

Shelley, Hookham, and one or two unknown friends, are noted. Besides this he wrote nothing, apparently, except a considerable fragment of an *Essay on Fashionable Literature*, of which a part has been printed in *Notes and Queries*.[1] The essay hardly warrants publication, although some of the paragraphs are interesting from a biographical standpoint. One is not surprised to find him scoring reviewers, the universities, the clergy, literary coteries, and fashionable laziness with an unsparing hand ; but many readers will be surprised to know that he speaks in praise of Scott, Wordsworth, and Coleridge, the last of whom he defends in detail from the attacks of *The Edinburgh Review*. One brief passage from the *Essay* deserves quotation :

" XXV. Fancy, indeed, treads on dangerous ground when she trespasses on the land of opinion— —the soil is too slippery for her glass slippers, and the atmosphere too heavy for her filmy wings But she is a degenerate spirit if she be contented within the limits of her own empire and keep the mind continually poring upon phantasms without pointing to more important realities. Her province is to awaken the mind, not to enchain it. Poetry preceded philosophy, but true poetry prepares its path.[2]

" XXVI. Cervantes, Rabelais, Swift, Voltaire, Fielding, have led fancy against opinion with a success that no other names can parallel. Works of

[1] *Notes and Queries*, Series XI., ii. 5–6 ; 62–3.
[2] Here follow in the manuscript the words, " See Forsyth." Peacock evidently meant to add a note from Forsyth's *Principles of Moral Science*.

mere amusement that teach nothing may have an accidental and transient success, but cannot of course have influence on their own times, and will certainly not pass to posterity. W. Scott's success has been attributed in a great measure to his keeping clear of opinion. But he is far from being a writer who teaches nothing. On the contrary, he communicates great and valuable information. He is a painter of manners. He is the historian of a peculiar and remote class of our countrymen who within a few years have completely passed away. He offers materials to the philosopher in depicting with the truth of life the features of human nature in a peculiar state of society, before comparatively little known.

" XXVII. Information, not inquiry ; manners, not morals ; facts, not influences, are the taste of the present day. If philosophy be not dead, it is at least sleeping in the country of Bacon and Locke. The seats of learning (as the universities are still called, according to the proverb, ' Once a captain, always a captain ') are armed cap-a-pie against her. The metaphysician, having lifted his voice and been regarded by no man, folds up his Plato and writes a poem." [1]

A more important literary work is first hinted at by an entry in the diary for August 4. " Looked over various books, fishing for a scheme for a romance. Rd. 3rd book of the Thebaid of Statius and some of

[1] Brit. Mus. *Addit. MSS.*, 36815, fol. 76–7. The punctuation, in the original almost lacking, has here been made to conform to the ordinary rules. Dr. Young's version in *Notes and Queries* is not quite accurate.

the old English Ballads." The next day : " Rd. 4th book of Thebaid, went on the river, but occupied the principal part of the day with meditating the scheme of a romance." And August 6 : " Could not read or write for scheming my romance. Rivers, castles, forests, abbeys, monks, maids, kings, and banditti dancing before me like a masked ball." On August 12 and 13, he speaks of reading " ballads about Robin Hood," but the diary says no more. His romance was very evidently, however, *Maid Marian*, which he took up seriously later in the year. Writing to Shelley on November 29, he called it " a comic Romance of the Twelfth Century, which I shall make the vehicle of much oblique satire on the oppressions that are done under the sun. I have suspended the Essay till the completion of the Romance."[1] Its completion, however, though it progressed rapidly to within three chapters of the end, was postponed until 1822, and the discussion of it belongs properly to the following chapter.

This delay was caused by a great change in Peacock's life. In all probability his financial circumstances had not been latterly of the best. A family tradition has it that he had lost heavily through going security for his friend Peter Auber. This may have been responsible for his ardent study of the reports which Birkbeck and Cobbett had sent back from America, apparently half in mind, during September, that emigration would be a possible solution of his difficulties. " The temptation to agriculturists with a small capital must be

[1] *Thomas Love Peacock : Letters*, &c., p. 81.

irresistible," Peacock wrote Shelley; "and the picture he [Birkbeck] presents of the march of cultivation and population beyond the Ohio is one of the most wonderful spectacles ever yet presented to the mind's eye of philosophy." [1] Financial pressure, likewise, rather than any burden of leisure, may have been responsible for his plan to organise a liberal review to counteract the influence of those already existing.[2] But he speedily decided to remain in England, and Hunt's *Liberal* took the place of Peacock's review among the "cuttings of futurity," when Auber, for gratitude or friendship, suggested employment at the India House. By the retirement of two employees from the office of the Examiner of the East India Correspondence, that department was heavily crippled. Moreover, the increase in business since the last organisation of the office in 1809 had rendered the staff, even with the retiring Rundall and Halhed, unable to cope with the demands made upon them. Consequently the Committee of Correspondence to the Board of Directors was ordered to prepare a report leading to the reconstitution of the Examiner's Office, It was perhaps largely through the recommendation of Auber, then Deputy-Secretary, that Peacock became one of the four men upon whom the choice of the Committee fell. The others were Edward Strachey, James Mill, and a former clerk in the same office, John Johnson Harcourt.

Peacock learned of the vacancy as early as October,

[1] *Thomas Love Peacock : Letters*, &c., p. 78.
[2] Shelley, *Letters*, p. 675.

and by November 5 had drawn up a paper on *The Ryotwar and Zemindary Settlements* which was presented to the Committee. At the end of November, however, he was not yet sure, and wrote Shelley that he had no intention of going to London at all, unless particular business called him.[1] Again, two weeks later, he said he was "rooted like a tree on the banks of one bright river."[2] Just after the beginning of the year, however, he was called to London to undergo a probationary period of six weeks' study. He lived with his mother at 5 York Street, Covent Garden, and, writing to Shelley, January 13, says, "I now pass every morning at the India House, from half past ten to half past four, studying Indian affairs. My object is not yet attained, though I have little doubt that it will be. It was not in the first instance of my own seeking, but was proposed to me. It will lead to a very sufficing provision for me in two or three years. It is not in the common routine of office but is an employment of a very interesting and intellectual kind, connected with finance and legislation, in which it is possible to be of great service, not only to the Company, but to the millions under their dominion."[3] His examination papers were returned to him with the commendation, "Nothing superfluous, and nothing wanting." Later Peacock used characteristically to say that he owed all his success in the world to his knowledge of Greek, which seems to have stood him in good stead at this examination.

[1] *Thomas Love Peacock : Letters,* &c., p. 81.
[2] *Ibid.,* p. 84.   [3] *Ibid.,* p. 86.

THOMAS LOVE PEACOCK

In the Court of Directors the new appointments were delayed when Charles Lloyd resigned the Assistant Examinership, to which he had been called February 3. On May 19, however, the Committee recommended that the office should take on four new "Assistants to the Examiner," who were to undergo a probation of two years, with a view to determining whether they should be made a part of the permanent establishment. Although Peacock ranked third on the list, his salary was fixed at only £600, to £1000 for Strachey, who was first, and £800 each for Mill and Harcourt, who were second and fourth respectively. As if partly to atone for this, Peacock's salary was to begin from the preceding Christmas. These appointments were confirmed April 10, 1821, and the salary of each man was raised £200. Not till then did their names appear on the Company's official lists.

His new occupation, of course, forced Peacock to move to London, but it made no very serious demands upon his time. He could still read in the early morning before he went to the office at ten; after four in the afternoon he was once more a free man. A letter from Leigh Hunt to Shelley tells how he spent his week-ends. "Hogg and Peacock generally live here over Sunday, when the former is not on the circuit; and we pass very pleasant afternoons, talking of mythology, and the Greeks, and our old friends. . . . You have heard, of course, of Peacock's appointment in the India House; we joke him upon his new Oriental grandeur, his Brahminical learning, and his inevitable tendencies to be one of the corrupt, upon which he seems to apprehend Shelleian objurgation. It is an honour to him that ' prosperity ' sits on him well. He is very pleasant and hospitable." [1] Shelley, far from reproaching Peacock for his indulgence in prosperity, was much pleased, and only irritated because he seemed quite unable to find out just what Peacock's work was. " What is it you do," he wrote, " at the India House ? Hunt writes and says you have got a *situation* in the India House : Hogg that you have an *honourable employment :* Godwin writes to Mary that you have got *so much or so much :* but nothing of what you do. The devil take these general terms ! " [2]

As the letter which Peacock wrote explaining his new duties was lost, his own testimony concerning these early days at the India House is not forthcoming. He found ample time, however, to render Shelley various services in London. He read the proof for *Rosalind and Helen.* In July 1819 Shelley sent Peacock a translation of the manuscript on which *The Cenci* story was founded, asking him for advice as to the best method of treating it. Peacock, who thought the theme one which might have been handled in the age of Massinger, but not since, returned suggestions which by no means met with Shelley's approval, but Shelley nevertheless enlisted his friend's further services in the endeavour to get *The Cenci* produced. Later in the same year *Prometheus Unbound,* concerning which

---

[1] *Correspondence of Leigh Hunt* (1862), i. 129.
[2] Shelley, *Letters,* p. 709.

they had already held correspondence, was put into Peacock's hands to await publication.

By July Peacock had taken a house at 18 Stamford Street, Blackfriars, "which, as you might expect from a Republican," Hogg cynically remarks, "he has furnished very handsomely." [1] Stamford Street was not in 1819 the long dingy thoroughfare it is now, but a short street running westwards from Surrey Street, as that part of Blackfriars Road was then called, and ending, only a few doors beyond Peacock's house, in an open field. To the new home came his mother, and thither, very soon, he took steps to bring the prime necessity of a well-established bachelor. His friends seem to have regarded it as more or less a matter of accident upon whom the choice would fall, if we may judge by a passage in one of Shelley's letters, omitted by Peacock and first published by Mr. Ingpen in 1909 : " If you had married Marianne I should never have seen much of you, and now I have at least a chance." [2] Who this Marianne was is unknown. She must not, of course, be confused with the other Marianne frequently mentioned in the correspondence of this group, Mrs. Leigh Hunt. She was evidently a friend of long standing, for Peacock had mentioned her in a letter to Hookham as early as 1810, and had been in correspondence with her, as his journal witnesses, eight years later. Whether the following letter, hitherto apparently unnoticed, from Leigh Hunt to Shelley, establish the identity or not, it at any rate throws some further light upon

[1] *Headlong Hall* (1891), p. 27.   [2] Shelley, *Letters*, p. 782.

Peacock's reputation as a lover : " Peacock has been reasoned by some mathematician out of his love for the opera, and is to read Greek, they say, instead on Saturday nights—the Dithyrambic, of course—to begin at seven precisely. What do you think of this *début* of mine in scandal ? But he glories in doing nothing except upon theory. He falls in love, as it were, upon a gravitating principle. His passion, literally, as well as metaphorically, is quite problematical. Let B be Miss Jenkins, &c." [1] The philosopher who fell in love by rule, now proceeded to woo by measure. Although he had heard nothing from Jane Gryffydh since 1811, he sent her, on November 20, a letter which was first published in opposition to the wishes of his family, but which, having become public property, may as well be quoted again in the correct form :

"It is more than eight years since I had the happiness of seeing you : I can scarcely hope that you have remembered me as I have remembered you ; yet I feel confident that the simplicity and ingenuousness of your disposition will prompt you to answer me with the same candor with which I write to you. I long entertained the hopes of returning to Merionethshire under better auspices than those under which I left it : but fortune always disappointed me, continually offering me prospects which receded as I approached them. Recently she has made amends for her past unkindness, and has given me much present good, and much promise of progressive prosperity, which leaves

[1] *Correspondence of Leigh Hunt,* i. 134.

me nothing to desire in worldly advantage, but to participate it with you. The greatest blessing this world could bestow on me would be to make you my wife : consider if your own feelings would allow you to constitute my happiness. I desire only to promote yours ; and I desire only you : for your value is beyond fortune, of which I want no more than I have. The same circumstances which have given me prosperity confine me to London, and to the duties of the department with which the East India Company has entrusted me : yet I can absent myself for a few days once in every year : if you sanction my wishes, with what delight should I employ them in bringing you to my home ! If this be but a baseless dream : if I am even no more in your estimation than the sands on the seashore—yet I am sure, as I have already said, that you will answer me with the same candor with which I have written. Whatever may be your sentiments, the feelings with which I now write to you, and which more than eight years of absence and silence have neither obliterated nor diminished, will convince you that I never can be otherwise than most sincerely and affectionately your friend.   T. L. PEACOCK.

" EAST INDIA HOUSE,
    " *November 20th,* 1819."

No comment upon this amazing proposal is so good as Shelley's, who declared it to be very like the conclusion of one of Peacock's novels. Less of the savour of improbability was the reply which came ten days later from Tan-y-bwlch, where Peacock's letter must have carried great, although apparently pleasant, consternation. Miss Gryffydh would not confess that she had remembered him as he seemed to have remembered her, but she had remembered him with some favour. To be sure, no one can make out from her letter whether she accepted him, but Peacock seems not to have been rebuffed by her prim answer. On March 22 of the following year, " Thomas Love Peacock, of the Parish of Christ Church, in the County of Surrey, Bachelor, and Jane Gryffdyh, of the Chapelry of Eglwysfach, in the Parish of Llanfihangel Geneu'rglyn in this County, Spinster," were married in the Chapel of Eglwysfach in Cardiganshire, and came directly to live in their new home.

To a very Peacockian courtship there succeeded a long married life, quite as much in keeping with Peacock's real character as was his proposal with his manner in the novels. As long as she lived, he gave his wife the most constant devotion, and, after she became an invalid, the most solicitous tenderness. In Wales the bride had been called, the story goes, " the beauty of Carnarvonshire." She must have lived in Carnarvon before Peacock met her. Mrs. Gisborne, who visited the Peacocks on her return from Italy, with a message from Shelley, wrote in her diary : " Mrs. Peacock seems to be a very good-natured, simple, unaffected, untaught, prettyish Welsh girl." [1] Further testimony as to her character and person during her early married life, save that she was tall, had fine lustrous eyes, and was a tolerable scholar,

[1] *Headlong Hall* (1891), p. 29.

there is none. Those who still remember her, remember her only as she appeared during her later years, when long illness had much changed her.

Now established in the world, with a substantial income, a handsome house, and a beautiful wife, Peacock became an exemplary citizen. Shelley complained that his friend's letters had fallen off in frequency,[1] and alluded to the same thing in his lines on Peacock in the letter to Maria Gisborne :

> " And there
> Is English Peacock, with his mountain fair,
> Turned into a Flamingo—that shy bird
> That gleams in the Indian air ;—have you not heard
> When a man marries, dies, or turns Hindoo,
> His best friends hear no more of him ?—but you
> Will see him, and will like him too, I hope,
> With the milk-white Snowdonian Antelope
> Matched with this camelopard ; his fine wit
> Makes such a wound, the knife is lost in it,
> A strain too learned for a shallow age,
> Too wise for selfish bigots ; let his page
> Which charms the chosen spirits of the time,
> Fold itself up for the serener clime
> Of years to come, and find its recompense
> In that just expectation."

Brought from a retired life at Marlow into a tolerably busy life in London, Peacock of course made new acquaintances, although not a great many. Edward Strachey and Horace Grant, both in the Examiner's Office, became his intimate friends. For the two Mills he cared less. The story is told that when Coulson asked him, " When I know Mill well, shall I like him—will he like what I like and hate

[1] *Letters*, p. 873.

what I hate?" Peacock replied, "No, he will hate what you hate and hate everything you like."[1] Peacock's low estimate of the science of political economy was not increased by his contact with his superior in office, but he refrained from publishing his *Paper Money Lyrics*, written in 1825, till after Mill's death, in order not to offend him. John Stuart Mill he always thought a greatly over-rated philosopher. When he introduced the youthful J. A. Roebuck to John Mill in 1824, and thus gave him the impetus to a long career of philosophical radicalism, he told him that Mill belonged to a "*disquisition* set of young men."[2] Later he introduced (Sir) Henry Cole also to Mill, a service for which Cole, as did Roebuck, always held himself vastly indebted to Peacock. Through the Mills Peacock met Jeremy Bentham, and was admitted once a week for years to dine alone with the father and prophet of Utilitarianism. Walter Coulson, Hogg, and Horace Smith, however, his old friends, still continued Peacock's best friends. Hogg and Coulson, who became, in 1822, editor of *The Globe*, and in 1823 editor of *The Globe and Traveller*, to which Peacock sometimes contributed, generally passed one evening a week with Peacock, who would repeat their jokes to Henry Cole as the two walked the next morning to the India House in Leadenhall Street, by Bankside and over Old London Bridge. Sir Henry Cole records in his diary that he went with his father to live in Peacock's Stamford Street house, April 15, 1826. Peacock had removed his family to

[1] *Calidore*, &c., p. 17.   [2] Roebuck, *Autobiography*, p. 25.

Halliford, and kept only two rooms for his own use. Cole was much attracted by Peacock, spent many evenings with him, made for him " tracings of Bacchic figures in the British Museum," and not infrequently went to the opera in Peacock's stead to take notes for the critiques which Peacock wrote.

Shelley made occasional claims upon his friend's time. Peacock read the proofs of *Prometheus Unbound*, not much to the satisfaction of its author. He also gave considerable attention to Shelley's ill-managed financial affairs, and was obliged to discourage him from hopes of a place in the India service : " I should not like your Indian project (which I think would agree neither with your mind or body) if it were practicable. But it is altogether impossible. The whole of the Civil Service of India is sealed against all but the Company's covenanted servants, who are inducted into it through established gradations, beginning at an early period of life. There is nothing that would give me so much pleasure (because I think there is nothing that would be more beneficial to you) than to see you following some scheme of flesh and blood— some interesting matter connected with the business of life, in the tangible shape of a practical man : and I shall make it a point of sedulous inquiry to discover if there be anything attainable of this nature that would be likely to please and suit you." [1] This was in October, but any inquiry Peacock may have made of course came to an end on Shelley's tragic death the following July. Peacock was found to have been

---

[1] *Thomas Love Peacock : Letters, &c.*, p. 92.

appointed joint executor of Shelley's will with Byron, and to have received a legacy of £500 and £2000 to be used for an annuity. Byron's absence abroad and his early death threw a great part of the business of settlement upon Peacock. Mary Shelley's unwarranted suspicion that he would be " very lukewarm and insensible " [1] in the affair was not justified, Godwin assured her.[2] In 1824 [3] and again in 1826 [4] it was Peacock who acted as agent between Mrs. Shelley and Sir Timothy in the negotiations which led to provision for the dead poet's children and widow, but he appears not to have been one of the guarantors for the volume of *Posthumous Poems* which appeared in 1824. As Beddoes, who was one, mentions Peacock in a letter written while the volume was undergoing preparation,[5] it may well be that he was concerned in the editing. Mrs. Shelley continued to feel a grievance on account of some boxes which had been left with Peacock in Marlow, and which he, on going to London, had deposited with Shelley's landlord, Maddocks. Maddocks, claiming a debt, had refused to restore them, and while Peacock was attempting their recovery, they disappeared.

Peacock's private life calls for little notice. In July 1821 was born his eldest child, Mary Ellen, " who grows and flourishes delightfully in this fumose and cinereous atmosphere." [6] During September of this year he went for a brief vacation in Wales, to

[1] Mrs. Marshall, *Mary Wollstonecraft Shelley*, ii. 34.
[2] *Ibid.*, ii. 51.   [3] *Ibid.*, ii. 121.   [4] *Ibid.*, ii. 150.
[5] Beddoes, *Letters*, ed. Gosse (1894), p. 24.
[6] *Thomas Love Peacock : Letters*, &c., p. 92.

pay a flying visit to his wife's family and to go once more over the scenes of his early rambles. His letters to his wife protest at the separation, and he resolves never to endure so long an absence from home again. A second daughter followed in March 1823, and later a son, Edward Gryffydh, and a daughter, Rosa Jane. In 1823 Peacock took a cottage at Lower Halliford for his mother, and soon moved his whole family thither. The cottage was enlarged by joining another to it, and remained his home to the end of his life, although for many years he came to Halliford only on Friday evenings, and went back Monday morning for the rest of the week. Not infrequently some of his friends from the City would come down with him. In January 1826 Edward Strachey and one or two others had done so, invited because Margaret, the second child, who had been very ill for some time, was now thought to be out of any danger. The men went out for a walk in high spirits, only to find on their return that the child, grown suddenly worse, had died during her father's absence. Both the parents felt the loss terribly. There were times, Peacock told Strachey, when the world could not be made fun of. He wrote for his child's gravestone at Shepperton the exquisite lines, " Long night succeeds thy little day," which constitute his finest serious lyric, and which Palgrave's selection for the second series of the *Golden Treasury* has made widely known.[1] The sorrow which called forth the

---

[1] It has been delightfully rendered in Latin elegiacs by E. D. A. Morshead (*Westminster Versions*, 1906, pp. 18–19).

poem, perhaps the more intense because of Peacock's total disbelief in human immortality, was aggravated by a quarrel which followed its composition. The vicar of Shepperton objected to the epitaph with tactless bigotry, on the ground that its sentiments in regard to a future life were not orthodox, and Peacock's temper, always hasty, flared up into bitter wrath.

Mrs. Peacock never recovered from her grief at the child's death. The loss of her health dates from the loss of Margaret, although it was some years before she became a complete invalid. Peacock's mother took the place of his wife in attending to the household. As she was already advanced in years, she was obliged to rely upon her son to an extent which hindered any literary work which he might otherwise have undertaken. Both he and his wife, however, were in part consoled by another little girl, Mary Rosewell, whose parents lived in Halliford. She first attracted their attention by her resemblance to the dead child, was brought to their house, finally adopted, and lived with Peacock, a devoted and unselfish daughter, until his death.

Although the India House interfered with Peacock's writing, it did not altogether put a period to it. He seems to say, in his letter to Shelley dated November 29, 1818, that he had written a political pamphlet which he meant to publish " about the meeting of Parliament," [1] but if he did so, it has been impossible to identify it. Near the end of 1819

---

[1] *Thomas Love Peacock : Letters*, &c., p. 81.

he wrote his paradoxical little essay, *The Four Ages of Poetry*, which came out as the last article in *Ollier's Literary Miscellany* at the beginning of 1820, and achieved notability by calling forth Shelley's impassioned *Defence of Poetry*. The ages of classical poetry, Peacock declared, should be arranged in an order which varies from the order of the ages of the world in having the age of iron first. Thus, the first is the bardic age ; the second, or golden, is the Homeric age ; the third, or silver, is the age of Virgil ; and the last is the brazen age of Nonnus. In England a similar progressive degradation has been observable. Shakespeare was the chief poet of the golden age ; Milton, the greatest English poet, stands between the golden and silver ages, combining the excellences of both ; the silver age was the reign of authority, the age of Dryden, Pope, Goldsmith, Collins, Gray ; and the age of brass, of course, is the age of Peacock's contemporaries, of Scott and the Lake school. The time has come when more useful learning has superseded poetic studies ; the poetry of the past, beautiful as it is, can now be read only at a sacrifice of time more wisely spent on other matters ; and it will not be long before all poetry will be held mere folly, and solid, practical learning will take its place.

It is interesting to note how the six months man of business erects an antimony of poetry and science, the very antimony of Wordsworth's own theory, as if to justify his transfer from poetical studies to the study of the practical world. An extract from a letter to Shelley on December 4, 1820, shows much the same attitude towards the subject : " Considering poetical reputation as a prize to be obtained by a certain species of exertion, and that the sort of thing which obtains this prize is the drivelling doggerel published under the name of ' Barry Cornwall,' I think but one conclusion possible—that to a rational ambition poetical reputation is not only not to be desired, but most earnestly to be deprecated. The truth, I am convinced, is, that there is no longer a poetical audience among the higher class of minds ; that moral, political, and physical science have entirely withdrawn from poetry the attention of all whose attention is worth having ; and that the poetical reading public, being composed of the mere dregs of the intellectual community, the most sufficing passport to their favour must rest on the mixture of a little easily intelligible portion of mawkish sentiment with an absolute negation of reason and knowledge. These I take to be the prime and sole elements of Mr. Barry Cornwall's ' Madrigals.' " [1]   But this, like the essay, is rather an attack upon contemporary taste than upon poetry itself. Few have loved poetry more than Peacock. " If I know the knight by the device of his shield," Shelley said in one of the cancelled passages of his *Defence*, " I have only to inscribe Cassandra, Antigone, or Alcestis on mine to blunt the point of his spear." [2] Starting with a pronounced dislike for most of his contemporaries, Peacock took a few of the ludicrous features of recent poetry, and elaborated them into

[1] *Thomas Love Peacock : Letters, &c.*, p. 90.
[2] *Memoirs of Shelley*, p. 208.

153

a systematic caricature of the whole art, exactly as he had produced his caricatures of actual men. His theory of poetical origins and developments was invented to suit his requirements. The entire essay had to be in keeping with this central idea, and it led him into statements which must not be scanned too closely. A reasoned criticism of *The Four Ages of Poetry* and any show of irritation at its opinions would be equally ludicrous. Poetry needs defence so little, and lacks defenders, of greater or less degree of reasonableness, so seldom, that its lovers may smile at the whimsical raillery with which the muse is here treated. Peacock is turning his back upon his real opinions when he asserts, at the close of the essay, that the growth of science, the pretensions of which he always ridicules, even the science of political economy, which he detested, will quite properly rid the world of all that constitutes the essence of poetry. If he had maintained merely that modern materialism had made poetry almost impossible, as did Macaulay's essay on Milton five years later, his contention might have seemed derived from his general attitude of scorn toward his generation. As it was, he rejected poetry voluntarily, on the grounds of use, in favour of the very " advances " in civilisation, the usefulness of which it was his custom to deny.

Shelley's *Defence*, as it now stands, shows little trace of being a reply to Peacock except in an over-emphasis upon the utility of poets. *The Four Ages* and its denunciation of poetry in general was sent to Italy along with the letter in which its author inveighed against Barry Cornwall. Shelley promptly set about a reply, and soon forwarded to England what he intended for the first of three parts of an essay which should answer his friend. He realised that he had taken a more general view of poetry than had Peacock. In fact, the two essays do not furnish a controversy at all. The allusions to Peacock which the *Defence* originally contained were struck out by John Hunt when he prepared the paper for *The Liberal*, and Mrs. Shelley later published the abridged version. So far as the argument is concerned, there is no more contest than ensues whenever easy mirth and intense seriousness are opposed. Peacock made merry with certain features of a noble art, and Shelley saw fit to answer his mirth with a lofty defence of the art itself.

Peacock had completed *Maid Marian* and brought it out by the beginning of 1822. *The London Magazine* for October and November of the same year contains an article *On the Poetry of Nonnus*, with considerable translations from the *Dionysiaca*, which Sir Henry Cole ascribed to Peacock,[1] an ascription which has recently been accepted by Dr. Young.[2] It is tolerably clear, however, that Cole had no reason for thinking Peacock wrote the essay except the fact that Peacock was exceptionally fond of Nonnus. A note which Cole sent to *Notes and Queries*,[3] some years after he had put the statement into print, asking whether the " Vida " articles in *The London Magazine*

---

[1] Cole, p. 21. [2] Young, *Life and Novels*, p. 19.
[3] Series V., vol. xi. p. 343 (May 3, 1879).

were by Peacock, confirms one in the belief that his previous judgment had been mere guess-work. Moreover, Peacock himself in 1862 sent Thomas L'Estrange a list of his periodical essays,[1] in which he says nothing whatever of this one. A single article, indeed, might have escaped his memory; an examination of *The London Magazine* shows that "Vida" contributed no less than nine articles to its columns from October 1822 to November 1823. Two are on Nonnus,[2] three on Quintus Calaber,[3] three are versions from the Greek tragic poets,[4] and one a general essay "On the Tragic Drama of Greece."[5] No one really familiar with Peacock's verse can think the translations his; the prose of these essays has none of his point; and the last-named contains opinions so at variance with Peacock's own that little further doubt can remain.

According to a statement in Coulson's *Globe and Traveller* for August 27, 1825, Peacock's clever verses *Rich and Poor ; or, Saint and Sinner*, had first been published in that paper "three or four years ago." An investigation of the file in the British Museum has resulted in a failure to discover the exact date. The poem, however, seems to have been very widely copied, but it was not generally known to be the work of Peacock.[6] The financial flurry of the winter of 1825–6 called forth *The Paper Money Lyrics*. Among his friends and associates Peacock was well known to be the author of the poems, which were handed about in manuscript

---

[1] Cole, pp. 32–34.   [2] vi. 336, 440.
[3] vi. 508 ; vii. 63, 199.   [4] viii. 262, 373, 503.
[5] viii. 625.   [6] See *Bibliography*.

and greatly enjoyed. But, for a reason already given, he kept them from the public until 1837. Then, a few having found their way into the short-lived *Guide*, edited by (Sir) Henry Cole, they were all collected in a privately printed edition of one hundred copies. Some of the parodies are clever, but they have lost a good deal of their zest with the disappearance of the spirit which combatted paper money as a dangerous Whig innovation. Peacock's opposition to paper money was a conservative prejudice which appeared early and lasted late, but it did not produce one of those rarest of rareties, a political poem which can hold the interest of a remote generation.

CHAPTER VII

"MAID MARIAN"—"THE MISFORTUNES OF ELPHIN"

THE third edition of *Headlong Hall* and the new *Maid Marian* were both in press by February 1822.[1] As the latter had been announced as printing a month earlier,[2] it had probably been completed some time near the close of the preceding year. There is nothing about the last chapters to indicate that they were composed after the rest of the book; but Peacock was careful to insert a prefatory note : " This little work, with the exception of the last three chapters, was all written in the autumn of 1818," in order to disarm the suspicion, likely enough under the circumstances, that his tale had been called forth by the great popularity of *Ivanhoe*, then three years before the world. The allusions to Peacock's romance in his diary of 1818 would furnish assurance of his good faith, even if it were doubted. There is, however, a still better proof of the independence of the two novels in their utter dissimilarity. The magnitude of *Ivanhoe*, the greatness of its issues, the intensity of its conflicts, the near approach to tragedy, the wide familiarity with mediæval manners, have no counterpart in the idyll of Sherwood Forest. *Maid Marian*, a mere

[1] *Blackwood's*, xi. 250.
[2] *British Critic*, New Series, xvii. 112.

burst of jovial laughter, sweetened with singing, and spiced with wit, took its origin in the mood of a man laughing at the nineteenth century from the standpoint of the twelfth. Slight as had been the limitations of verisimilitude forced upon Peacock by his tales of contemporary manners, here he was even freer. He could give his book an atmosphere of beauty and poetry and greenwood liberty which would have been out of place in the chronicle of a Mr. Escot or a Scythrop Glowry. At the same time, endless occasion for satirical comment upon the world, frail flesh, and the merry devils who rule it, remained. In Sherwood Forest might was avowedly right, though none the more so because there were no hypocritical philosophers or economists, Peacock would have said, to deny an obvious truth by a seemingly contradictory theory. The oppression of rulers, clerical gluttony and intolerance, and the slippery faith of the people, might furnish unpleasant obstacles to any belief that the Middle Ages had been an age of gold. Yet under the first Richard simplicity of manners was not merely a fashionable affectation, an out-of-door life was an easy possibility, and England still wore the name Merry England with some reason. From his new ground of attack Peacock could ridicule the reign of Richard I., because it was not more sensible, and he could cast oblique aspersions upon the Regency because it was so little like the twelfth century.

The great knowledge of English antiquity which Scott exhibited does not appear in *Maid Marian*. An occasional " gramercy " or " peradventure," with a few friarly "thou's" and "thee's," constitute practically all the archaism in a style of distinguished clearness and grace. There are no attempts at depicting the minutiæ of twelfth-century manners or costume. Such details as the drinking of canary, the wearing of miniatures, and walls hung with portraits, seem almost humorously anachronistic. The woodland scenes might have been localised in Windsor as well as in Sherwood Forest. For the most part, Peacock derived his details less from any first hand antiquarian knowledge of the period in which they took place, than from the ordinary traditional accounts of Robin Hood. His indebtedness to his sources of information appears to be tolerably simple. In making Robin Hood Earl of Huntington he follows an Elizabethan custom which had been discussed by Ritson in his *Robin Hood* (1795). The title, Earl of Locksley and Huntington, seems to be Peacock's own addition to Robin's nobility. Maid Marian is identified with Matilda Fitzwater, for whom King John is said to have had a guilty passion, on the authority of Munday and Chettle's two plays, *The Downfall,* and *The Death, of Robert, Earl of Huntington* (1601). These two plays furnish a considerable part of the basis of the novel. While Peacock may have done so, however, there seems no reason to say with certainty that he had read the old plays themselves. As neither had been reprinted since the quartos of 1601, as Ritson had given abstracts of both, and as Peacock's borrowings do not go beyond the extracts in Ritson's discussion, it seems safe to conclude that he may have

known the plays only in this form.[1] As to the other
incidents of the novel which could not have been taken
from the dramas, they can generally be traced to the
ballads of Ritson's collection.[2] It is quite within the
bounds of probability that Peacock, far from expending
much time in research, actually made use of Ritson,
and Ritson alone. If his library catalogue be trusted,
however, it must be owned that, although he had
several of Ritson's books, *Robin Hood* was not one
of them.

To indicate Peacock's sources is, of course, a service
of small importance, but it is interesting to note how
he shapes to his own purposes the material thus
gathered. His plot, although it has little dramatic

[1] The code of the outlaws in *Maid Marian* comes from a similar
code in the *Downfall*. In the play, too, Earl Fitzwater goes to find his
daughter and her lover in Sherwood Forest. The lines which Peacock
misquotes, as from an " Old Play," are given by Ritson from the
Downfall.

[2] Thus : the suit of the Abbot of Doncaster which brings the Earl
of Huntington to outlawry, is from the *True Tale of Robin Hood*,
although the abbot there is of St. Mary's ; Robin's relationship to the
Gamwells of Gamwell Hall and the origin of Little John are from
Robin Hood's Birth, Breeding, Valour, and Marriage ; the adventure
with the Abbot of Doubleflask repeats details from the ballads, *Robin
Hood and the Bishop of Hereford,* and *Robin Hood and the Bishop ;* the
rescue of young Gamwell from hanging, while based on incidents well
known in Robin Hood story, seems most likely to have come from
Robin Hood's Rescuing Will Stutly ; the ballad " Bold Robin has robed
him in ghostly attire," looks to *Robin Hood's Golden Prize* for a
source ; the story of the help which Robin gives Allen to recover his
bride varies little from the familiar ballad of Allen-a-Dale ; Sir William
of the Lee, the sorrowful knight of the last chapter, comes, though
his name does not, from the *Lytell Geste of Robin Hood,* which also
contributes several minor points to the narrative. These ballads, of
course, Peacock might have seen in *Robin Hood's Garland,* of which so
many editions appeared during the eighteenth century. A writer in *The
Globe* for December 4, 1822, who may have had the information directly
from Peacock, the editor's close friend, pointed out *Robin Hood's
Garland* and Ritson as the sources of the narrative.

structure or suspense, begins by being tolerably well knit. Toward the middle it descends to a succession of events, all wittily told, but still without any very marked connection. Robin Hood becomes a more dignified personage than the hero of the popular ballads. As Earl of Locksley and Huntington he never gets the worst of combats with pedlars and tinkers. In the meeting of Robin, disguised as a strolling minstrel, and Friar Tuck, it is the outlaw leader who throws his ghostly adviser into the water, and not the reverse, as in *Robin Hood and the curtall Fryer*. The characters of the piece have all been intellectualised into the sayers of witty things. This is especially true of Father Michael, *alias* Friar Tuck, who represents a far cleverer scoundrel than the holy clerk of Copmanhurst, and one quite as bibulous. Conversation in this Sherwood has the flavour of salon repartee. One must smile a little to see how much more deadly are the arrows of wit than the grey-goose shafts of the foresters. Though much fighting takes place, there is not in the whole book a single death, unless the man who fell into the water during the attack on the cottage in chapter xv. met his end there ; the tale does not tell. Serious wounds, even, are scarce. There is a great cracking of skulls, and the friar lays about him with mighty effect, but the fights all have the air of the bloodless conflicts that rage behind the footlights at comic opera.

In other respects as well, the novel has a pronounced operatic character. Answer meets question with the point and snap of the successful libretto.

"MAID MARIAN"

The spirits of the piece remain always high. There
are uproarious skirmishes; monks piled howling in " a
rolling chaos of animated rotundities," or battered
right and left with the irreverent eight-foot staff of
Friar Michael; sheriff's men driven before the winnowing wrath of the same cudgel ecclesiastic. The
exits from the scene of action often have the necessary
but ludicrous haste with which the butt of a pleasantry
tumbles from the stage in a farce. Dancing, singing,
shouting, the whiz of arrows, blasts from the hunting-
horn, laughter, flares of anger, and the constant mirth
of wine leave few pages unenlivened by their presence.
Life in the greenwood runs on as merrily as existence
in Arden, fleeting carelessly, without a recriminating
Jacques. The landscape wears a kind of painted
beauty. These capable foresters dwell " in the high
court of Nature, and in the midst of her own nobility,"
says the friar. " This goodly grove is our palace :
the oak and the beech are its colonnade and its canopy :
the sun and the moon and the stars are its everlasting
lamps : the grass, and the daisy, and the primrose,
and the violet, are its many-coloured floor of green,
white, yellow, and blue ; the May-flower, and the
woodbine, and the eglantine, and the ivy, are its
decorations, its curtains, and its tapestry : the lark,
and the thrush, and the linnet, and the nightingale,
are its unhired minstrels and musicians." [1] Rain and
cold, unwholesome nights or dreary days, never damage
the tints of a background bright as an unfaded tapestry.
The scenery itself seldom comes in for formal descrip-

[1] *Works*, ii. 55.

tion, but the whole book tastes of the open air in a reign of pastoral perfection. Nothing can mar the gaiety with which the outlaws go about their philanthropic pillaging. They are nowise dependent upon the pleasures of a capricious climate, able to numb the most skilful fingers with cold, or to melt resolution in the sun's rays. Their superb freedom suffers no drawback from an insistent penalty of Adam. As they are free from nature, so are they free from the encroachments of human authority. The sheriff of Nottingham, indefatigable as he is, cannot cope with the strategic Robin Hood and Little John. From a distance comes at times the noise of the lawless world, which Richard, off crusading in Palestine, has left to the tender ministration of John, the usurper; but the depths of Sherwood offer hospitable retreats into which no king's man can come. A security from dangers which actually menace heightens the sense of liberty in the forest. It is not wholly fanciful to feel that the brightness, and mirth, and ease of this life in *Maid Marian* reminds one of the lighted stage at the opera, all the brighter because there is darkness on every side.

The spirit of combined laughter and beauty which informs the novel finds frequent expression in the songs scattered through its pages, greater in number than in any of the other novels, and higher in the average of poetic excellence. It is a kind of apology for Dr. Gaster and Mr. Grovelgrub that Friar Tuck sings all but two of the songs, thus proving his claim to be minstrel as well as chaplain of the band, and the

most important character of them all. For, although
Robin Hood is a brave and generous captain, and
Maid Marian a sweet and gracious sovereign in exile,
Peacock evidently felt his prime fondness for the jolly
friar. He made him a fellow of the merriest fancy, as
well as valiant with staff and palate, whose spirits are
always ready to soar into song at a moment's notice.
The friar cannot long refrain from singing. If he
goes to tell a story, he must roar in the numbers
which will come. He evinces something of the same
compulsion to melody as does the hero of opera. He
can crack a jest or a crown in very vigorous prose, and
he can hold forth thus in his capacity as muscular
homilist; but when he has been a little warmed with
sack, or when there is love for the greenwood to be
uttered, he must give his feelings larger vent than sober
discourse will permit. His songs are an integral part
of the action in a sense that those of the other novels
are not. The latter for the most part are hilarious
anecdotes which heighten the merriment after the
departure of the ladies from a dinner-table, or sentimental ballads of the sort which young ladies seem
to have rendered to delighted companies in the days
when the Georges ruled. Such songs are seldom
particularly in keeping with their singers, and seldom
have anything to do with the progress of the story.
But the songs of Friar Tuck belong to the narrative;
they are speeches pitched in a higher key. One can
sometimes foretell the approach of one from a heighten-
ing of the spirit in the page that precedes it. Especially is this true in the operatic scene in the fourth

chapter, where Matilda, having indulged in a rapid
stichomythic dialogue with her father, bursts spontaneously into song and is followed by the friar,
himself already heated with wine and sympathy, until
their din extinguishes the angry exclamations of the
baron. Being partly in character, the friar's songs,
of course, are never sentimental. Even when he
ventures upon seriousness, he wears the quizzical smile
of a merry hypocrite ; and he proves himself the true
Church Militant when he sings :

> " A staff, a staff, of a young oak graff,
>   That is both stoure and stiff,
> Is all a good friar can needs desire
>   To shrive a proud sheriffe.
> And thou, fine fellôwe, who has tasted so
>   Of the forester's greenwood game,
> Will be in no haste thy time to waste
>   In seeking more taste of the same :
> Or this can I read thee, and riddle thee well,
> Thou hadst better by far be the devil in hell,
>   Than the sheriff of Nothinghāme." [1]

The novel was published in April.[2] Mrs. Gisborne,
writing in her diary, April 28, called it a " beautiful
little thing," but added that it had " not taken yet.
Ollier says the reason is that no work can sell which
turns priests into ridicule." [3] To judge by the scarcity
of reviews, it can hardly have made much of a stir.
The greater periodicals did not speak of it at all.
The Monthly Magazine called it amusing in a very
brief paragraph.[4] *The Literary Gazette*[5] and *The*

---

[1] *Works*, ii. 38   [2] *Monthly Magazine*, liii. 342.
[3] *Headlong Hall* (1891), p. 31.
[4] liii. 342–3.   [5] Nov. 23, p. 736 *ff*.

"MAID MARIAN"

Literary Chronicle [1] suffered it to lie unnoticed until
very late in the year, and then suddenly became
apologetic for their delay, on seeing the turn events
had taken. It seems that Charles Kemble, attracted
by features of *Maid Marian* which he thought would
go well in opera, called the attention of J. R. Planché
to the book. Planché promptly wrote a libretto,
based largely upon Peacock's story, but with certain
additions from *Ivanhoe* and various popular Robin
Hood ballads. He himself added some new songs,
mostly bad, and got Bishop to compose the music
for the piece. This was done without the formality
of securing any one's permission. Planché, when the
work had been completed, offered the refusal of the
libretto to Hookham, and seemed much surprised
that the publisher grew indignant, threatening to prevent the performance of the opera as an infringement
on his copyright. Accordingly Planché went to see
Peacock at the India House, and met with a cordial
reception. The novelist proved very willing to have
his tale made into an opera, and persuaded Hookham
likewise to agree. *Maid Marian; or, The Huntress of
Arlingford*, was announced for production early in the
season, but did not appear until the wags had begun
to say she would be an " old maid." [2] The performance was finally set for November 26,[3] postponed for
an unknown reason, and then given to a large and
eager audience on the night of December 3.[4] An

---

[1] iv. 775 (Dec. 7).   [2] *Literary Gazette*, Dec. 7, p. 779.
[3] *Ibid.*, Nov. 30, p. 763.
[4] *Literary Gazette*, Dec. 7, pp. 779–80 ; *Monthly Magazine*, liv. 550.

167

unusual splendour of scenery assisted the witty dialogue and somewhat commonplace music to make a fair hit, so that the piece was acted twenty-seven nights.[1] Charles Kemble, as Friar Michael, scored a decided success, even venturing upon the only song, it is said, which he ever sang on the stage, " The bramble, the bramble." Miss Tree took the part of Maid Marian, Abbot of Robin Hood, Farren of the Baron, Keeley of the ever-hungry Brother Peter, T. P. Cooke of King Richard, Egerton of Prince John, Baker of Sir Ralph Montfaucon, Pearman of Young Gamwell. Kemble's song, which had come down from *The Three Doctors* by the devious route of quotation in *Melincourt* and elaboration in *Maid Marian*, was particularly popular. Jovial Bob Swinney, in the second chapter of *The Great Hoggarty Diamond*, " was always . . . singing—

> " ' The bramble, the bramble
> The jolly, jolly bramble ! '

one of Charles Kemble's songs in ' Maid Marian,' a play that was all the rage then [Thackeray was writing in 1841], taken from a famous story-book by one Peacock, a clerk in the India House : and a precious good place he has too."

In writing his opera Planché boasted that he did Peacock the great service of increasing the sale not only of *Maid Marian*, " but of all the other novels by the same author, of which a second edition was speedily demanded." [2] As a matter of fact, no new edition of

---

[1] Genest, *English Stage*, ix. 196.
[2] Planché, *Recollections and Reflections* (1872), i. 46–7.

any of Peacock's previous works appeared for fifteen years, by which time he had written two more tales. It is possible that the publication of Planché's opera in the same year as its production may even have injured the sale of the novel quite as much as it helped it. We do not know, however, how large the edition was which met the needs of the hungry public until 1837. Certainly *Maid Marian* was excellently translated into German in 1823 as *Der Forstgraf; oder, Robin Hood und Mariane*, and twice into French, first by Mme. Daring in 1826, under the title *Robin Hood; ou, La Forêt de Sherwood*, and again in a better version by the translator of Scott, Louis Barré, at Brussels, 1855.[1] Planché's opera found its way to New York, where it was brought out at the Park Theatre, January 9, 1824, but failed of any particular success.[2]

The flattering reception of *Maid Marian* doubtless influenced Peacock in his choice of a romantic subject for his next tale, *The Misfortunes of Elphin*. At what time he had begun the study of Old Welsh is not certain. He quotes a Welsh triad in his letter to Hookham for March 22, 1810, and cites a Welsh ballad in a note to *The Philosophy of Melancholy*[3], two years later. His visits to Wales must have increased his interest in the language; perhaps more important was his marriage to a Welsh woman who is said to have been familiar with the ancient dialect of her nation. At any rate, a great deal more learning went into the

[1] This had been used by Anastatius Grün, in his version of *Robin Hood* (1864). See *Sämtliche Werke* (Hesse), Leipzig, ix. 24.
[2] Ireland, *New York Stage*, N.Y. (1866), i. 425.
[3] *Philosophy of Melancholy*, p. 78.

composition of *The Misfortunes of Elphin* than had
gone into *Maid Marian*. Sir Edward Strachey declares that Peacock " gave the Welsh legends with
careful accuracy. I heard him say that he had great
difficulty in getting at the true story of Taliesin's
birth, as more than one learned authority had con-
cealed his own ignorance on the matter by saying that
the story was too long to be told then ; and he was
proud of the fact that Welsh archæologists treated
his book as a serious and valuable addition to Welsh
history." [1] This testimony, however, must be taken
with more of an allowance for Peacock's habits of whimsical statement than Sir Edward seems to have made.
Whatever may have been his delight at the credit
given his book by trusting antiquarians, Peacock could
never seriously have claimed that he depended upon
sources any further than it suited his satiric purpose.
He avoids all that was supernatural in the account of
Taliesin's birth, although he lets the bard himself
tell the marvels in a song. " Where Taliesin picked
up the story which he told of himself, why he told it,
and what he meant by it, are questions not easily
answered. Certain it is, that he told this story to
his contemporaries, and that none of them contra-
dicted it. It may, therefore, be presumed that they
believed it ; as any who pleases is most heartily welcome to do now." [2] The same bard, instead of singing
his song of consolation to Elphin as soon as he has been
lifted, the merest baby, from the water, waits till after
years, when he is " on the safe side of prophecy."

[1] *Calidore*, &c., pp. 19–20.   [2] *Works*, ii. 178.

"THE MISFORTUNES OF ELPHIN"

The great storm which arises, in the original narrative, after Taliesin's song before Maelgon, finds no mention in Peacock. In fact, the mysterious warning which Elphin receives in the first chapter and which comes to both Elphin and Angharad in the second, is the solitary example of supernaturalism in the whole book. Other details are softened or varied with tolerable freedom. Peacock's learning appears less in any adherence to the narrative upon which he drew than in the amount of historical detail with which he enriches his pages. *Maid Marian* had been almost devoid of signs of wide reading in the history of the twelfth century. *The Misfortunes of Elphin* abounds in evidences that Peacock had acquired a considerable familiarity with what his contemporaries thought sixth-century life to have been.

As a brief indication of his indebtednesses, it will be sufficient to point out that he depends primarily upon the prose *Hanes Taliesin*, or History of Taliesin. This tale, as we know it, he had almost assuredly not seen ; in fact, he calls it a poem.[1] A fragment had been printed in *The Myvyrian Archaiology ;* [2] the part which deals with the finding of Taliesin had been translated and elucidated by Edward Davies ; [3] and the whole had been abstracted in Edward Jones' *Bardic Museum* (1802),[4] but the complete text did not

---

[1] *Works*, ii. 176. This may have been a confusion with the title, *Hanes Taliesin*, given by the *Myvyrian Archaiology* (1801, i. 19–20), to the song with which Taliesin answered Maelgon. Peacock's *Hanes*, however, is a poetical version of the account of Taliesin's birth and nurture.

[2] i. 17–19. [3] *British Druids* (1809), pp. 189–90 ; 213–14.
[4] Pp. 19–20.

appear until 1833, in *The Cambrian Quarterly*. There is no proof that Peacock was acquainted with the work in manuscript. The songs which he used as the basis for the loosest of paraphrases had all been included in the *Myvyrian Archaiology*, as had the triads which he frequently quotes. It may be noted, however, that he generally gives the triads in the English version of *The Cambro-Briton* (1820–22), of which he possessed a copy. With the story of Taliesin he unites two other legends : first, the one based on a triad of the Isle of Britain that Seithenyn the Drunkard let in the ocean upon the Great Plain of Gwaelod ; and second, that Queen Gwenyvar was stolen away by Melvas, a story which seems to have been first put into currency in the *Vita Gildæ*, ascribed to Caradoc of Llancarvan. Peacock's own contribution to the plot is the love of Taliesin for the fair Melanghel, daughter of his patron, whom he wins by rescuing her father from the prison of King Maelgon. Elphin is held in durance much more resolutely in *The Misfortunes of Elphin* than in the original story, apparently that he may thus assist in the romance of his daughter and the bard.

But if Peacock contributed few original incidents to the plot of his story, there can be no doubt that in the much more important matters of humour and satire the book which appeared in 1829 has to yield to nothing else that Peacock wrote. *The Misfortunes of Elphin* has enjoyed the same selection of its audience even from lovers of Peacock as the whole body of his work has enjoyed from the general audience of novel-readers.

" THE MISFORTUNES OF ELPHIN "

Although it was the first to win him notice in one of the great reviews, *The Westminster Review* for April 1829, it alone of all his tales was not reprinted after the first edition until his collected *Works* came out nearly half a century later. It fetched, indeed, during that time a handsome price at the bookshops, but such testimony proves nothing beyond the eagerness of the few. In part, the slight interest which a large number of readers feel in Welsh antiquity may be taken to account for the unpopularity of *The Misfortunes of Elphin*. Nothing in the book would entice the average novel-reading temper from fictions which deal more powerfully or more picturesquely with a better-known past. This shortcoming, however, does not account for the absence of enthusiasm among admirers of Peacock, who may generally be trusted to have a taste for antiquity which the Welsh scene of the novel need not displease. The truth is that *The Misfortunes of Elphin*, the quintessence of the Peacockian satirical spirit, suffers from the restraint put upon it by the exclusion of almost all else but satire. The romantic exuberance which had given *Maid Marian* popularity scarcely appears at all in Peacock's next book, although his theme was equally romantic, and his disposition toward the material not greatly changed. But there seems to have taken place, during ten years of official life, something of an evaporation of his high spirits. The style, the songs, the characters, the satire of *The Misfortunes of Elphin* are all drier than they had been in the idyll of Sherwood. The narrative never for a moment escapes, as that of *Maid Marian* had sometimes done, the full ironic control of the satirist. Such an intensity of satiric self-consciousness seldom occurs where there is no didactic purpose, and few readers probably escape the impression that the stern economy of emotion is sheer famine, and the dryness, flat aridity.

Yet if the style is dry, it has a finished clarity which Peacock never elsewhere excels. The passage which tells how Elphin looked out over his father's kingdom is one of the best examples of the brief descriptive touches with which Peacock varies his restrained style :

" The sea shone with the glory of the setting sun ; the air was calm ; and the white surf, tinged with the crimson of sunset, broke lightly on the sands below. Elphin turned his eyes from the dazzling splendour of [ocean to the green meadows of] the Plain of Gwaelod ; the trees, that in the distance thickened into woods ; the wreaths of smoke rising from among them, marking the solitary cottages or the populous towns ; the massy barrier of mountains beyond, with the forest rising from their base ; the precipices frowning over the forest ; and the clouds resting on their summits, reddened with the reflection of the west. Elphin gazed earnestly on the peopled plain, reposing in the calm of evening between the mountains and the sea, and thought, with deep feelings of secret pain, how much of life and human happiness was entrusted to the ruinous mound on which he stood." [1]

[1] *Works*, ii. 105. (The words within brackets were carelessly omitted from the edition of 1875, but are here restored from the first edition.)

And the last paragraph in the description of the flight from Seithenyn's ruined castle is another case in point :

" Thus they began their march. They had not proceeded far, when the tide began to recede, the wind to abate somewhat of its violence, and the moon to look on them at intervals through the rifted clouds, disclosing the desolation of the inundated plain, silvering the tumultuous surf, gleaming on the distant mountains, and revealing a lengthened prospect of their solitary path, that lay in its irregular line like a ribbon on the deep." [1]

In the matter of the songs, there can be no doubt that *The Misfortunes of Elphin* falls behind *Maid Marian*, and their excellence as a rule varies inversely with the degree of Peacock's indebtedness to his originals.[2] For the most part, however, he takes but

---

[1] *Works*, ii. 119.

[2] For the convenience of any one who may desire to compare Peacock's paraphrases with his Welsh sources, I give a list of the poems he used : (1) *The Circling of the Mead Horns* is from the *Hirlas* of Owen Cyveiliog (*Myvyrian Archaiology*, i. 265-7) ; (2) *The Song of the Four Winds*, from the *Englynion Duad* of Llywarch Hen (*Myv. Arch.*, i. 125-6) ; (3) The two songs of Gwythno, from the first two ascribed to him, *Gwyddneu ai Cant* and *Pan Ddaeth y Mor tros Gantrev y Gwaelod* (*Myv. Arch.*, i. 165) ; (4) *The Consolation of Elphin*, from Taliesin's *Llyma Dyhuddiant Elffin* (*Myv. Arch.*, i. 83-4) ; (5) *The Mead Song of Taliesin*, from his *Kanu y Medd* (*Myv. Arch.*, i. 22) ; (6) *The Song of the Wind*, very remotely from *Taliesin's Can y Gwynt* (*Myv. Arch.*, i. 38-9), by Peacock's acknowledgment, but with greater debt to the *Fustl y Beirdd* (*Myv. Arch.*, i. 26-7) ; (7) *The Brilliancies of Winter*, extracted from Llywarch Hen's *Y Gorwynion* (*Myv. Arch.*, i. 122-4) ; (8) *Merlin's Apple Trees*, from *Avallenau Myrddin* (*Myv. Arch.*, i. 150-4) ; (9) *The Massacre of the Britons*, from Aneurin's *Gododin* (*Myv. Arch.*, i. 1-14) ; (10) *The Cauldron of Ceridwen*, not from any single poem, but a poetical handling of the early part of the prose *Hanes Taliesin*.

the barest hint from the ancient pieces, content to
borrow a refrain or some odd hint if it suits him,
but under no apparent obligation to reproduce his
material with any degree of fidelity. By all odds the
best song of the lot is of course the superbly curt
War-Song of Dinas Vawr, which Peacock calls "the
sum and substance of all the appetencies, tendencies,
and consequences of military glory," and which is
altogether Peacock's own. It has been widely known
and quoted, never with more humorous effect than
when, in *Bentley's Miscellany* for June 1837,[1] a
variant version of it was gravely cited as a genuine
war-song of one of the North American tribes,
recently printed at Washington in the mythical
Indian Phœnix.

Among the personages of the book, one enjoys an
unassailed pre-eminence, equal to that of *The War-
Song of Dinas Vawr* among the songs. To the names
of Friar Tuck and Dr. Folliott must be added the
lofty title of Prince Seithenyn ap Seithyn Saidi,
Arglwyd Gorwarcheidwad yr Argae Breninawl, more
commonly known as Seithenyn the Drunkard, to complete the triad of the Three Principal Characters of
Peacock. If the millennium of temperance which
seems at times to threaten should ever so transform
taste as to make the Seithenyns of literature no longer
amusing, it may reasonably be expected that many
conservative gentlemen of a literary turn will see in
the change a cogent argument against the whole
millennial establishment, and will write invectives aimed

[1] i. 537-8.

at the present and elegiac lamentations for a past filled with Seithenyns. Indeed, few readers can resist the fascination of the vinous Achates of King Melvas. From the time when he shouts to Teithrin and Elphin, " You are welcome all four," until he subsides at the end of the story to the congenial rank of butler to King Arthur, he never once belies his true character as the thirstiest of men. Hot-throated as Tantalus, he has one course of action to follow, " Drink ; " he has one piece of advice to give, " Drink ; " he will medicine the whole world into deed, and reduce it to quiet when the time for deeds is over ; his Toryism is sloth ; his sloth is tipsy ; his judgments are refracted in the good liquor which submerges them till they drown ; his opinions hover between the prudence of the half drunk and the extravagance of the wholly drunk ; his reasoning staggers under the weight of wine ; he is a Mrs. Malaprop of logic, putting the right argument where the wrong should go ; he will not believe he is dead, and brings forward the best of proofs : " They have not made it known to me . . . for the best of all reasons, that one can only know the truth ; for if that which we think we know is not truth, it is something which we do not know. A man cannot know his own death ; for while he knows anything he is alive ; at least, I never heard of a dead man who knew anything, or pretended to know anything : if he had so pretended, I should have told him to his face he was no dead man." [1] And finally, since Seithenyn knows he was kept alive as the result

[1] *Works*, ii. 151.

of a long attempt to drink himself to death, he is resolved to persevere in his course, thus obviously approved by fortune, as long as there is still left in the world a drop of wine or a single golden goblet with which he can realise his motto, *Gwin O Eur,* " wine from gold."

The astonishing arguments with which Seithenyn combats the proposal for mending the embankment left under his charge are said by Sir Henry Cole, who was closely associated with Peacock during the composition of the book, to have been intended as a parody upon Canning's eloquence in defence of the British Constitution against the dangerous innovation of Parliamentary reform.

" Decay," said Seithenyn, " is one thing, and danger is another. Everything that is old must decay. That the embankment is old, I am free to confess ; that it is somewhat rotten in parts, I will not altogether deny ; that it is any the worse for that, I do most sturdily gainsay. It does its business well : it works well : it keeps out the water from the land, and it lets in the wine upon the High Commission of Embankment. Cupbearer, fill. Our ancestors were wiser than we : they built it in their wisdom ; and, if we should be so rash as to try to mend it, we should only mar it."

" The stonework," said Teithrin, " is sapped and mined : the piles are rotten, broken, and dislocated : the flood-gates and sluices are leaky and creaky."

" That is the beauty of it," said Seithenyn. " Some parts of it are rotten, and some parts of it are sound."

"It is well," said Elphin, "that some parts are sound: it were better that all were so."

"So I have heard some people say before," said Seithenyn; "perverse people, blind to venerable antiquity: that very unamiable sort of people who are in the habit of indulging their reason. But I say, the parts that are rotten give elasticity to those that are sound: they give them elasticity, elasticity, elasticity. If it were all sound, it would break by its own obstinate stiffness: the soundness is checked by the rottenness, and the stiffness is balanced by the elasticity. There is nothing so dangerous as innovation. See the waves in the equinoctial storms, dashing and clashing, roaring and pouring, spattering and battering, rattling and battling against it. I would not be so presumptuous as to say I could build anything that would stand against them half-an-hour; and here this immortal old work, which God forbid the finger of mortal mason should bring into jeopardy, this immortal work has stood for centuries, and will stand for centuries more, if we let it alone. It is well: it works well: let well alone. Cupbearer, fill. It was half rotten when I was born, and that is a conclusive reason why it should be three parts rotten when I die." [1]

This passage might reasonably be taken for the work of a Radical with ideas on the subject of progress, did not the whole book contradict any such opinion.

[1] *Works*, ii. 108–9. Peacock does not parody any specific speech of Canning so much as his general opinions, such, for instance, as were set forth in his address to his constituents at Liverpool, March 18, 1820, and in his speech in the House of Commons, April 25, 1822, on Lord John Russell's motion for a reform of Parliament.

THOMAS LOVE PEACOCK

Although it is drier than *Maid Marian,* more caustic, and far more worldly, *The Misfortunes of Elphin* differs little from its predecessor in the general method by which it holds up a picture of life in a blissful former age to shame the face of the nineteenth century. To take refuge from a distasteful present in the past, and there to impose upon oneself the safe and straitened bounds of a tower of fancy, is, of course, a common enough romantic scheme of escape from this world. Peacock, however, was too much of a scholar to believe that the past had really been perfect, and he clung too tightly to practical realities ever to be satisfied with the imagination alone. Whatever may have been his fondness for the colour and simplicity of the Middle Ages—and he had a genuine fondness for the period—he was as little minded to refrain from laughter at either the sixth or the twelfth century as at the one in which he himself lived. All had been packed with folly; all had offended against reasonableness in some way or other. But a good reason for defending the past was the cant of uninformed, complacent modernism which doubted that any one could have been really happy or virtuous before the days of the steam-engine and the science of political economy. If in these romantic novels Peacock seems particularly prone to champion outworn generations, it is largely because that was the best way of putting himself into the unpopular minority with which he preferred to take his stand whatever the point at issue. He is only a qualified romanticist; the standard by which he judges the modern world by no means coincides at all' points with the actual life of the past. His standard was still one of reasonableness, more or less abstract and bookish, a standard which he had acquired from the very Age of Enlightenment which most ridiculed the "Gothic Darkness" he now seemed to defend. Whenever the life he was portraying failed to coincide with his standard, he laughed at it ; but he laughed more heartily when he could point out to his fellow-subjects under the fourth George that many of their grievances had been lacking under Arthur, and that the blessings on which they were not infrequently wont to plume themselves had been by no means necessary to a very fair degree of contentment and efficiency. He is always critical ; always concerned with opinion. In *Maid Marian* he presents a neat social and political microcosm, a toy world, a laboratory experiment on the universe, where the whole terrestrial scheme is reduced to its simplest terms, and its workings studied by a relentless investigator. Thus cant and blind custom cease to hinder a right understanding of the real world, and the motives which actually impel kings, and priests, and robbers, and honest men, get called by their proper names. The England which he represents as the England of Richard I. deserves to be preferred to the present, Peacock maintains, even if for no other reason than the frankness with which it went about its roguery. In short, it is better to be a knave without disguise than to be a fool without just comprehension. And that, too, is the burden of *The Misfortunes of Elphin.* Let us make merry with these puppets of mortality, when and where we find them, reserving our verdict as to what is not foolish, and giving our admiration only to such actors in the human phantasmagoria as do not add to their frailties the additional weakness of pretending to be what they are not.

CHAPTER VIII

"WESTMINSTER REVIEW"—"CROTCHET CASTLE"
—"BENTLEY'S MISCELLANY"

IF *The Misfortunes of Elphin* represents a maturer Peacock than any of the first four novels, it must be remembered that over a decade had elapsed since the years 1815–18 during which he had composed them, a decade of active official life in a world which he had known but little before his India House appointment. At the Examiner's Office, of course, he was brought into close contact with the Philosophical Radicals who derived their Benthamism through James Mill. In no case, however, did Peacock form a close friendship with a member of the group. Grote, Austin, the Bullers, Roebuck, Albany Fonblanque, the Mills, Bentham himself—all of them Peacock knew, some of them well, none of them with real intimacy. One searches in vain for any considerable mention of him in the published memoirs or letters of the Utilitarians. It appears that he used to make one on the walking trips which James Mill frequently organised on Sunday, and that once when they, with some friends, were at dinner in a country inn where the beefsteak, being very tough, came in for round abuse, Mill gave a series of reasons which proved that it should be tender, and so declared that it was. "Yes," said Peacock, "but,

as usual, all the reason is on your side, and all the
proof on mine." [1] Of his relations with Mill only
one other incident seems to have been recorded. Just
after Jeremy Bentham's death, while his body, according to the provisions of his will, was being dissected,
Mill came to the Examiner's Office with the latest
news regarding the process. He told Peacock that there
had exuded from the head a kind of oil which experiment had found almost unfreezable. The Elisha of
the Utilitarians was of the opinion that such oil might
be used for oiling chronometers in high altitudes.
" The less you say about that, Mill," Peacock replied,
" the better it will be for *you* ; because if the fact once
becomes known, just as we see now in the newspapers
advertisements to the effect that a fine bear is to be
killed for his grease, we shall be having advertisements
to the effect that a fine philosopher is to be killed for
his oil." [2]

Leigh Hunt apparently considered that Peacock
had sympathies with the India House philosophers,
for he named him with the Utilitarians in the preface
to his *Poetical Works* of 1832 : " and last, not least,
the Utilitarians themselves are poetical ! . . . if you
want a proper Bacchanalian uproar in a song, you must
go to the author of ' Headlong Hall,' who will not
admire utility itself, unless it be jovial. It is a moot
point which he admires most, Bentham or Rossini."
To be accurate, not a quality characteristic of Leigh
Hunt, Peacock was far enough from being the singer

[1] *Calidore*, &c., p. 17.
[2] Sir M. E. Grant Duff, *Notes from a Diary*, 1851–1872, i. 60.

of utility. His was not the temper to belong to any
school whatever. Some of the doctrines of the
Utilitarians he shared. But his philosophy was eminently his own, and he never joined with his colleagues in the practical side of the radical programme.
A better testimony to his attitude toward his
fellow disputants may be found in some unpublished
verses which he wrote on the founding of London
University. Peacock was no friend to the scheme,
and he took great pleasure in pointing out an error in
the grammar of the inscription, where Gulielmus
Wilkins " appears as " Architectus " at the end of the
list of the founders.

> "By the favour of God, the great builder of earth,
> (Which favour we hope may be found of some worth,)
> This stone, in the ground with due mystery laid,
> By a Prince of the mason's original trade,
> A Prince whom the provident bounty of God
> Expressly cut out for a knight of the hod.
> 'Midst citizens, noisy with hand and with voice,
> Who, we clearly see, will be there to rejoice,
> Begins, at length, somehow, or sometime or other,
> A good job for this town, and each lecturing brother,
> And makes record, more lasting than pencil or pen,
> Of us twenty-five most illustrious men,
> Including our builder, who stands in his place,
> As just one of us, in the nominative case." [1]

The Utilitarians, however, were not without their
influence on Peacock's work. Through his acquaintance with their circle he became a contributor to *The
Westminster Review*, and there produced several

[1] Cole, p. 24. The verses are in part a translation of the inscription.
This explains most of the allusions.

articles which, while not greatly important as criticism, are interesting because Peacock appears in his own person, not as a caricaturist. The first was a review of Moore's *Epicurean*, October 1827, in which Peacock treated the book to a drastic examination of its facile ignorance in classical archæology and philosophy, its conceits, impossible images, silly sentimentality, and repeated flattery of received opinion. Significant is Peacock's defence of the Epicurean philosophy against the degradation of it by Moore :

" Epicurus taught that happiness is the end of life : that there is no happiness without pleasure : that all pleasure is in itself good, and that all pain is in itself evil ; but that present pleasure is to be avoided in the prospect of future pain, and that present pain is to be endured for the sake of future pleasure : that the true and only permanent pleasure of man is peace of body and mind : that the state in which the body is without pain, and the mind without perturbation, is the perfect health of the whole man : that the peace of the body is to be obtained especially by two means—Temperance, or a sober and continent life, to keep off corporeal diseases which arise mostly from the opposite vice, and Fortitude to endure them with a constant mind, and not exasperate them by impatience : that beyond this all that concerns the body belongs to medicine : that Philosophy is the medicine of the mind, that the two capital diseases of the mind are Cupidity and Fear, of which Care is the incessant adjunct, as Pain is of the diseases of the body ; the Cupidity, for instance, of honours and riches, and the Fear of the gods and of death ; and that these diseases being the offspring of ignorance and error, are to be cured by knowledge and reason."[1]

The real point of contact between Peacock and the Utilitarians is indicated by his modern application of Epicureanism.

"Thus Epicurus first taught, that general utility, or as Bentham expresses it, 'the greatest happiness of the greatest number,' is the legitimate end of philosophy; and it is curious to see the same class of persons decrying the same doctrines as impracticably dry, when the word utility precedes the word pleasure, and as too practicably voluptuous when the word pleasure precedes the word utility. So much are small minds the slaves of words."[2]

Having demolished him, Peacock leads Moore gently but firmly away from Attic pastures : " he could have found abundance of playthings for the grown children of society without dressing up in false apparel the chief of an Athenian School of Philosophy to play the fool and coxcomb for their entertainment. If he had wished to amuse the public with *ces Egyptiens si fameux par des monceaux de pierres*, and had left the Athenians alone, it would, at any rate, have been as innocent amusement as his previous florilegia in Ireland, Persia, and Paradise. But when he steps out of his way into the garden of Epicurus, and commits havoc among the roses planted by that illustrious philosopher,

'Qui genus humanum ingenio superavit, et omneis
Praestinxit; stellas exortus uti aetherius sol,'

---

he must be treated like a mischievous boy in a flower-garden, and turned back into the fields where he has been accustomed to pick nosegays with impunity." [1] There seems to be no absolute reason why Moore should not have trifled botanically in Athens as freely as in Paradise, or even in Ireland; but he happened to fall foul of a reviewer who united to a love of scholarly accuracy as ardent a championship of Epicurus as any disciple in the delectable garden.

Moore could scarcely have taken this review very kindly, and his anger was great when, three years later, the first volume of his *Letters and Journals of Lord Byron* was entrusted to the same unsparing hand. Peacock took pains to inform himself with care in the preparation of the review. It appears from correspondence still extant in the British Museum [2] that he applied to Hobhouse for assistance, and that from this application dates the beginning of the lifelong friendship between the two men. Hobhouse, however, thought it wiser that nothing which could be traced to him should go into the review, and Peacock accordingly confined his remarks to an exposition of Moore's shallowness. His treatment cannot escape the charge of spleen and occasional pedantry of criticism. What might have been more interesting, his full estimate of Byron's character, he reserved for the appearance of the second volume. But in consequence of Moore's quarrel with Bowring, then editor of the *Westminster*, over Peacock's strictures, [3] no review of

---

[1] *Westminster Review*, viii. p. 383.
[2] British Museum *Addit. MSS.* 36815, fol. 46–51.
[3] Bowring, *Autobiographical Recollections* (1877), p. 351.

the second volume ever appeared in that magazine,
and so Peacock's character of Byron is not to be found.

Peacock contributed two other articles to the
Westminster in 1830, one a review of *The Memoirs,
Correspondence, and Private Papers of Thomas Jefferson,*
in which he displayed an enthusiasm which he did
not often express for a contemporary, and another
a review of the Parliamentary reports on London
Bridge and *Chronicles of London Bridge. By an Antiquary* (1827), in which he once more asserted his
feeling for reverend age. Both appeared in October.
His partiality for Jefferson partakes of a fondness
which the eighteenth century had for Plutarchian
characters with a philosophical tendency to an extent
which an admirer of the great Democrat, from a
twentieth-century point of view, may not care to
applaud, but it was certainly genuine. More in
keeping with Peacock's ordinary character are the
proofs with which he lays bare the folly of erecting
a new London Bridge. He denied any sentimental
feeling in the matter, and went about his argument
with specific calculations to show that the removal
of the dam of the old bridge would flood half London.
" Logs of mahogany will swim about Bankside ;
kitchen fires will be extinguished in Lambeth ; cabbages will be submerged, and melon-frames floated
off at Millbank ; the Duchess of Buccleugh's beautiful
villa at Richmond will become a ' house of pleasaunce '
for Naiads : and our two-tailed friends will be set
paddling about Westminster Hall, and sending forth
sounds as choral, though not as musical, as those
which Aristophanes puts into the mouths of the

Frogs of the Styx." [1] It was plainly Peacock who wrote : " The old London Bridge was begun in 1176, and finished in 1209. It was built on such unscientific principles, that it ought to have been carried away before it was finished, when it was finished, and at any given time subsequently ; but partly by the awkward contrivance of barbarous men, partly by its own obstinacy, it has stood six centuries and a quarter, amidst the perpetual prophecies of disinterested engineers that it could not stand any longer : while one bridge after another, on different parts of the same river, in which no son of science had espied a flaw, has wilfully tumbled to pieces, by the sinking of the piers, or the yielding of the abutments, in despite of the most mathematical demonstrations of the absurdity of such a proceeding." [2]

Dr. Folliott himself might have spoken these words. When they were written, he had been conceived, and must have been nearly a completed figure in the Peacockian gallery of notables. The earliest discovered reference to *Crotchet Castle* is the announcement in *The Gentleman's Magazine* for January, 1831, that the novel was in the press.[3] A note in *The Examiner* indicates that it was published February 25.[4] The use in it of a quotation from *The Morning Chronicle* for December 20, 1830, seems to place its date of composition very late in that year. Most of the reviews were appreciative. *The Literary Gazette* called Peacock " the wittiest writer in England." [5]

---

[1] *Westminster*, xiii. pp. 408–9. [2] *Ibid.*, p. 402.
[3] *Ibid.*, CI. 70.   [4] Feb. 20, p. 126.   [5] Feb. 19, p. 115.

Albany Fonblanque reviewed it in the July *West-minster*, with a kind of official apology for satire directed against Liberals by a Liberal; *Fraser's*, possibly Maginn himself, treated it to a furious slashing. "Peacock is one of the people," said the reviewer,

"Marked with the indelible d—d Cockney blot,"

an "ignorant, stupid, poor devil, who has no fun, little learning, no facility, no *easiness*—a fellow whose style of thought is in the very contrary vein of the Rabelaisian—a dolt who thinks that the daily nonsense vomited up by all sorts of asses is something of moment, something worthy of even being satirised, instead of being spoken of in the same tone that we speak of the contents of nightmen's carts." [3] *Crotchet Castle* has generally enjoyed the reputation of being Peacock's maturest and most characteristic work.

In some respects, indeed, it is an epitome of all Peacock ever wrote. Its title might with justice be taken for the proper title to any of the novels. Nowhere else do his constitutional toryism and intellectual independence appear in such an admirable mixture. A decided gain in breadth and humanity is purchased by the loss of only a modicum of the high spirits which had danced on the pages of *Nightmare Abbey* and *Maid Marian*. Dr. Folliott lays out the astonishing highwaymen who attempt to stop him with as great a gusto as he disputes or goes to dinner, and the inimitable drinking song with which the equally inimitable Chapter VI. comes to a hilarious close remains

[3] *Fraser's*, iv. 17.

one of the very best examples of the joy in mere living which the early century had, but which seems to have left the world of letters when the new knowledge of good and evil came in at the mid-century. The strange fancifulness of the attack on Chainmail Hall seems less a barefaced thrust at probability than an ebullition of merriment. In *Crotchet Castle* Peacock surrenders enough of his customary preoccupation with opinion to free at least two of his characters from the leading-strings of abstract ideas. The worldly and fascinating Lady Clarinda suffers from no crotchet whatever. She owns to Captain Fitzchrome that he had once disturbed her dreams, and she secretly feels a sincere affection for him still, but she has deliberately made up her mind that the doctrine of love in a cottage is a doctrine for boarding-schools, and has no business in the head of a well-regulated young woman of this world. When the Captain takes her at her word, however, and discontinues his suit, she becomes properly regretful, and on the disappearance of her wealthier suitor, turns to her first love with an evident contentment which doubtless overjoyed the Captain, but which should not deceive the unenamoured reader, if there are such, into thinking that she would necessarily have permitted herself a similar consolation had young Crotchet kept his wealth. If Lady Clarinda seems more outright in her worldliness than many ladies who have never graced fiction, she is certainly more witty than a great many who have. Her skilful description of the guests at Crotchet Castle, besides serving as an admirable method of

introducing the company to the reader, bodes well
for the novel which she is writing and of which the
enterprising firm of Puffall may expect a satisfactory
sale. Miss Susannah Touchandgo is almost a foil to
Lady Clarinda. She will have none of the world
which has abused her by prompt neglect after the loss
of her father's fortune. Like Anthelia Melincourt she
has been nourished into sensibility by the poets of
Italy and relieves her solitude with Rousseau. In the
lonely seclusion of a Welsh farmhouse she grows into
familiarity with the nature about her until, " the
nymph of the scene," she has learned the secrets
of the mountains as had done the Lake Poets
whom her creator delighted to dishonour. When one
remembers Peacock, it is generally a satirical passage
that sticks in the memory ; but the scene in which
the antiquarian Mr. Chainmail comes upon his future
bride sleeping unperturbed on the brink of a precipice,
and waits in the warm, drowsy silence of the place for
her awakening, cannot easily be matched for real
romantic charm in the writings of professed foes to
romance. Peacock must have remembered tenderly
in his delineation of this mountain maid the lost love
of his youth. It is somewhat interesting, in this connection, to note that the picturesque dingle where
the meeting took place has a genuine original, a spot
called Llyn-y-Gygfraen, the Ravens' Pool, on the
Velenrhyd in Merioneth. " There is no chasm on
that river," Peacock explained in a letter to Mr.
L'Estrange, " which it is possible to leap over ; but
there is more than one on the river Cynfael, which

flows into the same valley. I took the poetical licence of approximating the scenes." [1]

The Reverend Doctor Folliott, "a gentleman endowed with a tolerable stock of learning, an interminable swallow, and an indefatigable pair of lungs," was said by Peacock to constitute his apology to the Church of England for the slender respect he had shown her pastors in his former novels. The good Doctor is not precisely a spiritual figure, but of the qualities of worldly fellowship he lacks few indeed. Intellectually, he stands for Common Sense, a quality which, despite much popular self-deception, gets personified quite as seldom as various more exotic qualities. Dr. Folliott's common sense consists largely in a safe and peculiar inaccessibility to ideas, except such as are recommended by an almost artless simplicity or a classical origin. An Epicurean love of peace lies at the root of his conservatism. He himself is disinclined to move, planted as he is on one of the pleasant places, and he thus has ample leisure to evolve witty sayings at the expense of grimy workers who go about shouting, "Progress." "Why should the world desire progress?" is a question which Dr. Folliott thinks satisfactorily answered by his own comment on the question, "I am comfortable." Dr. Folliott does not deal in sympathy except for himself. He is as tolerant of the sufferings of others as he is of their weaknesses. He dreams no dreams; he hunts no phantoms. He would define wise as prudent or practicable, referring, in both synonyms, to material self-interest. A good

[1] Cole, p. 34.

dinner will quiet most social unrest. Any reformer who is not cured by old wine must assuredly be a lunatic. If he could, the Doctor would make all men happy, for thus his own existence would become more pleasant. As he cannot render himself completely blissful, however, by any such omnipotence, he sees no good reason for rendering himself less happy because his condition is not perfect. Whatever folly the world may be going to suffer from, it will never suffer from his meddling with its course. Clearly, such a man has admirable traits, although it is hard to see anything essentially Christian in his general position. When he adds to these qualities an excellent wit which can turn into laughter all pretence and high-flying fancies, and strong prejudices to give a delightful bias to his wit, Dr. Folliott becomes a figure who does not require for his persistent fame the credit of cousinship to a character in one of the most brilliant of novels. Dr. Middleton of *The Egoist* is not more witty or original than Dr. Folliott.

Chief among the victims of Dr. Folliott's displeasure is the " learned friend," who never appears in person, but who is pilloried as the arch-champion of the march of mind in the great crusade which the Steam Intellect Society is leading against popular ignorance, and who, after having declared that he will never take office, becomes an official and Sir Guy de Vaux at the same time. The " learned friend " is of course Lord Brougham, who had organised the Society for the Diffusion of Useful Knowledge in 1825, and in November 1830 was made Lord High Chancellor with the title Baron Brougham and Vaux. Peacock's own distaste for the conceit and officiousness of Brougham crops out in the mirth which the Doctor has at the Chancellor's expense. One should guard against the assumption, however, that Dr. Folliott's gibes at the whole trend of reform in 1830 are drawn directly from Peacock's private opinions. It will be remembered that Canning's opposition to the same movement had made him the target for ridicule in *The Misfortunes of Elphin,* and that one of the principal charges against Moley Mystic in *Melincourt* had been that he opposed the spread of education very much with Dr. Folliott's arguments. " In the questions which have come within my scope," Peacock said to L'Estrange in the above-quoted letter, " I have endeavoured to be impartial, and say what could be said on both sides." In *Crotchet Castle* this is generally true, although Peacock seems to give his sympathy, so far as it can be detected, to a conservatism which was just then in the minority. The notable thing is that all this proceeds from a man who was eminently familiar with the whole body of liberal ideas, who contributed to the chief liberal organ of the day, and who was ordinarily considered to be a member of the powerful body of radicals who took their cues from the Examiner's Office. Nothing gives so good an idea of Peacock's actual position as to call him the Court Jester of Utilitarianism. Like a jester, he belonged to the Court. He was informed in all its gossips and in the secrets of its policies. He was daily companion of its prince and great men, and admitted to their councils if he cared to come. If his equality to any of them in learning seems little like a jester, his superiority to all of them in wit restores the truth of the simile. Like the jester he seems to pay little heed to the larger issues that confront the Court. He keeps his sober opinions in his motley cap and shakes his bauble at the solemn courtier who makes a system out of half an idea. He takes to himself the full jester's privilege of distorting a man's principles in order to laugh at the man. He has no hesitation in speaking as frankly as he will to the most dignified masters of the Court. He mocks, he flouts, he jeers, he contradicts, and he mimics their foibles to their very faces, all without loss of office.

The Philosophical Radicals who read *Crotchet Castle* may have recognised various sly hits which it is quite impossible to appreciate now. Mr. MacQuedy (Mac Q.E.D., the son of a demonstration) is very obviously intended for a caricature of John Ramsay MacCulloch, who had been since 1828 professor of political economy in London University, and who, in spite of his dictatorial manner and pronounced Scotticisms, had done much to make the dismal science fashionable. An instance of the liberties which Peacock took with MacCulloch appears from an incident related by Sir Edward Strachey. Peacock came one day into the room of Edward Strachey, senior, and exclaimed in mock anger : " I will never dine with Mill again, for he asks me to meet only political economists. I dined with him last night, when he had Mushet and MacCulloch, and after dinner, Mushet took a paper out of his pocket, and began to read : ' In the infancy of society, when Government was invented to save a percentage—say, of $3\frac{1}{2}$ per cent.'—on which he was stopped by MacCulloch with, ' I will say no such thing,' meaning that this was not the proper percentage." [1] Two or three years later the incident was presented in *Crotchet Castle*, when Mr. MacQuedy began :—

" Nothing is so easy as to lay down the outlines of perfect society. There wants nothing but money to set it going. I will explain myself clearly and fully by reading a paper. (*Producing a large scroll.*) ' In the infancy of society——'

The Rev. Dr. Folliott.—Pray, Mr. MacQuedy, how is it that all gentlemen of your nation begin everything they write with the ' infancy of society ' ?

Mr. MacQuedy.—Eh, sir, it is the simplest way to begin at the beginning. ' In the infancy of society, when Government was invited to save a percentage —say two and a half per cent.——'

The Rev. Dr. Folliott.—I will not say any such thing.

Mr. MacQuedy.—Well, say any percentage you please.

The Rev. Dr. Folliot.—I will not say any percentage at all.

Mr. MacQuedy.—' On the principle of the division of labour——'

The Rev. Dr. Folliot.—Government was invented to spend a percentage.

Mr. MacQuedy.—To save a percentage.

[1] *Calidore*, &c., p. 18.

The Rev. Dr. Folliott.—No, sir, to spend a percentage ; and a good deal more than two and a half per cent. Two hundred and fifty per cent. ; that is intelligible." [1]

At this point Mr. Toogood breaks in upon the argument with a paper of his own, and he is followed by one guest after another, each desirous of edifying the company with an important composition, until Dr. Folliott is obliged to threaten them with one of his sermons and thus reduces them all to quiet again.

Mr. Philpot, a rapt geographer who is full of enthusiasm for the steam navigation of rivers, and Mr. Trillo, who worships the opera, are sly reflections of Peacock himself in his respective capacities of India official and operatic critic. Mr. Toogood, the co-operationist, stands for Robert Owen ; Mr. Wilful Wontsee, for Wordsworth ; Mr. Rumblesack Shantsee, for Southey ; Mr. Skionar, for Coleridge ; Mr. Ramsbottom, the zodiacal mythologist, perhaps for Mr. Newton of Bracknell. The remaining characters may have had living prototypes, but they are so slightly presented that it seems impossible to establish their identities. The point, of course, is the ridicule of the opinions themselves ; the people who hold them come in but incidentally for laughter.

In discussing a novel of Peacock's one is likely to fall into the error of giving information which should go rather into notes for the novel than into an exposition of its general characteristics. Possibly the time may come when these tales may be printed with

[1] *Works*, ii. 218.

the desideratum of an accurate text, and with sufficient annotation to make clear the topical allusions. It may be questioned, however, whether any beside *Melincourt* would gain much by the process. Certainly Peacock does not deserve to become an established minor classic, if he depends too far upon any such factitious aid for his appeal. His satire, only moderately valuable to the student or historian of manners, and innocent of any direct intention to instruct, must look for its longevity to the success with which it renders ludicrous perennial foibles. Whenever a satirist girds at an object of ridicule, however ridiculous, which is soon to pass out of memory, he has probably encumbered himself with so much dead weight in the race for posterity's favour. *Crochet Castle*, in the main, is free from such lumber. The Morbifics and Henbanes and Trillos are good enough specimens of the cranks of our acquaintance to make them amusing, and they are nowhere allowed to indulge in disquisition to any tiresome length. The worldly experience which renders Peacock more charitable in the treatment of his characters than he had been in the earlier novels, has taken away some of the sharpness of the wit and refined the caricature. There is a complete social amenity among the personages of the piece which makes the atmosphere in *Crotchet Castle* much more tranquil than in *Headlong Hall*. Everywhere appear the evidences of a dignified retirement from commotion. The characters never take themselves so seriously as to imperil the quiet of the scene. Even the irascible Dr. Folliott is the very pink of blunt courtesy toward the opponents whom he demolishes in leisurely rotation. His real function seems that of the jovial priest of some Epicurean garden, where the inhabitants are quite unconscious, or at any rate careless, of what the rest of the world does, but where they are all exceedingly well-informed as to what the silly world, including themselves, thinks. Except in the two love affairs, the novel seldom gives a line to anything that is not purely an intellectual matter. But the dialogue is rich with acute observation and laughing worldly wisdom. As in the plays of Congreve and Sheridan, the characters atone for a lack of human quality in their own persons by being the mouthpieces for much comment which gives a spectator confidence that they have seen the world, even if from an unassailed distance.

The man who could write *Crochet Castle* must have deserved the reputation he had among his few intimate friends of being a genuine wit. But the justice of the reputation can be confirmed by little which has survived him except the novels. Even after he had become, as he was by 1830, a man with a tolerably well established literary reputation, his circle of intimates remained as small as ever. He abstained painstakingly from letter-writing, and he managed to find no one able or inclined to serve as his Boswell. For the same reasons, and because of the absence from his life of any incident of note, it is impossible now to throw much light upon the personal chronicle of his later years. It is known, however, that he occasionally wrote operatic critiques for Coulson's *Globe and Traveller*, and that after Albany Fonblanque accepted the editorship of *The Examiner* in 1830, Peacock became a regular contributor to its musical columns. He left behind him a collection of newspaper clippings which give most of the notices and which seem to indicate that his work as operatic critic belongs chiefly to the years 1830–34. To judge by these, his contributions to *The Globe and Traveller* were neither numerous nor frequent, and his *Examiner* notes contain little that is characteristic of the " Author of Headlong Hall." To judge by what we have, he possessed wide and accurate musical scholarship, a tolerable catholicity of taste, few enthusiasms, and a love for simplicity and restraint in music as in poetry. Malibran he admired with absolute devotion ; for Grisi, whose first appearance he recorded, he had an almost equal fondness. " There has never been anything perfect under the sun except the compositions of Mozart," he wrote in *The Examiner* for February 10, 1833. He was particularly fond of the ballet, especially during the days when Taglioni was in her prime. " Dancing," he wrote on July 13, 1832, " as we had before seen it, we now perceive to have answered OVID's description of ' beating the ground alternately with the feet.' If such has been dancing, TAGLIONI's is flowing into attitudes of grace, and making sensible the loveliness of motion—it is on the music she seems to move, sporting (as Gay's song has it) ' on seas of delight,' waving, buoyant, and sparkling." As might be expected, Peacock was severe upon historical inaccuracy or blunders in the staging. He found annual opportunity to defend the costumes of the ballet from Philistine aspersion. " *The Morning Herald*," he wrote February 20, 1831, "has begun canting about the dresses of the female dancers. *The Times*, according to custom, will not begin canting till after Easter, when it will be sure of the largest audience." He objected to the presence of a director in full view of the audience, and continually scored Costa's habit of striking the score with his baton, thus keeping up a ceaseless " phlatto-thratto-phlatto-thrat," as Peacock named it out of Aristophanes. His sincerest censure, however, was invariably aroused by the practice of cutting up operas at the will of the management. To him an operatic score, just as it had come from the hand of the composer, was sacred, and he had no mind to excuse trespass in the matter. Almost all innovations he contested, and when, early in 1835, he reviewed the Earl of Mount Edgcumbe's *Musical Reminiscences* in *The London Review*, the decadence of the ballet and the triumph of the conductor had estranged him so much that he gradually renounced the opera as he had done in 1819. This time it was final, and the centre of the first row in the pit, where he always sat, frequently with his daughter Mary, knew him no more.

The death of his mother in 1833 contributed to his withdrawal from periodical criticism by throwing upon him many of the domestic cares which his invalid wife could not assume. His mother's loss he mourned inconsolably, and he himself ascribed to it his long literary silence. When she died he had perhaps already begun the fragment which has recently

been published [1] with the title, *The Lord of the Hills.*
The paper bears the watermark 1833. Increasing
duties at the India House, however, as well as the death
of his mother, must have been responsible for his
failure to complete the novel. Even these did not
put a period to his writing till after his succession to
James Mill as Chief Examiner in 1836. When in
1834 the philosophical Radicals found it necessary to
secede from *The Westminster Review*, and projected a
new organ of their own, Peacock agreed to become one
of the contributors. John Stuart Mill, writing to
Albany Fonblanque for a promise of assistance in the
venture, told him they had everybody worth asking
except Bulwer, and included Peacock in the list.[2] To
the two volumes of *The London Review* which appeared
during 1835–36, Peacock contributed four articles, but
he apparently ceased to write for it on its merger with
the original *Westminster*. There is an amusing reference, however, to his reputation as a reviewer in a letter
which Mill wrote to his co-editor, John Robertson,
in 1837. "Moore," he said, "if favourable, is not
worth doing; if unfavourable, Peacock should do it."[3]
As nothing of Moore's was reviewed, Robertson apparently gave him the compliment of a judgment which
kept him out of Peacock's hands.

Besides the review of Lord Mount Edgcumbe's
book, there is another musical article, on Bellini, which
appeared in January 1836. More notable are the two

[1] *Thomas Love Peacock : Letters,* &c., pp. 215–33.
[2] Albany Fonblanque, *Life and Letters* (1874), p. 39.
[3] *Atlantic Monthly,* "John Stuart Mill and the London and Westminster Review," lxix. 58.

essays, *French Comic Romances* and *The Épicier*. The first was published in July 1835, the second the following January. Both constitute a kind of prolegomena to a considerable discussion of Paul de Kock which Peacock promised, but which he seems never to have written. It is unfortunate that he did not, for he would probably have given a full account of his own critical ideals. Even as it is, he offers some interesting opinions on the subject of comic fiction. He thought that the combined spirit of comedy and ridicule had had much more influence upon social progress than was commonly supposed. Even reformatory folly had not been able to destroy the advances toward freedom of inquiry which each wave of reform had actually accomplished, and in which it was remarkable that some of the most honest and self-sacrificing agents had been the writers of comic fiction. " We are here speaking, however," he says, " solely of the authors of the highest order of comic fiction—that which limits itself, in the exposure of abuses, to turning up into full daylight their intrinsic absurdities—not that which makes ridiculous things not really so, by throwing over them a fool's coat which does not belong to them, or setting upon them, as honest Bottom has it, an ass's head of its own. Ridicule, in the first case, the honest development of the ridiculous *ab intrà*, is very justly denominated the test of truth : but ridicule, in the second case, the dishonest superinduction of the ridiculous *ab extrà*, is the test of nothing but the knavery of the inventor. In the first case, the ridicule is never sought ; it always appears, as in the comic tales of Voltaire, to force itself up obviously and spontaneously: in the second case, the most prominent feature of the exhibition is the predetermination to be caustic and comical. To writers of the latter class most truly applies the axiom—*homines derisores civitatem perdunt.* But an intense love of truth, and a clear apprehension of truth, are both essential to comic writing of the first class. An intense love of truth may exist without the faculty of detecting it; and a clear apprehension of truth may co-exist with a determination to pervert it. The union of both is rare; and still more rare is the combination of both with that peculiar ' composite of natural capacity and superinduced habit,' which constitutes what is usually denominated comic genius." [1]

In theory, at any rate, Peacock regarded the writing of his novels as a more or less serious attempt to apply to his generation a genuine test of ridicule. Commenting upon the great difference, in respect to the embodiment of opinion in fiction, between Pigault-Lebrun and Paul de Kock, Peacock gives what he probably thought the reason for his own unpopularity. Pigault-Lebrun had lived while men were full of interest in ideas, when they believed in them, and demanded that their literature be informed with them. Paul de Kock, on the contrary, steers clear of everything even resembling an idea, because the public no longer requires such a commodity, and men of letters meet the demand. Peacock must have been thinking that he himself had refused to fall in with the wants

[1] *London Review,* ii. 72.

of the public which required Paul de Kocks and
Walter Scotts, and that he had suffered accordingly.
His article, *The Épicier*,[1] arraigns a generation which
depends upon the grocer for all its necessities, and
which, in Peacock's opinion, had given its whole
government into his hands. In such a state of society
there must be none of the perturbing yeast of ideas
which can disarrange, even by a centime, the price
of sugar or fish-sauce. No public alarm, however
inevitably the result of an attempt to distribute justice
with greater fairness, can seem to the *épicier* to justify
any disturbance of commercial confidence. His life—
that is, his immediate prosperity, depends upon the
maintenance of business peace, and consequently he
has developed the normal impregnability of his apprehension into an unwieldy bulk of stupidity which
smothers ideas from all the rest of the world. Against
such a spirit Peacock's novels had been able to make
little headway.

The last literary work he did before he was sub-
merged by India House duties was in connection with
Bentley's Miscellany, which, under the editorship of
Charles Dickens, began its merry career in January
1837. The magazine had been planned by Richard
Bentley the preceding October, and Dickens had been
engaged as editor in November.[2] On whose initiative
Peacock became a contributor does not appear, but

---

[1] Dr. Young (p. 19) was the first to call attention to this article.
It was not mentioned by Peacock, but the signature "M. S. O.," the
same as that appended to those undoubtedly his, together with internal
evidence, renders the ascription a matter of no doubt.

[2] *The Times*, Dec. 8, 1871.

he was probably solicited by Bentley, who desired to secure for his venture all the best-known names in wit's commonwealth. An advertisement in *The Athenæum* for December 3 gives a list of the various contributors who had already promised, but Peacock's name is not among them. On January 7 the *Athenæum* advertisement puts him second in the list, between Theodore Hook and Father Prout. To the first number he contributed a cheerful ballad, *The Legend of Manor Hall*, and to the second number his *Recollections of Childhood*. These contributions of his were probably responsible for the fact that Bentley issued, about the beginning of 1837, a new edition of four of Peacock's tales in a single volume of the *Standard Novels and Romances*. On February 18 it was announced in *The Athenæum* that *Headlong Hall*, *Nightmare Abbey*, and *Maid Marian* would appear ten days later. Some arrangement seems, however, to have been made with Hookham, and on March 18 Bentley advertised that *Crotchet Castle* would be included in the volume, and that all would be published March 24. Peacock was named in the advertisement, but the book itself bears only the pseudonym, " The Author of Headlong Hall." There are some slight changes in the text and a highly characteristic preface. Peacock appends in a note to *Crotchet Castle* his poem, *The Fate of a Broom*, which, aimed at Lord Brougham, had been written in March 1831 and published in *The Examiner* for the following August 14.

Whether Peacock met Dickens, or whether he ever attended any of the monthly dinners which Bentley gave for his contributors, cannot be ascertained. As he did not keep up his contributions, he probably saw little of those who became regular producers for the *Miscellany.* His connection was not severed as quickly as has always been assumed, however, for there are three hitherto unnoticed pieces of his in the volume for 1838. Two [1] are unacknowledged poems from *The Paper Money Lyrics,* of which some had appeared in *The Guide,* and all had been privately issued the year before ; the other may be quoted in full, as it has never been reprinted, and as it constitutes Peacock's farewell to the Muses for a dozen years.

" THE NEW YEAR

Lines on George Cruikshank's Illustration of January in the Comic Almanack for 1838.

BY THE AUTHOR OF ' HEADLONG HALL.'

A great philosopher art thou, George Cruikshank,
In thy unmatched grotesqueness ! Antic dance,
Wine, mirth, and music, welcome thy New Year,
Who makes her entry as a radiant child,
With smiling face, in holiday apparel,
Bearing a cornucopia, crowned and clustered
With all the elements of festal joy :
All smiles and promises. But looking closely
Upon that smiling face, 'tis but a mask ;
Fitted so well, it almost seems a face ;
But still a mask. What features lurk beneath,
The rolling months will show. Thy Old Year passes—
Danced out in mockery by the festive band—
A faded form, with thin and pallid face,
In spectral weeds ; her mask upon the ground,

---

[1] *Bentley's Miscellany,* iv. 140, 239.

THOMAS LOVE PEACOCK

And Amalthæa's horn reversed, and emptied
Of all good things—not even hope remaining.
Such will the New Year be: that smiling mask
Will fall; to some how soon! to many later:
At last to all! The same transparent shade
Of wasted means and broken promises
Will make its exit; and another Year
Will enter masked and smiling, and be welcomed
With minstrelsy and revelry, as this is."

---

[1] *Bentley's Miscellany*, iii. 104 (Jan. 1838).

CHAPTER IX

INDIA HOUSE

THE biographer of a man whose reputation depends chiefly upon his writings perhaps too often assumes an attitude of indifference toward the other chapters of the author's life. Fielding, the justice, Chaucer, the civil servant, Wordsworth, the distributor of stamps, are personages over whom most readers hurry with impatience to get at the authors of *Tom Jones*, *The Nonnes Preestes Tale*, and *Michael*. So with Peacock, whose hold on posterity owes but little to his having been a trusted official of the great company which so long manipulated the left arm of the British Empire. At the same time, although his career was largely devoid of important political relations which might give it general interest, it is quite impossible to appreciate his true character unless one knows something of his life as a model man of business, who was entrusted with large responsibilities, shared many political secrets, exhibited notable capacity and had it recognised, and who, scorner as he was of his commercial generation, actually contributed to some of the " advances " for which the generation had a habit of praising itself.

The details of his appointment have already been given. An examination of the Court Minutes of the

Board of Directors has shown by what steps he rose to his subsequent high rank. When Strachey, Mill, Peacock, and Harcourt were first appointed, the Committee of Correspondence reported that they thought it best to select no Assistant-Examiner for the present, but to call all of the new men Assistants to the Examiner. It appears, however, from the report of May 19, 1819, that the four men were kept on probation, not alone with a view to testing their fitness for becoming members of the permanent establishment, but with a view to finding out which of them deserved selection for the post of Assistant-Examiner. Whether the candidates themselves appreciated this rivalry, there is no way of knowing. Harcourt, as an experienced employee of the office, did work of a general nature ; Strachey drafted the despatches for the department of Justice, Mill, of Revenue, and Peacock, of Public Works. But when, on the recommendation of the Committee of Correspondence, all four appointments were confirmed by ballot in the Court of Directors, April 10, 1821, it was not thought advisable to decide the question of succession, because, the Committee reported, there seemed no reason to anticipate any speedy vacancy in the Examinership. The Committee recommended that Strachey, Mill, and Peacock, " besides continuing to prepare the Correspondence in those Departments in which they have hitherto been employed, be required to co-operate in the ordinary routine of the duties of the office, as well as to contribute their assistance on any extraordinary occasion on which their services may be deemed useful : and to conform generally to the rules which are applicable to the other officers of the Establishment." From this it would appear that the three candidates had hitherto enjoyed certain immunities, but the nature of them can only be inferred.

Two years later, April 9, 1823, Mill received the appointment as Assistant-Examiner, and his salary was raised from £1000 to £1200. At the same time Peacock, who had been receiving £200 less than Mill from the first, was awarded an increase of his salary to £1000. His new income, " a mark of the Court's approbation of the talents and services of Mr. Thomas L. Peacock," was to begin from the preceding Lady Day. On December 8, 1830, William McCulloch having retired from the Examinership, James Mill became Examiner, and Strachey and Peacock, although no Assistant-Examiner was appointed, became Senior Assistants at £1200 each, again an increase for Peacock. Mill's promotion probably made some changes in the nature of Peacock's duties ; at least he testified two years later before a parliamentary committee that he now examined the revenue despatches from Bengal, Madras, and Bombay.[1] On February 17, 1836, Strachey having died, Peacock became Assistant-Examiner at £1500, and he succeeded to the place vacated by James Mill's death on July 27, with a salary fixed at £2000, the salary which Mill had been drawing at the time of his death, but £100 more than that official had been awarded on his first promotion.

[1] *Report from the Select Committee on the Affairs of the East India Company* (1831–32): *Minutes of Evidence*, iii. 1.

McCulloch's salary had been £2300 in 1819 ; Peacock's seems never to have been increased. After his retirement from the office, March 28, 1856, his pension was £1333, 6s. 8d. Dr. Garnett asserts that Peacock received from time to time extraordinary grants of money, as did the two Mills.[1] The records of the India House show that such gifts were made to John Stuart Mill, but neither to his father nor to Peacock.

From an early date Peacock seems to have busied himself with the problem of a shortened route of communication with India. By his own testimony,[2] this concern of his began in 1829. Thomas Waghorn, then a young British sailor, had been sent by a committee of merchants in Madras and Calcutta to induce the Government or the India Company to promote steam navigation on the Red Sea. Waghorn met with considerable opposition, but was finally allowed to make a test voyage in October 1829. On the suggestion of one of the Directors of the Company, Peacock had already begun to study the problem, and by September of that year had drawn up an extensive *Memorandum respecting the Application of Steam Navigation to the internal and external Communications of India.*[3] Certain queries of his as to the relative merits of the Egyptian and the Syrian routes were transmitted the same year through the Earl of Aberdeen, then Foreign Secretary, to Consul-General Barker at Alexandria, and were there put into the hands of Capt. F. R. Chesney, who had been sent on a political mission

---

[1] *Headlong Hall* (1891), p. 36.
[2] *Report from the Select Committee on Navigation to India* (1834), p. 1.
[3] *Ibid., Appendix*, pp. 1 *ff.*

to Egypt. Chesney was much struck by the " compre-
hensiveness, sagacity, and forethought," [1] of the queries,
and accordingly began his preliminary investigations
along the lines suggested by Peacock. When Chesney
returned to England in the autumn of 1832, he met
Peacock, and discovered that the Senior Assistant to
the Examiner had already done a good deal to pave the
way for steam communication. " My visits to the India
House . . . led to an introduction to Mr. Peacock,
one of the leading people in the Examiner's Office. I
found that he was deeply versed in the ancient history
of the Euphrates, and that he had not only been the
first to bring this line of communication with India
forward, but that he had collected in a thick book
every private notice he could find of that river,
whether contained in Gibbon, Balbi, or any other
work." [2] The preceding February and March Peacock
had been summoned before the Parliamentary Committee on the Affairs of the East India Company.[3]
He had reported concerning the voyage of the *Enter-
prise* by the Cape of Good Hope seven years before,
and had expressed his preference for the Euphrates
route as one better than that by the Red Sea. Chesney,
like Waghorn, encountered much inertia, but he had
stout supporters, among them Peacock, who persuaded
him to publish his *Reports on the Navigation of the
Euphrates* early in 1833. Finally a Select Committee
of the House of Commons on Steam Navigation to
India opened its session, June 9, 1834. Chesney

[1] Chesney, *Narrative of the Euphrates Expedition* (1868), p. 4.
[2] *Life of Chesney*, ed. Lane-Poole (1893), p. 261.
[3] *Report of Select Committee on the Affairs of the East India Company :
Minutes of Evidence* (1832), ii. 119–30 ; iii. 1.

records in his diary : " At 12 the Steam Committee commenced its labours with Peacock, who answered all things clearly and quickly, giving a general idea of the whole question as to economy and policy, &c." [1] Peacock's evidence shows a vast amount of information, both ancient and modern, on every possible subject connected with the route to India. He clearly preferred the Euphrates to the Red Sea route, but admitted that both would be useful. He doubted that the application of steam to India navigation would benefit trade, but he thought it a very important matter for the mails, and politically important as a move to forestall Russia in the Euphrates Valley and the Persian Gulf, before it should be too late. In the Appendix to the Report are printed the papers which Peacock submitted in support of his testimony. As a result of the Committee's Report, Parliament set aside £20,000 for an expedition to the Euphrates, and Chesney was put in command. Part of the credit for the conception of the famous expedition which Chesney led must be given to Peacock, who may have emphasised the contradiction involved in his appearance as the champion of steam by writing a review of the Report for his much-scorned *Edinburgh Review* the following January.[2]

[1] *Life of Chesney*, p. 272.
[2] This ascription cannot be made with certainty. Cole (p. 26) says Peacock wrote an article on steam navigation in the *Westminster* in 1835. As no such article appeared, Dr. Garnett (*Headlong Hall*, 1891, p. 35) felt justified in ascribing to Peacock the one in the *Edinburgh*. It may have been Peacock's. The opinions are in accord with his, but the style is too merely business-like to yield internal evidence for naming any author.

INDIA HOUSE

July 1834 saw Peacock appear again as the Company's representative. James Silk Buckingham, then member for Sheffield, had been expelled from India eleven years before because of censure of the India Company in his *Calcutta Journal*. He claimed that his expulsion had been illegal, and he had certainly lost very heavily by it. Not a few of Peacock's friends, among them Bentham, Coulson, Bowring, Hobhouse, had expressed their opinion that Buckingham had been unjustly treated. He appealed to Parliament for redress from the Company, and in 1834 secured a hearing before a Select Committee on the Suppression of the Calcutta Journal. He conducted his own case, while Peacock, unassisted, represented the India Company. He established the grounds of the Company's action with the skill of an experienced barrister, displaying a wide and minute knowledge of all the questions involved, and presenting his arguments with his accustomed lucidity. Irrespective of the merits of Buckingham's contention—the Committee recommended that the Company should reimburse him for his losses—it is obvious that Peacock had the same right to conduct his employers' case as has any barrister to act for a client. Certainly his arguments do not suffer by comparison with the petition which John Stuart Mill drew up for the Company in 1858, when Palmerston's Bill for the Better Government of India, with its intention to dethrone the Company, was pending.

Two years later Peacock defended the Company again before the Select Committee on Salt, British India, when the Company's right to the salt monopoly was being contested by the merchants of Liverpool. He held that the Liverpool interest merely desired to secure for themselves a privilege which the Company already possessed, and he had no compunction in doing all he could to defeat them. The Company triumphed.

His final appearance as witness for the Company was before a Select Committee on Steam Navigation with India in 1837. His testimony was the longest given. It differs from his earlier evidence by the fact that he had changed his mind on some few minor points, but more notably by the admission into it of various characteristic remarks which suggest the Peacock of the novels. " I am not aware that it would be any benefit to the people of India to send Europeans amongst them," he said.[1] Indeed, he was of the opinion that such a course would have a sinister effect upon the " morals and domestic habits " of the Hindoos. Commenting upon the influence which increased intercourse would have in persuading Indian students to come to England, he speaks with the tongue of Dr. Folliott : " I think interest will overcome prejudice anywhere." [2] Obviously the Examiner did not feel called upon to repress his private notions as the Assistant-Examiner had done.

It was partly due to Peacock's recommendations and efforts that the India Company took a prominent share, first in the experiment of sending out vessels propelled by steam alone, and second, in the substitu-

[1] *Report from the Select Committee on Steam Navigation* (1837), p. 55.
[2] *Ibid.*, p. 57.

tion of iron for wood in their construction. The *Atalanta* and *Berenice*, built as a result of the report from the Committee of 1834, were larger than any which the Company had so far employed in its Red Sea service. Peacock laboured unremittingly to have them sent around the Cape, and was thoroughly justified by the results. The first vessel which navigated the Indus, and the first three iron vessels ordered for the Company's service, were in part constructed from designs presented by the Examiner of Correspondence. In 1839 the Secret Committee consulted with Peacock as to the extension of the use of iron vessels, and, acting on his advice, ordered six new vessels of iron. Four, the *Nemesis*, *Phlegethon*, *Ariadne*, and *Medusa*, were built by the Lairds of Birkenhead, and, to keep the Company's ownership secret, were sent out in the name of the makers. Peacock persuaded the Company to despatch the *Nemesis* and *Phlegethon* under steam around the Cape, instead of sending them out in pieces as had been done formerly. He then turned his attention to the *Pluto* and *Proserpine*, which were built in London under his personal supervision, and which he tested on repeated experimental voyages before they too were sent out by way of the Cape. All of the six except the *Ariadne* saw service in the Chinese war.[1]

Peacock, who took great delight in his share in maritime improvements, always called the ships his " iron chickens." As his activities were largely secret, and as he has left practically no personal record, it is

[1] Clowes, *Royal Navy* (1897–1903), vi. 288.

difficult to get at the truth concerning these years.[1] It is known that he contributed two letters to *The Times* for November 3 and 7, 1838, in which he explained the recent failure of the *Semiramis* to complete a journey from Bombay to the Red Sea during the summer monsoon, but these throw no light upon his own personality. A characteristic letter which he wrote to " J. H.," an unidentified correspondent, on the Russian question in the same year has been preserved, and may here be quoted from his granddaughter's *Biographical Notice :*

" MY DEAR SIR,—No European power that intends to march through Central Asia need care about the actual possessors of the divisions of nominal supremacy. Belong Herat to whom it may before an European army walks up to it, it belongs to that army from the moment of its approach. So with the whole country from the Mediterranean to the Indus. As to the establishment of local interest by diplomacy, I consider it mere child's play. If we do not mean to fight in Central Asia, we may as well leave the field to Russia, who certainly does mean to fight there some time or other. If we do mean to fight under any conceivable circumstances, let us conceive those circumstances and see how we mean to fight. Surely we shall begin by sending troops up the Indus. Indian troops from India, but European troops, how ? I say down the

[1] The principal, and almost the sole, authority for this part of his career is a MS. *Memorandum as to the part taken by the late Thomas Love Peacock, Esq., in promoting Steam Navigation*, written by John Laird in 1873, and preserved by Mrs. Clarke.

Euphrates. Then let us retain our present pre-occupation of that river, which we can now do without offence, and make our pre-arrangements quietly but surely. I have been thinking of sending you a memorandum on the grounds and modes of proceeding, but on mature consideration, with which recent circumstances have had something to do, I cannot originate anything, or suggest the origination of anything, on the matter, or on any matter connected with the East India Company's Steam Navigation.

. . . . . .

" P.S.—Did it make any difference to Alexander whether Darius had a satrapy more or less ? "[1]

Beyond these bare details very little can be recovered which presents Peacock to the life in his official capacity. Like the two Mills, he was always punctual in his attendance at the Company's office in Leadenhall, where, in a spacious office up two flights of stairs, he attended to his duties when they demanded attention, but still found much leisure for his literary studies. His advocacy of shortened steam communication disturbed his leisure in more ways than by occupying him with an extraordinary duty. When the route had finally been shortened the Indian mails came monthly instead of twice yearly as before, and the Examiner's Office no longer had to work furiously for a brief period and then yawn through several months of idleness. It was during the earlier days of his service for the Company that Peacock wrote the

[1] *Works*, i. xliv.

lines on the way they spent their time which are said
to have excited the wrath of Charles Lamb :

> " From ten to eleven, ate a breakfast for seven :
> From eleven to noon, to begin 'twas too soon ;
> From twelve to one, asked ' What's to be done ? '
> From one to two, found nothing to do ;
> From two to three began to foresee
> That from three to four would be a damned bore."

The first line has reference to the fact that the Company gave breakfast to the members of the permanent
staff who arrived by ten o'clock.

An unsubstantiated family tradition has it that
one of Lord Ellenborough's grievances against the
Company was that the order for his recall had been
written by a " novel-writing clerk." As Peacock was
Examiner at that date, Ellenborough was probably
correct, but Peacock, of course, was not in any way
responsible for the policy of the recall. From the
journal of Sir M. E. Grant Duff it appears that he
met Peacock during the winter of 1851-52, and
later was often in his company. " I saw a good
deal of Mr. Peacock about this time," he says in an
entry for April 1853, " and enjoyed his society ex-
tremely. He was utterly unlike anybody I have ever
seen before or since." [1] It could be wished that some
of the people who shared this opinion of Peacock's
unique qualities had left us better proof than the un-
supported testimonials which come so tantalisingly to
any one desirous of knowing more about him. The

[1] *Notes from a Diary*, 1852-1872, i. 41.

curious, however, are obliged to look less upon his biography than upon his books.

That aloofness from acquaintance which partly explains his fate with posterity may be illustrated by the recollections of Mr. P. A. Daniel, who was a junior clerk in the Examiner's Office during the later years of Peacock's work there. He remembers that Peacock was invariably kind to his subordinates, but that he never entered into the intimacy with them which John Stuart Mill allowed himself. Mill used to come to the outer room where the clerks had their desks, both before and after his succession to the Examinership, and talk with the young men before the fire which always burned there in chilly weather. Peacock never did this. Unless they were sent for, the clerks saw their chief only when he arrived in the morning and was ushered to his office with great ceremony by the uniformed messengers who stood at the outer door. New employees of the Office were always questioned closely as to their classical proficiency. Peacock's own writings were little known among the clerks, although *A Goodlye Ballade of Little John*, which was first published in 1875 as of uncertain date, but was actually written soon after the appearance of Lord John Russell's *Letters to the Bishop of Durham on Papal Aggression*, November 1850, circulated in manuscript among the younger men, with some illustrations by Mr. Daniel. *The Paper Money Lyrics* still enjoyed a similar circulation among the members of the Office staff up to the time of Peacock's leaving it.

Practically the only close friendship Peacock formed

as a result of his official position was with John Cam Hobhouse, Lord Broughton. Apparently they first met in 1830 or thereabouts; by the end of his life Peacock saw almost no one else. His necessary absence from his home throughout the week for a long time kept him in touch with several friends in London. After he gave up the Stamford Street residence he had chambers in the Adelphi, where, by a touch so Peacockian as almost to seem a matter of his own invention, his cook cherished a tame kangaroo in the kitchen. But when the London and South-Western Railway had made daily transit to Lower Halliford possible, Peacock grew even more recluse. He was driven in a fly each morning from his house, just off the green in Lower Halliford, to Walton Station, and thence proceeded up to London with Sir John Easthope and several old acquaintances whom business took on the same journey. At the end of the day's work he came down again as swiftly as the first train would carry him, perhaps not one whit the less satisfied with the speed of the locomotive because he was wont to ridicule the passion for speed in his novels. Mrs. Peacock's long illness had brought on an intense nervousness which made it necessary for her husband to safeguard her from any worry or excitement. If he left home at all, it was to visit Lord Broughton at Erle Stoke, Westbury, where he was always made enthusiastically welcome by the whole family. It is testimony to the real kindliness of his character that he should have been the close friend of Lord Broughton's young daughters as well as of their father. There

INDIA HOUSE

is allusion to this in some unpublished verses which
Broughton sent to Peacock at an uncertain date,
presumably about 1840.

"*Ad, or in Titum Amarcellum Pavoniam* [*sic*].
Peacock! examiner of all things East,
Thinks I've forgot his promise; not the least!
He said—for all his sayings I remember—
'I'll be at Erle-Stoke some time in December.'
December's come, alas! and almost gone;
But he, oh, shameless mortal! lingers on,
With no pretext—no, no pretext at all,
Not e'en a decent play or opera stall,
Lost in collections, puzzled by P.C.'s,
And hopes I'll take excuses such as these.
These may deceive some simple folk, but I,
Who know the hogs of Epicurus' stye,
And like them, as a Christian well may do,
Though hateful to Mahometan and Jew,
Protest against such shuffling, and declare
He's tired of pleasure that he once could bear;
Yes, autumn sports, and Christmas and her pie,
And all her revels, pass unheeded by;
No more he's solaced by the simple sight
Of little listeners, silent with delight
At many a tale, to them, at least, unknown,
Gay, witty, innocent, and all his own.
No more his Babrian studies, idly broke
By visits to the dingle in a cloak;
No more they charm him, and, preposterous now,
He calls it duty to forget his vow;
Nay, more, e'en here in town we never meet,
Though living only in another street,
He will not come to Berkeley Square: myself, I
Have never managed yet to reach th' Adelphi.

Such is the fate of every hapless host—
Poor creatures, all their pains are more than lost!
Heaven sent them railroads to entice them more,
In vain! all vote a country life a bore;

THOMAS LOVE PEACOCK

The man is well enough—knows how to keep
A place where any one may eat and sleep,
Has beagles, takes you out to hunt or course;
But what is that to me, who hate a horse?
And, Lord! how dull the eternal round to me
Of breakfast, luncheon, dinner-time, and tea!
Never alone, and then, the more to tire,
Comes the prim parson and the sleepy squire,
The lord-lieutenant, and, oh, worst of all!
The county member, and the county ball!
True, but d'ye think they're worse than Leadenhall?

Come, come, if only for a change, come down,
The world's away, and London's out of town,
And all the sixteen sages that of late
Sat fixed in Downing Street to save the State,
To Dan and to the devil leave the nation,
And quit for three whole weeks their high vocation;
You, too, shut up your shop and make it known
That India's old enough to walk alone;
Leave the dull wilderness of paragraph,
For better nonsense, and an honest laugh,
And care—'twas said by some illustrious joker—
No more for Ali Cawn than Ali Croaker.
In short, just keep your promise to the text,
And be at Erle Stoke upon Thursday next." [1]

The death of Lord Broughton's daughter Julia in
1849 Peacock honoured with some affecting verses. One
of the two Greek poems which he is known to have
written celebrated a whitebait dinner at Lovegrove's,
Blackwall, in 1851, at which both he and Lord
Broughton were present. During a visit at Erle
Stoke the next year news came to Peacock of his
wife's sudden and totally unexpected death. The
grief which he felt at this drove him still more into

[1] Cole, p. 30-31.

a studious retirement. In the endurance of pain Peacock had little of the Stoic and less of the Christian. He would not pretend that suffering gave no hurt ; he did not believe that it was bestowed as a righteous discipline. His natural pride, as well as his philosophy, counselled fortitude, but fortitude he thought he could best practise in his study, where the resolute exercise of his mind would leave as little time as might be for the pain which he could not forget.

CHAPTER X

"FRASER'S MAGAZINE"—"GRYLL GRANGE"— TRANSLATIONS—DEATH

The Edinburgh Review for January 1839 contained a suggestive and valuable article on Peacock by James Spedding. Just ten years elapsed before any of the works there recommended to the public's attention seemed to call for republication, and then it was in the form of a reissue of the Bentley volume. Miss Harriet Love, Peacock's cousin, later said that he had written her in 1840 that a new work was in the press. She thought it had been *The Pilgrim of Provence*, but of that only a very few slight fragments were preserved.[1] They indicate that he had meditated another mediæval subject, perhaps even before *The Misfortunes of Elphin*, and had hesitated between the form of a play and a novel. More considerable are the fragments of a translation of *Prometheus Bound*, which extends to line 152, but was never published.[2] So far as the world was concerned, Peacock maintained complete literary silence for a dozen years. He returned to the world of letters that had once yielded him a recognised position, and which, though not clamorous, had never entirely forgotten him, with some characteristic essays in *Fraser's Magazine*, the first of which

[1] Brit. Mus. *Addit. MSS.*, 36815, fol. 152–8.
[2] *Ibid.*, fol. 89–93.

appeared at the head of the number for December 1851. This piece, *Gastronomy and Civilization,* has not hitherto been cited as Peacock's, but there can be no doubt that it was very largely his work. The initials " M. M." with which it was signed, stand for Mary Meredith, Peacock's eldest daughter, then two years the wife of a man who causes her father's later years to be a matter of curiosity, as Shelley does the earlier ones. Mary Ellen Peacock had married, in January 1844, Lieutenant Edward Nicolls, who met a tragic death by drowning within three months. In 1847 or 1848 Mrs. Nicolls, then living with her brother, Edward Gryffydh Peacock, in London, made the acquaintance of George Meredith, recently returned from Germany, very young, very poor, very ambitious. The first record which has been preserved of their friendship is a recently discovered manuscript periodical, *The Monthly Observer,* which was originated by Meredith, and which was edited in successive months by a number of young friends, of whom Meredith and Mrs. Nicolls were two. The contributors included all of the group, Edward Gryffydh Peacock, Austin Daniel (Mr. P. A. Daniel), a Mr. St. Croix, who belonged to a family of Peacock's friends in Chertsey, a Mr. Charnock, who wrote under the pseudonym of " Aretched Kooez "—a wretched quiz— Mrs. Nicolls, and Meredith. The magazine was begun presumably in 1848. The numbers 11, 13, 14, 16, and 17, which were recently sold by Messrs. Sotheby, Wilkinson, and Hodge (December 1, 1910), cover the period from January to July 1849. Whether the

THOMAS LOVE PEACOCK

earlier numbers are in existence has not been discovered, but *The Monthly Observer* probably did not continue its course beyond No. 17, for on August 9, Meredith and Mrs. Nicolls were married at Lower Halliford and departed for a brief stay abroad before returning to take up residence at Weybridge. The great disparity in the ages of the two novelists was nearly sufficient of itself to prevent any intimate friendship between them. Moreover, Peacock was not very strongly drawn to his gifted son-in-law, who had been educated in Germany, which Peacock hated, and who disturbed the old pagan with a lack of concern in the Greek mythology only a little less than by his somewhat eccentric and impetuous habits. At the same time, one feels that the references to Goethe in Peacock's later writings may owe something to Meredith, and there can be little doubt that Meredith's admiration for Peacock bore fruit in a genuine influence. While still at Weybridge Meredith dedicated his *Poems* of 1851 to " Thomas Love Peacock, Esq., . . . with the profound admiration and affectionate respect of his son-in-law." In all probability, Peacock had assisted in the publication of the volume, which was issued by J. W. Parker & Son. The " Son " of this firm, J. W. Parker, junior, was a close friend of Peacock's. This too may account for the fact that one of Meredith's earliest identified poems, *Invitation to the Country*, appeared in *Fraser's Magazine*, then published by Parker & Son, in August of the same year. Peacock did more for his son-in-law. When it became apparent that Meredith's struggle against poverty at Weybridge was almost too severe for him, Peacock invited him to bring his wife to her father's house, and, after the birth there of Arthur, the only child of the union, in 1853, took a cottage on the green in Lower Halliford, and installed the family in it. There Meredith wrote *The Shaving of Shagpat*, which he read during its progress to his little step-daughter with a view to discovering whether it would be effective as a child's story. The marriage proved an unhappy one. Mrs. Meredith was seven years her husband's senior, and he only twenty-one when they were first married. They gradually became alienated, and did not live together at all during the latter part of her life—she died in 1861. Their last meeting, by her daughter's recollection, was in the autumn of 1858. The separation, of course, put a deep gulf between Peacock and Meredith, and neither saw anything of the other afterwards.

Gastronomy and Civilization may have been begun by Mrs. Meredith ; she may, indeed, have held the pen, but the learning and opinions of the article are those of her father. Internal evidence would be sufficient to ascribe it to Peacock, were not such proof made unnecessary by the fact that Mrs. Clarke knows it to have been a joint production, written in Peacock's study, under his direction, and with his constant assistance. Capable as Mrs. Meredith undoubtedly was, she was scarcely scholar enough to have done the work unaided. Readers of *Gryll Grange* will recognise in *Gastronomy and Civilization* a number of details which later found their way into the novel. Briefly, the burden of the essay is that the art of eating wisely and well goes with an advanced state of civilisation; that under republican forms of government the discipline of the palate has generally been more severe than under monarchies ; that simplicity, indeed, is the hall-mark of good taste in the gourmet ; but that society at dinner is indispensable. " We have recorded, as historical evidence, that the most incorruptible republicans were austere and abstemious ; but it is still a question whether they would not have exercised a more beneficial influence, and have been better men, if they had moistened their throats with Madeira, and enlarged their sympathies with grouse." [1] The main body of the work is taken up with a learned and sympathetic account of various banquets which have gladdened old times.

Presumably this collaboration brought Peacock into the notice of *Fraser's* as a possible contributor. At any rate, the next year he began a series of articles called *Horæ Dramaticæ*, in which he planned to deal with various vexed problems of the classical drama, not according to any systematic method, but rather after the easy manner of the novels. His first paper was on *Querolus; or, The Buried Treasure*, the sole extant Latin comedy outside of the work of Plautus and Terence. In Peacock's day the play had been published but once since 1619 (in 1829), and Peacock gives an extended description of it, with several spirited metrical translations.[2] This most erudite of

[1] *Fraser's*, xliv. 609.
[2] The form of these versions is said by Dr. Garnett, it seems on insufficient evidence, to have been suggested by Maginn's Lucianic comediettas in *Fraser's* in 1839. See Art. " Maginn," *Dict. Nat. Biog.*

his *Horæ Dramaticæ* appeared in March. It was
followed the next month by *The Phaëthon of Euripides*,
containing some admirable translations of the choric
fragments. Then, however, leisure seems to have
failed, for the third and last number of the series was
delayed till October 1857, when he made the congenial subject, *The "Flask" of Cratinus*, occasion for
characteristic remarks on the Bacchic inspiration of
poetry. Both tragedy and comedy, he was inclined
to think, had suffered from the gradual increase of
water-drinking, and the absence in the new comedy
of such figures as Aristophanes, in later tragedy of
such poets as Æschylus, and in nineteenth-century
humour of such giants as Rabelais, must be accounted
for by the loss of convivial habits. This essay belongs
in Peacock's philosophy with *Gastronomy and Civilization* and the drinking songs of the novels. It is note-
worthy, however, that he closes his remarks with a
concessionary praise of temperance which an en-
thusiast for prophecy might consider a foretoken of
Peacock's New Comedy of *Gryll Grange*.

After his retirement from the India House, Peacock
was at liberty to write as much as he would. That
very month, March 1856, he wrote a preface for the
new edition of *Melincourt* which Chapman and Hall
published at about the same time as *The Shaving of
Shagpat*. The same year saw the republication in
cheap form of all the novels except *The Misfortunes
of Elphin*. At the close of his *Melincourt* preface he
hints at a new work which might treat contemporary
problems as *Melincourt* had done those of four decades
previous, but *Gryll Grange*, if already planned, did

not see its completion at once. In the meantime he continued his contributions to *Fraser's* with an article, *Chapelle and Bachaumont,* in April 1858, and another, *Demetrius Galanus,* in November. The former contains some English versions that almost deserve to be called worthy the originals. The least satisfactory of them, perhaps, is the one by which Peacock renders " Sous ce berceau, qu'Amour exprès," but as the poem is easily the gem of the whole work, he may be forgiven for falling short of what could have been desired. A comparison may prove interesting. The French is as follows :—

> " Sous ce berceau, qu'Amour exprès
> Fait pour toucher quelque inhumaine,
> L'un de nous deux, un jour au frais
> Assis près de cette fontaine,
> Le cœur percé de mille traits,
> D'une main qu'il portoit à peine
> Grava ces vers sur un cyprès :
> Hélas ! que l'on seroit heureux,
> Dans cet beau lieu digne d'envie,
> Si, toujours aimé de Sylvie,
> L'on pouvoit, toujours amoureux,
> Avec elle passer la vie."

Peacock's version :

> " Beside this brightly gushing spring,
> Within this ever-verdant bower,
> By Love expressly made, to bring
> Some cruel fair beneath his power,
> One of us two, in noontide hour,
> With heavy hand, from heavy heart
> Pierced through by passion's keenest dart,
> Engraved these verses on a tree :

'Sylvia! how blest would be his lot,
Who, loving and beloved by thee
Unchangeably from day to day,
In this most enviable spot
Might wear his earthly time away!'"[1]

Except for a weighty and characteristic review of
Müller and Donaldson's *History of Greek Literature*
which appeared the following March, and his *Newark
Abbey*, November 1860, Peacock contributed nothing
more to *Fraser's* beyond *Gryll Grange* and the Shelley
Memoirs and letters. The *Memoirs* have been, from
first to last, the cause of a considerable amount of
discussion, mostly intemperate. In June 1858, when
the earliest of them appeared, Middleton, Trelawney,
and Hogg had just come before the public with their
own widely differing accounts of Shelley, no one of
which satisfied Peacock. He considered, and justly,
that he had as good a knowledge of Shelley as any who
had dealt with him. He himself had often been
solicited to undertake a biography of his friend, but
had steadily refused. " No man is bound to write
the life of another. No man who does so is bound
to tell the public all he knows. On the contrary,
he is bound to keep to himself whatever may injure
the interests or hurt the feelings of the living, especially
when the latter have in no way injured or calumniated
the dead, and are not necessarily brought before the
tribunal of public opinion in the character of either
plaintiffs or defendants. Neither if there be in the
life of the subject of the biography any event which

---

[1] *Fraser's*, lvii. 504.

he himself would willingly have blotted from the
tablet of his own memory, can it possibly be the duty
of a survivor to drag it into daylight. If such an event
be the cardinal point of a life ; if to conceal it, to mis-
represent it, would be to render the whole narrative
incomplete, incoherent, unsatisfactory alike to the
honour of the dead and the feelings of the living—
then, as there is no moral compulsion to speak of the
matter at all, it is better to let the whole story slumber
in silence." [1] With this conception of the biographer's responsibility, Peacock attempted to correct
such errors as he thought had been admitted to the
earlier accounts. Hogg's book, which Peacock called
an autobiography, not a life of Shelley, had been
particularly displeasing, and led to a breach between
the men which Peacock's own remarks did not heal.
Trelawney, personally antipathetic to Peacock, had
not known Shelley at all in England, and Middleton
was an irresponsible literary person. Peacock went
about his task with a deliberate restraint which has
been objected to as downright coldness and lack of
sympathy. Probably no subject on earth could have
warmed Peacock to the point of incandescence which
passes for sympathy among Shelley worshippers, but
certainly the dispassionate tone of his comments does
not become less dispassionate from any desire to correct
the excessive laudation by which Shelley was already
beginning to be misrepresented. Peacock's idea as to
what he owed the public, as one of the last surviving
friends of a great poet, may be questioned. Since

[1] *Memoirs of Shelley*, p. 2.

"GRYLL GRANGE"

Shelley was going, willy-nilly, to become one of the most eagerly discussed figures in English literary history, Peacock might have done genuine service by greater loquacity. But one cannot blame him for refusing to pamper what he would have called a depraved curiosity. If he is censured at all, it must be on grounds which concern the candour and accuracy with which he set forth the facts he was willing to communicate. Assuredly Peacock remembered Shelley only with the greatest kindness. To the end of his days, even though he admitted to private friends more than he had been minded to write concerning Shelley's violent temper and the personal qualities of Mary Shelley which had prevented Peacock's feeling for her the fondness he had felt for Harriet, still he was invariably as friendly to Shelley's memory as he could have been to his living presence. He used always to speak of Shelley with the warmest affection, as of one whose personal charm had been almost unearthly. On one occasion he became very angry because a member of his family impetuously declared that Shelley must have been merely a liar, or he would never have suffered from the hallucinations which Peacock explained away. He never varied in his readiness to defend either Shelley or Harriet from injustice or uncharitable interpretation.

In some details of his account Peacock was wrong. Subsequent researches have unearthed facts which he could not have known, facts which he knew or remembered only imperfectly, and facts which he preferred to leave untouched. His judgments, however, have

237

not been greatly invalidated by this new information. The question of the hallucinations to which Shelley was undoubtedly subject is still a matter for pathology. Even if the attack on Shelley at Tanyrallt, which Peacock flatly discredited, does seem in the light of recent discoveries to have been a real one, not a fiction,[1] there is still ample evidence for the opinion that Shelley found it difficult to distinguish between what had happened to him and what he thought might have happened. In the more important matter concerning which Peacock's judgment has been censured, that of Shelley's separation from his first wife, Peacock's testimony still holds its ground for all the unchivalrous willingness on the part of Shelley's defenders to asperse the character of Harriet in order to shield her husband. Sir Percy and Lady Shelley, who had asked Peacock to write the *Memoirs*, were greatly dissatisfied with the results. Richard Garnett took issue with Peacock[2] with a degree of asperity which he afterwards had the good taste to regret. Since then half a century has elapsed, and there is still no proof that the mutual agreement to a separation which Peacock declared could not have existed, ever did exist. There will probably never be any concurrence of opinion regarding Shelley's character so long as critics persist in belonging

[1] Miss Margaret Croft learned in Wales that a certain Welsh farmer, Robin Pant Evan, confessed to having committed the assault with a view to frightening Shelley from the neighbourhood. Shelley had been in the habit of shooting sick sheep, and the farmers not unnaturally failed to sympathise with him in his humanitarianism. See " A Strange Adventure of Shelley's," *Century Magazine*, October, 1905, pp. 905–9.

[2] "Shelley in Pall-Mall," *Macmillan's Magazine*, June 1860 ; *Relics of Shelley* (1862); pp. 145–74.

to one or other of the parties which have immemori-
ally divided the world into temperamental Platonists
and temperamental Aristotelians. Dr. Garnett was
on one side, Peacock was on the other. Matthew
Arnold, rather than Shelley's official biographer,
ranged himself on the side which Peacock had chosen.

The Shelley articles appeared in five separate
instalments during the years 1858–62. During the
year 1860, *Gryll Grange* was published as a serial in
Fraser's. Peacock's return to novel-writing after
thirty years, and at the age of seventy-five, is a notable
proof of the strength and vigour of mind which he
retained to the last. He began several novels before
he could hit upon a plan which suited him. One was
a story with the scene laid at Chertsey ; one opens at
St. Catharine's Chapel, near Guildford ; one has a
classical setting ; another rejoices in the two characteristic titles, one of which he would probably have
discarded, *Boosabout Abbey* and *Pottledeep Priory*. A
fifth, which may, however, have been subsequent to
Gryll Grange, he planned to call *Cotswold Chace*. But
all these, like various odds and ends which he had conceived during his India Company days, remain mere
fragments, while *Gryll Grange* was pushed to its conclusion. People who knew Peacock during the latter
days of his life are inclined to prefer *Gryll Grange* to
all the others on the ground that it, better than any,
represents his personal characteristics. The Old
Comedy days of *Maid Marian* had been long outlived.

Although nothing is known of the composition of

Gryll Grange, it must have been well under way by
February 1860, when an advertisement in *The Athenæum* announced that *Fraser's Magazine* for April
would contain the first part of the new novel. Peacock
would hardly have undertaken serial publication on the
terms which other Victorian novelists accepted—that
is, of binding themselves by a beginning to furnish so
much monthly till the end. There are no signs of
haste in *Gryll Grange*, nothing to mar the air of deliberate leisure which his books always possess. To all
appearances, Peacock wrote slowly, but with a care
which made revision little necessary. This last novel
is only slightly shorter than *Melincourt*, but the undoubted tedium of the earlier novel finds no counterpart here. The most frequent objection to it has been
a charge of pedantry because of the bits of quaint
erudition with which it is packed. Generally these
are fragments of whimsical learning which Dr. Opimian
has gathered by the reading of many years, and which
he is likely to bring forward in illustration of any
point which may arise, or which Mr. Falconer finds
necessary to quote in general confirmation of his
priggishness. Pedantry, of course, is a relative term.
If one looks at *Gryll Grange* with the eyes of an ordinary
novel-reader and attempts to criticise it according to
the ordinary rules for such works, it is fair enough to
say that the multifarious references which punctuate
its pages do make it look rather like a treatise than a
novel. The answer, of course, is that *Gryll Grange*
is not to be judged by the principle which would find
it a highly pedantic proceeding if, say, *Silas Marner*

exhibited a tendency to prove every tenth sentence with a classical footnote. The concern of *Gryll Grange* is not with the portrayal of normal beings, in whom a constant habit of citing Greek, Latin, Italian, French, and English writers is no matter of daily business. *Gryll Grange* exists largely for the sake of these remote allusions. Peacock delighted in them and the opinions which they bolster up, and he chose the persons of the little comedy with deliberate reference to their general fitness to serve as mouthpieces for many strange things. All of the characters appear to be unfashionably learned, but, after all, only Dr. Opimian and Mr. Falconer make much parade of knowledge. Mr. Falconer, to be sure, carries off his part somewhat ungracefully, for he is young and in love. If Dr. Opimian, however, expounds at great length his reasons for believing that the Vestal Virgins let their hair grow again after their admission to the order, his firm conviction that Venus Calva was no bald Venus, and his personal notion as to the complexion of Cleopatra ; if he talks to Harry Hedgerow of ' Proslambanomenos ' and ' agistor,' to that amorous swain's considerable surprise ; and if he radiates quotations from dozens of recondite sources, he at least does it without any effort and without any violation of the type he is made to represent. One might nearly as well censure Athenæus for pedantry as *Gryll Grange*. Indeed, Mr. Gryll seems a kind of Hampshire replica of the Laurentius who gathered about him the learned guests of *The Deipnosophists*, while Mr. Falconer, Mr. MacBorrowdale, and Dr. Opimian might fittingly have taken places at that most protracted of banquets.

The minute learning of *Gryll Grange* is but a sign of the age of its author, an example of the attraction facts have for restless minds which have tried all theories, been satisfied with none, and come back to the safe grounds of the facts from which all theories take a beginning. Of a piece with this is the constant attention paid to the noble art of dining. " For, indeed," Friar Tuck had said long before, " I do find in myself certain indications and admonitions that my day has past its noon ; and none more cogent than this : that daily of bad wine I grow more intolerant, and of good wine have a keener and more fastidious relish. There is no surer symptom of receding years." [1] Wine and dinners in *Gryll Grange* have become a consolation, however, and are no longer a mere stimulus to hilarious mirth. In the whole novel there is not a single drinking-song. There are none of the swift passages at arms which so often made the latter end of a dinner boisterous in *Headlong Hall* or *Melincourt*. Mr. MacBorrowdale refuses absolutely to indulge in any argument at table, maintaining that such an occasion is the time of times for good humour and is not to be disturbed by mental effort. Peacock had been greatly quieted in spirit in thirty years. Very worldly he still

[1] *Works*, ii. 83. Readers of Rabelais will recognise in this a pleasant imitation from book iii., chapter 28, where Panurge says : " Vray est que en moy je recongnoys quelque signe indicatif de vieillesse. . . . C'est que je trouve le vin meilleur et plus a mon goust savoureux que ne souloys : plus que ne souloys je crains la rencontre du maulvais vin. Note que cela argue je ne sçay quoy de ponent, et signifie que le midy est passé."

"GRYLL GRANGE"

is, but his judgments are tempered with the kindness of an old man. Mr. Gryll represents a landed gentleman less ridiculous than Squire Headlong, less despicable than Sir Simon Steeltrap; Dr. Opimian is a softened Dr. Folliott; Mr. MacBorrowdale, a Scotchman and an economist, still has his creator's sympathy. It is as if Peacock were determined in *Gryll Grange* to make honourable amends to all the persons he had laughed at in his little world of satire. Lord Curryfin illustrates an interesting advance in portraiture over any character Peacock had yet drawn. There takes place an actual development in him, from the time when he first makes his formal bow as a laughable lord telling fishermen about fish till he turns out to have been merely an able young man bitten by a pantopragmatic fad. His humanity is not very convincing, but at any rate it has a little of the complexity which most of Peacock's people, terribly limited as they are to a single idea, almost always seem to be without.

To say that *Gryll Grange* has a personage more than ordinarily lifelike is, of course, to praise Peacock for a quality upon which his excellence does not primarily depend. Learning, humour, wit, fancy, satirical point, not truthful characterisation, make his reputation. *Gryll Grange* has more learning than any other of the novels, and perhaps as much humour as any beside *Maid Marian*. But the wit has lost some of its pungency from the very fact of its having been made gentler. Bitterness scarcely appears; irony seldom. Dr. Opimian says the wittiest things he has to say

243

with little spleen. Like Dr. Folliott, he represents common sense, but he is sweetened with a charity which extends even to a kindly appreciation of the romantic Mr. Falconer, and does not seem out of place in the midst of the strange world of *Gryll Grange*, where satire and fancy are inextricably blended. The general irresponsibility of the plot is nothing to be wondered at in Peacock, nor is there novelty in the stately love affair of Lord Curryfin. But all that concerns Mr. Falconer is sheer Watteau. What can we say of a satirical novel, written at the beginning of the "strident sixties," in which there struts, as here, a young Englishman who has seven beautiful maidens in a lonely tower to minister to him, all without any offence to Victorian propriety; a young man learned in everything worth knowing, a Liberal with a powerful fondness for antiquity, and with a devotion to St. Catherine which comes very close to hagiolatry? Mrs. Opimian, respectable matron, takes the position that Mr. Falconer ought to be looked after. But Peacock feels an obvious tenderness for him, and vindicates him amply from Mrs. Opimian's suspicions. Other novelists have frequently enough made their favourite characters prigs, and Peacock does this with amazing success. In reality he admired priggishness as little as he thought the fallible world full of heroes. That he could have produced such a personage in this wise old age of his, must be attributed to the strong vein of romantic idealism which never left him. The seven fair maidens in the tower, needless to say, were merely a pleasant imagining,

as was likewise the extraordinary accident by which
the seven rustic suitors won the maidens without any
crossed loves among them. But the homage which
Mr. Falconer pays St. Catherine had a genuine original
in Peacock himself. How this came about, with what
unknown passage in his life it may be connected, no
one now knows. It is certain, however, that he read
repeatedly Aretino's *Vita di Santa Caterina, Vergine
e Martire* (Venetia, 1636), and that he collected such
accounts of her life, and such prints and engravings
representing her, as he could acquire. During his later
years not a few of his casual associates actually believed that he had become a Catholic, confusing with
a religious, what was certainly never more than an
æsthetic, feeling. To an unusual degree Peacock was
devoid of the religious spirit. If he had any belief
at all, his friends said, it was in the Greek mythology.
Mr. Falconer spoke almost directly in Peacock's person
when he said, explaining his quaint worship : " I feel
the necessity of some such devotion, to fill up the
void which the world, as it is, leaves in my mind. I
wish to believe in the presence of some local spiritual
influence ; genius or nymph ; linking us by a medium
of something like human feeling, but more pure and
more exalted, to the all-pervading, creative, and pre-
servative spirit of the universe ; but I cannot realise
it from things as they are. Everything is too deeply
tinged with sordid vulgarity. There can be no intellectual power resident in a wood, where the only
inscription is not ' *Genio loci*,' but ' Trespassers will
be prosecuted ; ' no Naiad in a stream that turns a

cotton-mill; no Oread in a mountain dell, where a railway train deposits a cargo of Vandals; no Nereids or Oceanitides along the seashore, where a coast-guard is watching for smugglers. No; the intellectual life of the material world is dead. Imagination cannot replace it. But the intercession of saints still forms a link between the visible and invisible. In their symbols I can imagine their presence. Each in the recess of our own thought we may preserve their symbols from the intrusion of the world. And the saint, whom I have chosen, presents to my mind the most perfect ideality of physical, moral, and intellectual beauty," [1] This is as near as Peacock comes to confessing that dreams often lay next his heart. Satirist he was to the end, still proud, still reserved, still ready to laugh at the world of other men in their vain pursuit of bubbles. But he was not a mere intellectual machine, dwelling perpetually in the dry places of satire.

The satire in *Gryll Grange* is directed at the pretensions of science, at newspapers, at innovations in the methods of serving dinner, at reforming zeal, at " bestowing the honours of knighthood, which is a purely Christian institution, on Jews and Paynim," at the whole American continent, all its people, acts, and customs, at postprandial orators, at the scholarship of poets, at spirit-rapping, just then a fad also celebrated by Browning in *Mr. Sludge the Medium*, at The National Association for the Promotion of Social Science, and at competitive examinations. The

[1] *Works*, ii. 326.

Social Science Association Peacock called the Pantopragmatic Society, thus adding another to the list of
words with which he has enlarged the English vocabu-
lary.[1] His chief shots are at Lord Facing-both-ways
(Lord Brougham) and Lord Michin Malicho (Lord
John Russell). "The stone which Lord Michin
Malicho—who was the Gracchus of the last Reform,
and is the Sisyphus of the present—has been so
laboriously pushing uphill, is for the present deposited
at the bottom in the Limbo of Vanity. If it should
ever surmount the summit and run down on the other
side, it will infallibly roll over and annihilate the
franchise of the educated classes ; for it would not
be worth their while to cross the road to exercise it
against the rabble preponderance which will then have
been created." [2] This is from the creator of Seithenyn
ap Saidi, ludicrous defender of the faith in things as
they are. To competitive examinations for the Civil
Service Peacock returns more than once. He had been
brought into contact with the system toward the close
of his East India career, and he found much fault
with it, not as a method necessarily bad in itself, but
as a test which had little to do with finding out the
actual fitness of the candidates for the posts they
were seeking " I saw the other day," said Dr. Opimian,

[1] By the testimony of the *New English Dictionary* the list includes
mastigophoric, noometry, antithalian, inficete, excubant, kakistocracy,
hylactic, adoperation. The *Century* gives veridicous, titubancy,
titubant. To these half-whimsical pedantries may be added the un-
garnered Aristophanic mintages jeremitaylorically, tethrippharmate-
lasipedioploctypophilous, osteosarchaematosplanchnochondroneuromu-
elous, osseocarnisanguineoviscericartilaginonervomedullary.

[2] *Works*, ii. 376.

" some examination papers which would have infallibly excluded Marlborough from the army and Nelson from the navy." [1] In the amusing comedy, *Aristophanes in London*, which Dr. Opimian and Mr. Falconer write for production at Gryll Grange, seven competitive examiners are made to reject, in an examination for a military career, the shades of Hannibal, Oliver Cromwell, and Richard Cœur-de-Lion.

This play within the play gives the essence of the satirical spirit of the whole book. Gryllus, summoned by the Spirit-rapping Society from a nap of three thousand years, is confronted with all the glories of the modern world, to see if he will still retain his ancient preference for the state of beasthood to that of humanity. A series of reformers, each the advocate of some cause for modern self-congratulation, answers all the questions he has to ask, but, as might be expected from so true a pig of Epicurus' herd, Gryllus decides that the old way of life was best, and stays no longer than for supper. Whether Peacock meant it for a sly apology to Liberals that his arch-Tory was a Gryllus, remains a question for dispute.

Gryll Grange appeared in book form February 23, 1861,[2] and attracted very moderate notice. *The Athenæum*, for example, did not review it at all. *The Saturday Review* for March 16 gave it genuine praise. Peacock, of course, had not been so nourished upon praise as greatly to mind if none came. Apparently he already planned a collection of his miscellaneous pieces, perhaps on the suggestion of his friend the

---

[1] *Works*, ii. 361.   [2] *Athenæum*, 1861, p. 272.

younger Parker, but this plan was never executed. He soon turned his attention to a translation of *Gl'Ingannati* of Curzio Gonzago, one of the two Italian comedies frequently suggested as possible sources for *Twelfth Night*. Peacock, who gave a careful English version of most of the play, with connecting narratives, and discussed *Gl'Inganni* as well in his preface, was under the erroneous impression that he was for the first time making the plays known to Shakespearean scholars. As a matter of fact, J. P. Collier had already commented at length on *Gl'Inganni* in 1839,[1] and Joseph Hunter had shown the existence of both plays six years later.[2] Peacock's translation, however, has become an accepted and useful tool in Shakespearean studies.[3] It was published at the end of the summer, 1862,[4] along with a new solution of the *Ælia Lelia Crispis* enigma, which, while ingenious, leaves that puzzle still unsettled.

This closed Peacock's active career as an author. During the three years and a half of life which remained to him he did not put pen to paper except in the composition of such notes, telegraphic in length, as he found it necessary to write to a few friends. He kept up his normal course of life nearly to the end, in dignified retirement on the banks of the river he had panegyrised in his youth. Thackeray, in 1850, had been at a country house (it must have been Lord

---

[1] *Further Particulars regarding Shakespeare* (1839), pp. 10–24.
[2] *New Illustrations of the Life . . . of Shakespeare* (1845), i. 391–8.
[3] Dr. Furness reprinted it in the notes to his New Variorum *Twelfe Night* (Phil. 1901), pp. 341–59.
[4] *Atheænum*, Sept. 6, p. 305.

THOMAS LOVE PEACOCK

Broughton's, though he does not say so), and had written to Mrs. Brookfield describing the guests, among them " Peacock—did you ever read *Headlong Hall* and *Maid Marian ?*—a charming lyrical poet and Horatian satirist, he was when a writer ; now he is a white-headed jolly old worldling, full of information about India and everything else in the world." [1] The acquaintance thus formed led to the exchange of several letters between the two, but never became intimate. Thackeray speaks of Charles Villiers as having been present on the same occasion, and at a later visit there, Peacock discovered, as might have been expected, that he disliked Disraeli intensely. There, too, he probably met Macaulay, who records in his journal for December 31, 1851, that they had tired each other out in Greek, and found they were " both strong enough in these matters for gentlemen." [2] Peacock's stays at Erle Stoke were pleasant intervals in a life varied by much domestic unhappiness. The tragic death of Lieutenant Nicolls, the re-marriage of his eldest daughter and the marriages of his two younger children in opposition to his wishes, the instability of his son, the death of his wife, the death of two children of his daughter Rosa, her own death soon after, the separation of George and Mary Meredith, the death finally in 1861 of Mrs. Meredith, all these were blows to try to the uttermost the laughing philosopher who followed Epicurus. Another might have sought forgetfulness in society, but Peacock pre-

---

[1] *Letters of W. M. Thackeray*, ed. Mrs. Brookfield (1877), p. 100.
[2] Trevelyan, *Life and Letters of Lord Macaulay* (N. Y., 1876), iii. 254.

ferred to find it in the congenial world of books. Every morning he continued to rise at five and read till breakfast, then to pass the whole day in his library unless the summer season took him out to the river or to the pleasant garden which ran down to the very edge of the Thames. When he was in his library, no one dared to disturb him except his privileged grand-daughter, whose invasions of his privacy he always forgave. Thackeray, who had been so pleased with Peacock at Lord Broughton's that he came later to call, was taken up boldly by that same granddaughter to Peacock's study. He was received with courtesy, but later Peacock was furious that he had been disturbed, even though it was by the great satirist. Possibly he had been reading Aristophanes. Peacock was somewhat given to fits of sudden anger in his old age, and was always a little dreaded by the members of his household. Variations in the ordinary domestic programme put him out of temper exceedingly. He could be peppery with offenders if he were irritated. A characteristic incident tells that two neighbours were rowing by the house one evening, and that one of them, not quite sure of their locality, asked the other in a tone of voice which should have been modified : " Is this old Peacock's ? " Before his companion could reply, a strong voice called from the garden, " Yes, this is old Peacock's, and this is old Peacock," and " old Peacock " stepped irately out of the shadow.

But these little ebullitions of temper were only occasional, and for the most part Peacock was kindness personified. His servants felt the warmest affection for him. Children considered him the best of play-mates. Even the pets about the place had reason to feel his tenderness, for he would never allow them to be disturbed, and made bird-shooting or birds'-nesting unpardonable offences. Robert Buchanan, the only man of the new literary generation whom Peacock saw after his daughter's separation from Meredith, has left some pleasant memorials of these last years. It seems that Buchanan, while still a young student in Scotland, had become acquainted with Peacock's work and desired to know more of him. " I was prompted to write to him, expecting (I remember) to receive but a cold response from one who, to judge him by his works, was too much of a Timon to care for boy's homage. I was agreeably disappointed. The answer came, not savage like a rap on the knuckles, but cordial as a handshake. Afterwards, when I was weary, ' climbing up the breaking wave ' of London, I thought of my old friend and determined to seek him out. Mainly with the wish to be near him, I retreated to quiet Chertsey, and thence past Chertsey Bridge, through miles of green fields basking in the summer sun, and through delightful lanes to Lower Halliford, I went on pilgrimage, youth in my limbs, reverence in my heart, a pipe in my mouth, and the tiny Pickering edition of Catullus (a veritable ' lepidum libellum,' but, alas, far from ' novum ! ') in my waist-coat pocket. And there at Lower Halliford I found him . . . seated on his garden lawn in the sun, with the door of his library open behind him, showing such

delicious vistas of shady shelves as would have gladdened his own Dr. Opimian, and the little maiden
[Clari Leigh Hunt, who spent much of her time with
Peacock latterly] reading from the book upon his knee.
Gray-haired and smiling sat the man of many memories,
guiding the utterances of one who was herself a pretty
two-fold link between the present and the past, being
the granddaughter (on the paternal side) of Leigh
Hunt, and also the granddaughter (on the maternal
side) of the Williams who was drowned with Shelley.
Could a youthful student's eyes see any sight fairer ?
. . . And this old man had spoken with Shelley, not
once, but a thousand times ; and had known well
both Harriett Westbrook and Mary Godwin ; and had
cracked jokes with Hobhouse, and chaffed Procter's
latinity ; and had seen, and actually criticised, Malibran ; and had bought ' the vasty version of a new
system to perplex the sages,' [1] when it first came out,
in a bright, new, uncut quarto ; and had dined with
Jeremy Bentham ; and had smiled at Disraeli, when,
resplendently attired, he stood chatting at Hookham's
with the Countess of Blessington ; and had been face
to face with that bland Rhadamanthus, Chief Justice
Eldon ; and was, in short, such a living chronicle of
things past and men dead as filled one's soul with
delight and ever-varying wonder." [2]

Buchanan, like all who knew Peacock in these days,
testified to the sweetness of his disposition and his

---

[1] Byron's description of Wordsworth's " Excursion." [Buchanan's
note.]

[2] *Look around Literature*, pp. 164–5.

" delicious personality." " It was rest and inspiration indeed," the Scot wrote elsewhere," to pass from the roar of Grub Street and the strident sixties into the peaceful atmosphere of the brave old pagan's dwelling, to drink May Rosewell's cowslip wine, and to boat on the quiet river with Clari Leigh Hunt, a bright-eyed little maid of fifteen and Peacock's special pet. It was under Peacock's influence that I wrote many of my pseudo-classic poems, afterwards gathered together in my first volume, ' Undertones.' " [1] Buchanan speaks amusingly of the vehement antipathy to tobacco which made Peacock refuse to let any one smoke near his house, but he does not tell, what there can be no harm now in telling, that Peacock caught his young friend smoking on the premises and irrevocably banished him. The cause of his dislike for tobacco was partly an intense dread of fire. He would never allow more than a few matches in the house at a time, and they must be carefully guarded to prevent accident. The house in which he lived had been formed by throwing two cottages together, and, being a rambling structure, seemed to Peacock as susceptible to fire as it certainly was to water. During flood-times the Thames took liberties with the garden and the lower part of the house, often driving the family to the upper floor. Peacock had a gauge with which he was accustomed to take daily observations of the river's height, and he recorded the changes of the weather as carefully as had Captain Hawltaught in *Melincourt*. These duties, with the daily ordering of dinner, which he performed

---

[1] H. Jay, *Robert Buchanan* (1903), p. 103.

with the masterly skill born of long practice and a keen
interest in the matter, took nearly all the time which
Peacock spent away from his library, which looked out
across the river. His state appearance was at dinner, a
great and ceremonious occasion in the Peacock household. It was here that his talk flowed most freely, but
the quaint erudition he displayed, and the stories he told
with such ability, by the testimony of all who knew him,
seem to have left no record. Peacock was as delicately
epicurean in his fondness for a good table as any of
his own clergymen. He had a deep-rooted objection
to tea in the afternoon, because he declared that it
spoiled dinner. He never failed in the worship which
he declared was due Bacchus. After dinner he would
fall asleep in his chair, then later, aroused from his nap,
would go again to his study. He once told Thackeray
that he no longer read anything but Greek, but the
last year of his life he began for the first time to read
Dickens, and was frequently found in fits of laughter
over *The Pickwick Papers*, although, on the whole, he
preferred *Our Mutual Friend*. He was particularly
taken with Lizzie Hexham, whom he declared to be his
ideal of womanhood. It is proof of the vigour of his
old age that he never wore glasses to the day of his
death, severe as had been his use of his eyes for more
than seventy years.

Latterly Peacock grew very much attached to the
observance of old-fashioned ceremonies at which he
might have laughed in his early novels. Dinner was
the occasion of one of them. An unpublished letter
from his cousin Harriet Love tells how he always cele-

brated August 15 by having for dinner "a stubble goose, and no others," and when it came to the table he would repeat over it, before he began the carving, at which he excelled, the lines from the Prologue to *The Cokes Tale* in which the "stubbel-goos" is mentioned. More picturesque was his keeping of May Day. The children of the village would assemble early in the morning at the parsonage for a sermon. Then they would visit different houses of the neighbourhood in smaller parties, and would finally come altogether to Peacock's house at eleven, where the stately old gentleman, still erect at eighty, bright-eyed as in his youth, his white hair a nimbus about his merry countenance, would receive them, and stand smiling while they marched about the garden to display the garlands of flowers which they had brought. To every child he would give a penny, and more to those whose flowers showed the best taste in their arrangement. In his garden was crowned the Queen of the May—generally one of his own granddaughters—and then the day's festival would end with songs and dances.

Buchanan, Mr. Howes of the Adjutant-General's office, Thomas James Arnold, a Westminster magistrate, and his own family were practically the only people Peacock saw the last four or five years. With a few more he was in correspondence, but they were mostly kinsmen or close friends of other days. An unpublished letter to Thomas Hookham, dated April 3, 1862, and now in my possession, says : "I have been in London only three hours since the 23rd day of

TRANSLATIONS

December 1860. I have been very well all this time, which I ascribe to staying at home, and leading as quiet a life as circumstances allow. I am sorry you have not been equally so : but I think it impossible to be well in London, since air and water have been poisoned by gas." Between 1860 and 1862 he wrote a few letters to a Mr. Thomas L'Estrange of Belfast, an ardent admirer, but they contain little beside bare biographical or bibliographical details. Peacock was never a good letter-writer. He excused himself by saying that he feared he might fall into habits of hasty composition. The true reason was rather a habit of self-restraint which held him back from the easy confidences that good letter-writing demands. This partly appears in two letters to Lord Broughton, the first an undated fragment, which are here quoted from the *Biographical Notice*, with slight corrections from the manuscript of the former.

" DEAR LORD BROUGHTON,—I return the letter with many thanks for the communication. It is an affecting reminiscence. I very much regret not having seen more of Mr. Baillie. The little intercourse I had with him was most agreeable to me.

> " ' Encore une étoile qui file,
> File, file, et disparait.'

" I have had too much occasion of late to recall these beautiful lines of Béranger. The last winter made fearful havoc among my few friends of my own generation, and among some of the generation below me.

257

THOMAS LOVE PEACOCK

I am sorry to think that you have had cause to say the same.

"Yesterday you attended your old friend's funeral. Soldiers who 'Follow their dead comrade to the grave' march slowly to solemn music, but they return in quick time to the liveliest measures the band can play. The last duty has been paid to the dead : what remains belongs to the living. Therefore, turning from sad to comic realities I will tell you a good story.

"Our parson is evangelical, and holds forth weekly against rowing and fishing on Sunday. The other day, going into church, he saw two bargemen unloading gravel. He asked them, 'if they could not do their work on a week-day ? ' They said, 'They could not afford to lose their day's work.'—'How much was their day's work worth ? '—'Three and sixpence a piece.'—'If they would leave off work for the day, to go into church, he would give them five shillings each and a Bible.' Readily accepted. He went into his house, which is close to the church, and returned with ten shillings and two Bibles. The bargemen followed him into the church, where they behaved very decorously, receiving some unctuous admonitions on the sin of unloading gravel on Sunday. After church, they went to a public-house, where they dined, and sat over their host's good liquor till the time for afternoon service. The parson, proceeding to it, saw them reeling away together, arm-in-arm, flourishing their Bibles with their disengaged hands, and singing at the tops of their voices—

"'The parson's a jolly good fellow.'"

TRANSLATIONS

" DEAR LORD BROUGHTON,—There is an often-quoted saying of Dr. Johnson : ' If you do not go on making new friends as old ones drop off, you will find yourself alone in the world.' I have seen Lord Mansfield and Lord Campbell severally cited as men who had wisely acted on this dictum. Perhaps lawyers can do it. The doctor spoke more to my mind when he asked, ' What can replace a friend of twenty years' standing ? ' And Voltaire still more so when he wrote to Madame du Deffond, ' You have lost two old friends ; can you replace them ? *Pas même l'ombre.'* Orlando, standing alone by the fountain of Roncesvalles, with his dearest friends and his favourite horse lying dead at his feet, is visited by the Archangel Gabriel, who says to him amongst other things :

> " ' Ma se tu vuogli ancor nel mondo stare,
> Iddio ti dara ben di nuovo gente,
> E tremerà di te la terra e il mare :
> Ma perchè il nostro Signor non si pente,
> Quí che son morti non posson tornare.'
> —PULCI, xxvii. 143.

" Orlando does not accept the offer—he wishes to follow those that are gone. I have more pleasure in reading through books which I have read and admired before than in reading anything new. The three last old works which I have so gone through were ' Rabelais,' Chaucer's ' Canterbury Tales,' and the ' Morgante Maggiore.' I have, however, read Miss Knight's ' Autobiography ; ' Windsor and its neighbourhood, and the old royal family, were so familiar to me from my earliest days, that I seemed in reading it to live

259

over again in the associations of my youth. I have not, for a long time, read anything that pleased me so much ; but I am not sure how much may belong to the book and how much to old associations. She is a very accomplished woman. Her ' Latium ' has long been a favourite book with me. My son is at present in Paris. He intends to return in about a month and take a house near the British Museum. I shall have a special apartment, and shall be in town occasionally. In the meantime the abomination I entertain for gas and tobacco prevents my taking up my quarters there even for a night. Science has greatly multiplied the old metropolitan horrors ; ' incendia, lapsus Tectorum assiduas, et mille pericula sævæ Urbis.' When I have που στω, I hope I may see you. I earnestly wish to do so.—Vale, nostri memor, Tuus ex animo,

"T. L. Peacock." [1]

Toward the end of the year 1865 a fire broke out in the roof of Peacock's bedroom, and he was hurriedly removed to his library for safety. He had been infirm of late, and the shock came severely upon one whose dread of fire was almost morbid. He could not assist in putting out the flames, but when the curate of the parish, with the kindest intentions, urged him to seek shelter in a neighbouring house, the resolute old pagan shouted, " By the immortal gods, I will not move ! " and move he did not. The books which he had thus defended, however, could not hold him much longer, for the maladies of old age were gaining quickly upon

---

[1] *Works,* i. xci.-xcii.

his strength. After that night he hardly left his bed again. The doctor said he had been worn out by his years, and that there was nothing to do but to lessen the pain. He suffered severely from intestinal cramps, and his granddaughter remembers that, as she sat by his bedside only two days before his death, she heard him, pagan to the last, calling upon the immortal gods with reproaches because they persisted in tormenting one who had served them for a lifetime and never wavered in the service. But the gods were deaf, and Peacock died very quietly on January 23, 1866. He is buried in the New Cemetery at Shepperton, where a plain stone, erected not far from the entrance by his cousins Harriet and Henry Love, bears this inscription :

SACRED
TO THE DEARLY LOVED
MEMORY OF
THOMAS LOVE PEACOCK, Esq.
LATE OF THE EAST INDIA
COMPANY'S HOME SERVICE
BORN AT WEYMOUTH
OCTOBER 18, 1785
DIED AT LOWER HALLIFORD
JANUARY 23, 1866.

Peacock's personal appearance is best represented by the photograph, made in 1857, which serves as frontispiece to the present volume. He protested with characteristic vigour against having it made at all. A singularly handsome man, the signs of self-indulgence in his face are more than made up for by the genial kindliness of every feature. He was careful, though somewhat old-fashioned, in his dress, particularly fond of wearing a long cloak, or rather cape, the skirt of which he would throw across his shoulder in chilly weather, and look out at the world as proudly as if he were an Athenian citizen. The portrait by Mr. Henry Wallis, now in the National Portrait Gallery, is not a satisfactory likeness, robbing Peacock as it does of the look of benignity which he almost always wore, and bestowing upon him a ruddiness of complexion quite the opposite of the fine clear pallor of his old age.

CHAPTER XI

REPUTATION—CONCLUSION

HAVING stolen out of the world with much the same
stealth as he had lived in it for over eighty years, the
man who had already become, by the suffrage of a few,
an established minor classic, eluded the claque of the
ordinary necrologist as he had eluded bores for a lifetime. But there was not wanting judicious comment.
" Rated among novelists," said *The Athenæum*,
" Peacock, in one respect, counts for little. He never
tried for plot ; he had small descriptive power. Rated
as a satirist who shot Folly as it flew, and could exhibit
the philosophies and paradoxes of the time with an
epigrammatic keenness, and withal a genial recognition
of all that is best, highest, and most liberal, he demands
no common praise, and will hold no common place
whenever the story of ultra-liberal literature shall come
to be written."[1] James Hannay published in *The North
British Review* for the following September an admirable paper, *Recent Humorists : Aytoun, Peacock,
Prout*, for which George Meredith and various friends
furnished most of the biographical facts. These,
however, were scanty, and half a century has not seen
any notable increase in their number. Peacock had
been one of the closest friends of Shelley ; he had

[1] *Athenæum*, Feb. 10, 1866, p. 208.

lived for years in intimate daily contact with the Philosophical Radicals, and had written for the *Westminster* and the *London* reviews; he had been one of the humorists who had helped launch *Bentley's Miscellany* upon its hilarious course; he had been among the regular contributors during a famous decade of *Fraser's Magazine;* he had been for half a century "The Author of Headlong Hall," and had added to it six other novels, of which only one was in any way inferior to it, and none less characteristic. Yet the present biography, with its enforced paucity of contemporary reference to Peacock, shows how seldom he had been on the tongues or pens of the men who have left the record of the times. Such mention of him as exists seldom lacks praise of his wit and learning. There can be no doubt that he made his fame, among the three generations he knew, less than it might have been had he not so deliberately limited his circle of associates. In such a case his books were obliged to find their way unassisted to the readers they secured. But his reputation as an author has steadily increased since the day when the outraged *British Critic* consigned *Melincourt* to hopeless oblivion until Mr. Arthur Symons, one of his latest critics, declared that "Peacock's novels are unique in English, and are among the most scholarly, original, and entertaining prose writings of the century." [1]

It will be noticed that the thin thread of Peacock's fame crosses few examples of direct influence. Mr. E. H. Coleridge is of the opinion that Lord Byron's

[1] *The Romantic Movement in England* (1909), p. 230.

REPUTATION—CONCLUSION

' Literary Eclogue,' *The Blues*, may have been written as the result of a reading of *Melincourt* and *Nightmare Abbey*.[1] As Shelley, writing to Peacock about August 10, 1821, less than a week after Byron is known to have finished the piece, mentions Byron's fondness for *Melincourt*, the opinion seems plausible. Certainly, the character Vamp of *The Blues* came from *Melincourt*. Conjecture has it, somewhat loosely, it is to be feared, that Thackeray was thinking nearly as much of *Maid Marian* as of *Ivanhoe* when he composed *Rebecca and Rowena*. There can be no doubt that another novel of almost the same date as Thackeray's burlesque, the deservedly long-forgotten *Maid Marian, the Forest Queen*, of J. H. Stocqueller, was written with an eye on Peacock. Stocqueller was an industrious compiler, who extended his professional methods to the creation of novels, and in this case borrowed from *Maid Marian* with an unsparing hand. He took over bodily the whole constitution of Sherwood Forest, and quoted more than once from Peacock's lyrics with no other acknowledgment than the convenient label, " Old Song." Robert Buchanan freely owns that he wrote his *Undertones* with the influence of Peacock upon him. In the work of a much greater man, George Meredith, there have not been wanting readers to find traces of his father-in-law's novels. James Thomson, " B.V.," called attention to this as early as 1879 in his review of *Richard Feverel* for Cope's *Tobacco Plant*.[2] Meredith himself, it seems, never acknow-

---

[1] Byron, *Works : Poetry* (1898–1904), iv. 569.
[2] M. B. Forman, *George Meredith* (1907), p. 82.

ledged, perhaps never felt, any such direct indebtedness as critical ingenuity has sought to point out. He did admire Peacock as a man, and he admired particularly his literary high spirits. But until Meredith's early life has become less a mystery than it is at present, his critics can easily go astray in the attempt to show how far he derived from Peacock the traits which they have in common. So far as details go, the humorous management of a medieval subject in *Farina* may recall *Maid Marian* and *The Misfortunes of Elphin*, *The Rajah in London* of *One of Our Conquerors* might have been a reminiscence of *Aristophanes in London*, and Dr. Middleton of *The Egoist* could hardly have been drawn had there been no previous Dr. Folliott or Dr. Opimian. These instances, however, which a quick judgment might easily multiply, probably do nothing more than confirm the opinion which sees in the two novelists a similarity of intellectual temper sufficient to account, not only for these slight resemblances, but for matters of real importance. Many of the salient characteristics of Peacock's work, his darting wit, his sudden fancies, his pungent criticism of contemporary life, his genuine love of beauty, appear again in Meredith, but the younger man, more passionate, opulent, and powerful, has glorified them until they are lost in the flame of his brilliant achievement. Keen influence hunters may see in the stories which make up Dr. Garnett's delightful volume, *The Twilight of the Gods* (1888), especially in the semi-mythological tale which gives the book its title, and in *The Poet of Panopolis*, symptoms of the crackling laughter with which their author's studies in Peacock had made him conversant. The first scene of Tennyson's *Foresters* seems to contain, in the conversation between Sir Richard Lea and Marian, certain obvious reminiscences of the similar argument between the baron and his daughter in chapter iv. of *Maid Marian*. Finally, the only instance in which it appears that a book has been directly modelled upon the Peacockian pattern is Sir Edward Strachey's *Talk at a Country House* (1895), which makes so little concealment of the fact as to admit Mr. Foster from *Headlong Hall* as one of the disputants. The host of the symposium rejoices that Mr. Escot has not come with his quondam opponent and opposite.[1]

To point out significant expressions of critical opinion and of general knowledge of Peacock is of greater value in the history of his reputation than to indulge in the dangerous and thankless task of finding influences which may be merely fanciful. When Peacock died, he was probably as little known as any man of equal rank whose work in English letters had been done since 1750. His fame might be expected to have been highest during the decade 1830-40, and yet Maclise did not include him in his *Gallery of Illustrious Literary Characters*, which appeared in *Fraser's* from 1830-38, although John Galt, Mrs. Norton, James Morier, Miss Landon, David Moir, and Alaric A. Watts achieved the dignity of ample notice. Spedding's essay in *The Edinburgh Review* for January 1839 never once mentions Peacock's name. Five years

[1] Pp. 4-5.

later the first edition of that famous repository of
literary judgment, Chambers' *Cyclopædia of English
Literature*, had the briefest mention of him as J. L.
Peacock and an extract from *Maid Marian*. A tolerable article in *The United States Magazine and Democratic Review* (New York), June 1845, shows that in
the United States Peacock, whose *Headlong Hall* and
Nightmare Abbey had just appeared in a popular
American series, was clearly identified with his novels,
for all *Rhododaphne* still continued to be thought the
work of Dabney. New issues of the novels in 1849
and 1856, with the return to authorship in *Fraser's*,
were not sufficient to restore Peacock his proper
initials in the second edition of Chambers' *Cyclopædia*
(1857–60).[1] *Men of the Times* gave him a highly inaccurate notice in 1862, which Thomas L'Estrange
corrected three years later. Hannay, in the essay of
1866, first recorded Thackeray's admiration of Peacock's songs as among the best of the age. The next
year Frederick Locker included *The Fate of a Broom*,
" In his last binn Sir Peter lies," *Rich and Poor*, and
Love and Age, in *Lyra Elegantiarum*, with brief comment on the remarkable freshness of Peacock's best
verses.[2] Except for occasional gossip in *Notes and*

[1] The same *Cyclopædia* dismisses Matthew Arnold, already the
author of *The Strayed Reveller, Empedocles, Poems* (1853–55) and *Merope*,
in a curt paragraph, without a line of quotation ; it devotes pages to
such singing contemporaries as Caroline Bowles, Thomas Aird, Philip
James Bailey (of cisatlantic notoriety), Frances Brown, Charles Swain,
Thomas Ragg, Eliza Cook, and James Hedderwick.

[2] Swinburne, reviewing the later edition of *Lyra Elegantiarum*,
declared that he thought " the riper and richer humour of Peacock as
superior to Praed's as dry champagne to sweet, or a Sultana grape to
a green gooseberry." (*Studies in Prose and Poetry* (1894), p. 101.)

Queries, and two essays in 1873, one by Mr. C. W. Hutson in *The Southern Magazine* (Baltimore) for February, and another by Mr. George Barnett Smith in *The Fortnightly Review* for August, the name of Peacock was allowed to rest in peace till Cole's edition of 1875 furnished the occasion for comment from various critics above the standard of the average reviewer, an anonymous writer of good ability in *The Edinburgh Review* (July), Robert Buchanan in *The New Quarterly Magazine* (April), James Davies in *The Contemporary Review* (April), and Mortimer Collins in *The St. James Magazine* (August). Five years later Mr. Edmund Gosse wrote an introduction for the selection from Peacock in Ward's *English Poets*, naming him a "prose humorist of incomparable vivacity," and praising his poetry as well. Mrs. Oliphant, in her *Literary History of England in the End of the Eighteenth and Beginning of the Nineteenth Century* (1882), contrives to indicate a distaste for Peacock under the cover of faint praise, but in spite of her dissentient voice there appeared in the *Encyclopædia Britannica* in 1885 an article on Peacock which, to resort to a primitive method of criticism, is nearly as long as that on Thomas Hood, is as long as that on Gay, and longer than those on Prior, Churchill, or Praed. It was written by Richard Garnett, and marks an important day for Peacock's reputation. Dr. Garnett's labours on his behalf have already been cited in the preface to the present biography. The next year Professor Saintsbury contributed his first essay on Peacock to *Macmillan's Magazine* for April, and thus allied himself with Dr. Garnett as one of the men who have done most to keep Peacock from neglect. An edition by Dr. Garnett in 1891 was followed by one under the editorship of Professor Saintsbury in 1895–97. In the latter year Professor Herford included in his *Age of Wordsworth* a criticism of Peacock which, though brief, has been equalled by no other. Since then Peacock has been steadily assuming a rank which he can hardly lose while minor wits and poets maintain an audience. A glance at the *Bibliography* will show a steady output of his works which may surprise even readers who know him reasonably well. Within the past decade Dr. A. B. Young has devoted much energy to publishing facts concerning Peacock's life and works, and letters received during the writing of the present book attest to the fact that Peacock counts among his readers a devoted, if small, body of admirers in three continents. He who ridiculed the universities is studied as an English classic at Oxford ; hater of all things German, he has at least twice been made the subject of extended research in Germany; satirical reviler of Scotland and America, he has found in both readers who yield to none in their degree of attachment, and in one, by an irony which would have delighted him, his biographer.

When an author still continues to be read after a lapse of eighty years—for Peacock's proper literary period was 1816–31—and bids fair to hold his position, although nine out of ten of the persons who make up what is called the reading public have never heard of him ; when not a few readers whose taste is ordinarily most catholic find it impossible to get on with him at all, and others install him enthusiastically in a sort of private Paradise of Dainty Devices for their own literary pleasure, some explanatory comment seems to be called for.

The redoubtable Beetle, of Mr. Kipling's *Stalky and Co.*, having been given the run of the Headmaster's library, there found, among other more or less savoury literary messes, some " little tales of a heady and bewildering nature, interspersed with unusual songs—Peacock was that writer's name." A similar bewilderment has fallen upon readers more sophisticated than Beetle, at the first introduction to " that writer." In the first place, the novels probably suffer from being placed in a class of writings to which they belong only by a vague external resemblance. The novel-reader finds in them little which conforms to his notion of what a novel should be like, little plot, little attempt at characterisation, little " human interest," no passion. He probably feels that the persons of the story indulge in protracted gossip of which he is not invited to partake any more than he is asked to share in their frequent banquets. Even if he be interested in the opinions which form the staple of these arguments, he finds it confusing to perceive that Peacock, although himself concerned with opinions to the exclusion of almost everything else, does not seem to care for any one in particular, but plays them against each other, weighing out alternate victories with easy impartiality, and finally dismissing them all with a song or a glass of wine. There is always the difficulty of fitting preconceived modes of thought to the eccentric angles of Peacock's little world. Everywhere there is tipsy-turvy : laughter extinguishes reverence, words play tricks with logic, wine leaves sobriety lurching, up go the heels of dignity, and folly splits its sides at the jest, wit is as unpartisan as it is unerring, irony shows its head where it is least expected, humour bestows its caresses where it will. A woman may be an angel—an intellectual angel in a pelisse and a poke-bonnet—or she may be an abstraction to be treated with the mockery generally meant for men. A man may be a man, a lay figure, or an ape ; presumably he is a fool. It takes good self-possession not to feel that the reader is being treated with some of the contempt from which wit can scarcely be disassociated in the minds of most people. And Peacock's public is treated with contempt in the sense that he pays only the slightest attention to its tastes or desires. He wrote his books for his own pleasure, to a degree unusual even in wilful England. Thus he was bent on pleasing an audience of the smallest proportions. " He was utterly unlike any one I have ever met before or since," said one of his friends. Wilfulness, a strong bent towards singularity, was one of his most prominent intellectual qualities. To it was due his choice of the novel as the form which gave him the greatest latitude of expression. It showed him a hospitality which he could not easily have found elsewhere. Neither the drama, the lyric, the long poem, nor the essay would have afforded him such facilities. In the novel he could indulge himself in the dialogue which would have been his chief staple as a writer of comedy ; he could add lyrics at his will; and though he took no opportunity to include long poems, yet he could make his personages deliver as many oral essays as he pleased. The novel gave him leisure, without the attention to plot which a comedy would have demanded, to record his observations of human character in the terms of the caricaturist. Peacock's eye for "humours," as the seventeenth century called them, never slept. His judgment had in it a peculiar turn which seems almost obliquity of vision. He saw the world by twists and angles. As in scholarship he delighted in fantastic learning, so in his novels he neglected normal human beings to sport with eccentricity.

This does not mean that Peacock's comprehension, his sober judgment both of men and books, could not often be just, but so far as his own literary work went, he limited himself to a narrow field out of which he did not try to stray. He deliberately avoided discussion of the larger problems which confront serious thinkers. Lofty speculations, all that concern the origin and destiny of mankind, he turned away from. The world is in the hands, it was his habit to say, of Necessity, before whom Jupiter and his successors are alike helpless. What have men to do with gods or the business of gods? They sit in "tranquil abodes which neither winds do shake nor clouds drench with rains nor snow congealed by sharp frost harms with hoary fall," and have as little care for the men beneath their feet as men have power to draw them down to earth. It is better for men to think only of the time that passes too rapidly, and best if they regard its flight with eyes undimmed by gazing into mysteries. The poetry of faith, intense devotion to ideals too high ever to be realised, magnificent sacrifices where there is no hope, these Peacock comprehended only from a distance, and left to other hands. And even in the world to which he confined himself he did not pretend to be a guide. His apparent denial of moral responsibility repels many who might otherwise, forgiving an occasional obviousness in his satire or lack of point in his ironic criticism, still find his books delightful. It seems almost as if to him the Me of existence were the power to ridicule, and the Not-Me the state of being ridiculous. A speech of Friar Tuck may serve as a text for Peacock's sermon to his readers. " None shall laugh in my company, though it be at my expense, but I will have my share of the merriment. The world is a stage, and life is a farce, and he that laughs most has most profit of the performance. The worst thing is good enough to be laughed at, though it be good for nothing else ; and the best thing, though it be good for something else, is good for nothing better." [1] A man who holds such doctrine has made out of laughter an inaccessible seat from which he will despise the world and be as lonely on his merry throne as the desolate sublime, if there is bitterness mixed with his mirth. In Peacock, however, there is little bitterness. His pessimism was the theme of his daily talk, but it was a half-humorous pessimism, laughing at a hundred things which bitterness would have made him hate. If he despised his generation, it was due chiefly to the

1 *Works*, ii. 86.

consciousness of his intellectual superiority to the huzzas of the rabble. " I am more afraid of deference to popular clamour than I am of anything under heaven," he said before one of the parliamentary committees.[1] From the first Peacock felt out of touch with the world he lived in. The fact has given him a reputation for Toryism which cannot be properly said to have characterised his intellect. That he was constitutionally a lover of the past, there is no denying ; but to think that his intelligence was submerged by devotion to antiquity, is an error. Nearly the only friends he had were liberal thinkers. His seal bore the line from Horace, " Nec tardum opperior nec præcedentibus insto " (I neither follow in the rear, nor pursue those who run before me). He considered that his intellectual position, as a sensible man, was indicated by the motto. When, in *Crotchet Castle* and *Gryll Grange*, the present seems to suffer rough handling, it is done less to prove its inferiority to the past than to prove the superiority to either of a common-sense world of simplicity and peace, which, of course, never existed, but which Peacock created from the fragments of the ancient world. It was its offences against peace which made him score the doctrine of progress. That the world needed to be made better, he had no doubt ; it was difficult for him to see in the midst of the reforming spirit which surrounded his later life, that anything was being done by the very generation which actually achieved so much. To fall into paradox,

[1] *Report from the Select Committee on Steam Communication with India* (1837), p. 56.

if he had not been so detached from his contemporaries, he would have been more so ; that is to say, but for his intellectual liberalism, he would have been temperamentally driven to an affection for pre-revolutionary days which might have spoiled utterly the independence which generally marks his ironic criticism.

If one judges Peacock by the highest qualities of literature, loftiness to inspire, wisdom to instruct, nobility to incite, or beauty to enchant, one will simply depreciate him, as by such standards one must, for failure to achieve excellence in directions to which he never turned his attention. He fully accepted his limitations, at any rate after he had reached maturity, and confined his efforts resolutely to the field in which he was proficient. Subtracting from his praise still further, and without argument, the power to amuse as Scott or Cervantes amuses, there still remains excellence, a little narrow, somewhat unvaried, but still excellence that amounts to supremacy in a type which requires no mean ability. Satire of a restricted kind, bristling with eccentricities of opinion and originality of expression which repel the normal intelligence ; without didactic intention to a degree which estranges sober thinkers ; with a sharpness of wit and a nicety of learning lost upon casual readers— such satire must look to an audience composed of individuals who unite to liberality of opinion, quickness of perception, and extent of learning, either a temper as full of crotchets as Peacock's, from the testimony of his novels, seems to have been, or else a capacity for sheer enjoyment in the exercise of wit, who or what may be its objects, as great as Peacock, by the testimony of his life, actually had. Peacockians are wont to plume themselves upon a taste denied to the vulgar as if it conferred upon them some peculiar credit. The credit, as a matter of fact, may belong quite as much to a congenital singularity of perception as to an intelligence sophisticated enough to find in caprice and whim a pleasant diversion after long pedestrian inquiry for firm grounds of opinion.

Eccentric, unreal, bookish, the novels of Peacock undoubtedly are. They partly atone for these shortcomings by the most careful literary craftsmanship. Without a notable sense for form, Peacock never goes, even when he is on the uproarious trail of Rabelais, beyond due limits. This is ascribable partly, of course to the lack of an opulent invention, but partly to the austere restraint which marks the whole body of his work. This reticence made him unlikely to strive for eloquence ; it also kept him from becoming diffuse in an age of verbiage. Especially is this evident in his nature descriptions, a form of writing which has suffered notoriously from false elevation. Peacock never dwells long upon a bit of landscape, but his hand is unerring. *Melincourt* has one of the best of these, a description of a sunset over Lake Windermere : " The sun sunk behind the summits of the western mountains : the clouds that, like other mountains, rested motionless above them, crested with the towers and battlements of aërial castles, changed by degrees from fleecy whiteness to the deepest hues of crimson.

A solitary cloud, resting on an eastern pinnacle, became tinged with the reflected spendour of the west : the clouds overhead spreading, like a uniform veil of net-work, through the interstices of which the sky was visible, caught in their turn the radiance, and reflected it on the lake, that lay in its calm expanse like a mirror, imaging with such stillness and accuracy the form and colours of all around and above it, that it seemed as if the waters were withdrawn by magic, and the boats floated in crimson light between the mountains and the sky." As truthful, and more stately, is the exordium of *Crotchet Castle.* " In one of those beauti-ful valleys, through which the Thames (not yet polluted by the tide, the scouring of cities, or even the minor defilement of the sandy streams of Surrey), rolls a clear flood through flowery meadows, under the shade of old beech woods, and the smooth, glossy [2] greensward of the chalk hills (which pour into it their tributary rivulets, as pure and pellucid as the fountain of Ban-dusium, or the wells of Scamander, by which the wives and daughters of the Trojans washed their splendid garments in the days of peace, before the coming of the Greeks) ; in one of those beautiful valleys, on a bold, round-surfaced lawn, spotted with juniper, that opened itself in the bosom of an old wood, which rose with a steep, but not precipitous ascent, from the river to the summit of the hill, stood the castellated villa of a retired citizen." [3] Whether Peacock dresses his landscape in such Ciceronian splendours as these, or

---

[1] *Works*, i. 184.   [2] " Mossy " in the first edition.
[3] *Works*, ii. 185.

compresses his wit into the short, swift sentences of his dialogue, he is always restrained, polished, clear. His narrative style is so light, though strong and adequate, that he can pass from it to the wittiest conversation without any apparent break. He does not strive for epigram, but abounds in quotable passages. Even at the risk of attracting too much attention to itself, his prose never dwindles into mere flatness, unenlivened by fancy or original turns of expression. His songs, for the most part, are only intensified prose, and to increased brevity they add increased polish and clearness, and a freshness of phrase secured by skilful avoidance of the " poetic " diction into which he sometimes falls when the mood which produces the poem is not a vigorous one. His prose is consecutive, but in verse he could not go beyond a few lines without the loss of his singing garments.

It is to his adroitness in maintaining a point of view, and to his care as an artist, rather than to his mental or moral power, that Peacock owes his place in English literature. In that literature, and his fame will reach few who do not read it with native eyes, he seems to belong to a class which he exhausts, standing alone in laughter as Landor stands in wrath. Inferior to Lamb in personal charm and humour, far to the rear, when it comes to scope, of Fielding, Thackeray, Meredith, Mark Twain, he can by no means be ranked with the ephemerides. Among the wits in whom the first half of the century abounded he enjoys the pre-eminence of having given his work a classical finish that bodes well for the permanence, if not for the extent, of his fame.

THOMAS LOVE PEACOCK

Few books in the course of English laughter are as compact of sense and learning as the little edition of 1837 which contained *Headlong Hall, Nightmare Abbey, Maid Marian,* and *Crotchet Castle.* That year saw the completion of a work which begins a new chapter in mirth, but *The Pickwick Papers* obscured no minor humorist who seems more likely to endure side by side with the great Dickens than Peacock. The slightness of his output, which has enabled a twentieth-century printer to include all the novels in a single small volume, serves only to rank him with the fastidious of the literary tribe who forestall the winnowing action of time voluntarily. One who desires to assign Peacock a rank among his contemporaries will probably put him with Hood, when Hood was not merely journalistic, and with Praed. To go to periods with which Peacock has more in common, he is like Gay and Prior, or Congreve and Sheridan. But these unsatisfactory attempts at classifying prove nothing beyond the often-repeated contention that Peacock is unique. He derives little from any predecessor and bequeaths little to any follower. Except indirectly through Shelley, he exerted small influence upon thought and letters. At the same time, he belonged to a liberal movement in English thinking which has changed the face of belief, and he was perhaps the keenest satirist the English romantic movement had to endure.

Witty men are likely to be suspected of some innate coldness of heart. Peacock, indeed, had a large share of the sardonic in his make-up, and he was almost devoid of mental and spiritual humility. But he did not lack either tenderness or earnestness. He loved truth, he hated injustice ; he was upright in business, charitable to the unfortunate, affectionate toward his family and friends. The tenderness which occasionally finds exquisite reflection in his lyrics arose from a sensitiveness of spirit which appears but indirectly in his books. That romantic melancholy, bordering upon sentimentalism, which he had manifested in his youth, had been an outward sign of the shocks which he felt at contact with reality. To them he attempted to give voice in his early poems, but his pride asserted itself, and, retreating from the dangerous grounds of sentiment, he took up a position from which he could defend himself against all attacks with the unconquerable weapons of laughter. His old sensitiveness persisted. It lent his work an occasional touch of pathos and frequent passages of delicate beauty. His pride persisted, and it imposed upon him cautious restraint, ironic aloofness, satiric scorn. Almost all the apparent contradictions in his character can be understood if they are looked upon as the results of an endless opposition within him of sensitiveness and pride. The use which he made of laughter secured him immunity from many a disturbing incident which could not overcome his mirth, and it gave him fame. But because he laughed without responsibility he belongs less with the writers of power than with those of whom laughter has exacted a great, as of all laughter exacts a certain, penalty.

BIBLIOGRAPHY OF PEACOCK'S
PUBLISHED WRITINGS

NOTE—*Of the items marked * no copy has been discovered.*

1800. Is History or Biography the more improving study?
The Juvenile Library (February), i, 54 *ff*. [Re-
printed by W. E. A. Axon, *The Library* (January
1901), New Series, II. 69–71.]

1804. *The Monks of St. Mark. (Dated September.)

1806. Palmyra, and other Poems. London.

1810. The Genius of the Thames : a Lyrical Poem. London.

1812. The Philosophy of Melancholy. London.
The Genius of the Thames, Palmyra, and other Poems.
London.

1814. Sir Proteus : a Satirical Ballad. London.
A letter in *The Morning Chronicle*, April 8, signed " P."
Sir Hornbook ; or, Childe Launcelot's Expedition. A
Grammatico-Allegorical Ballad. London. [A third
edition appeared in 1816, a fifth* in 1818. It was
reissued in a series called "The Home Treasury,"
edited by Sir Henry Cole under the name Felix
Summerly, in 1843, 1846,* and 1855.]

1816. Headlong Hall. London. [Second edition,* 1816,
and third edition, 1822.]
Prologue to " The Faro Table ; or, The Guardians," by
John Tobin. London.

1817. Melincourt. London. 3 vols.
The Genius of the Thames, Palmyra, and Other Poems.
Second Edition. London.
Melincourt. 2 vols. Philadelphia.

1818. Rhododaphne ; or, The Thessalian Spell. London.
Nightmare Abbey. London.

BIBLIOGRAPHY

Rhododaphne ; or, The Thessalian Spell.   Philadelphia.
[This text was reprinted in *The Southern Literary Messenger*, June and July 1843.]
[A French version* of Melincourt is said to have appeared in this year, but a careful search made for me in the principal libraries of Paris by Mr. B. Woodbridge has failed to find a copy of the book.]

1819. *Nightmare Abbey. New York. (? See above, page 127.)
*The Round Table ; or, King Arthur's Feast.   London.
[This date is uncertain, but it cannot be far from correct.   See *Notes and Queries*, Series IV. xii. 207–8, and *Works*, iii. 213–21.]

1820. The Four Ages of Poetry.   Ollier's Literary Miscellany in Prose and Verse, pp. 183–200.   London.

1822. Maid Marian.   London.

1823. Der Forstgraf ; oder, Robin Hood und Mariane.   Jena.

1825. Rich and Poor ; or, Saint and Sinner.   *The Globe and Traveller*, August 27.   [An editorial note says that the verses had appeared in the same paper " three or four years ago," but the files in the British Museum do not verify the statement.]

1826. Robin Hood ; ou, La Forêt de Sherwood.   Paris.

1827. Review of Moore's " Epicurean."   *Westminster Review* (October), viii. 351–84.

1829. The Misfortunes of Elphin.   London.

1830. Review of Moore's " Letters and Journals of Lord Byron," vol. i.   *Westminster Review* (April), xii. 269–304.
Review of " Memoirs, Correspondence, and Private Papers of Thomas Jefferson."   *Westminster Review* (October), xiii., 312–35.
Review of " Chronicles of London Bridge."   By an Antiquary, &c., *Westminster Review* (October), xiii. 401–15.

1831. Crotchet Castle.   London.
The Fate of a Broom.   *The Examiner*, August 14.

BIBLIOGRAPHY

1834. Memorandum respecting the Application of Steam Navigation to the internal and external Communications of India; Steam Navigation in India and between Europe and India; Estimate of the probable Expense of placing Two Iron Steam Vessels on the River Euphrates at Bussora, and navigating the same from Bussora to Bir and back. *Report from the Select Committee on Steam Navigation to India* (1834), *Appendix*, pp. 1–12. [Some fragmentary notes by Peacock may also be found on pp. 12–41.]

1835. Review of "Report of the Select Committee on Steam Navigation to India (1834)." *Edinburgh Review*, (January), lx. 445–82. [This cannot be ascribed with certainty to Peacock.]

Review of the Earl of Mount Edgcumbe's "Musical Reminiscences." *London Review* (April), i. 173–87.

French Comic Romances. *London Review* (October), ii. 69–84.

1836. The Épicier. *London Review* (January), ii. 355–65.

Bellini. *London Review* (January), ii. 467–80.

1837. The Legend of Manor Hall. *Bentley's Miscellany* (January), i. 29–32.

Recollections of Childhood. The Abbey House. *Bentley's Miscellany* (February), i. 187–90. [Reprinted in *Tales from Bentley*, 1859, i. 89–96.]

Headlong Hall. Nightmare Abbey. Maid Marian. Crotchet Castle. London. [Bentley's *Standard Novels and Romances*. Reprinted in 1849.]

Paper Money Lyrics. *The Guide :* The Three Little Men, April 22 ; Proemium of an Epic, May 21 ; Pan in Town, May 28 ; A Mood of My Own Mind, June 4 ; Chorus of Scotch Economists, June 11 ; The Wise Men of Gotham, and Love and the Flimsies, June 18.

Promotion by Purchase and by No Purchase. *The Guide* (April 29).

Rich and Poor, or, Saint and Sinner. *The Guide* (May 6).

BIBLIOGRAPHY

Paper Money Lyrics. London. [A complete edition of these poems, privately printed. It includes Byp and Nop, The Fate of a Broom, and Rich and Poor as well.]

1838. The New Year. Lines on George Cruikshank's Illustration of January, in the Comic Almanack for 1838. *Bentley's Miscellany* (January), iii. 104.

Love and the Flimsies. *Bentley's Miscellany* (August), iv. 140.

Chorus of Bubble Buyers. *Bentley's Miscellany* (September), iv. 239.

1845. Headlong Hall and Nightmare Abbey. New York. [In Wiley and Putnam's *Library of Choice Reading*.]

1851. Gastronomy and Civilization. *Fraser's Magazine* (December), xliv. 591–609. [This was the joint work of Peacock and his daughter, Mrs. George Meredith.]

1852. Horae Dramaticae. Querolus, or the Buried Treasure. *Fraser's Magazine* (March), xlv. 291–302.

Horae Dramaticae. The Phaëthon of Euripides. *Fraser's Magazine* (April), xlv. 448–58.

1855. *Maid Marian. Translated by Louis Barré. Bruxelles.

1856. Melincourt, or Sir Oran Haut-Ton. London.

Headlong Hall and Nightmare Abbey. London.

*Maid Marian and Crotchet Castle. London.

1857. Horae Dramaticae. The 'Flask' of Cratinus. *Fraser's Magazine* (October), lvi. 482–88.

1868. Chapelle and Bachaumont. *Fraser's Magazine* (April), lvii. 502–11.

Memoirs of Percy Bysshe Shelley. *Fraser's Magazine* (June), lvii. 643–59.

Demetrius Galanus. Greek Translations from Sanscrit. *Fraser's Magazine* (November), lviii. 596–608.

Review of Müller and Donaldson's History of Greek Literature. *Fraser's Magazine* (March), lix. 357–77.

1860. Memoirs of Percy Bysshe Shelley. Second Paper. *Fraser's Magazine* (January), lxi. 92–109.

BIBLIOGRAPHY

Unpublished Letters of Percy Bysshe Shelley. *Fraser's Magazine* (March), lvi. 301–19. Postscript to the Shelley Letters. (May), lxi. 738.

Newark Abbey. *Fraser's Magazine* (November), lxii. 598.

Gryll Grange. *Fraser's Magazine* : Chap. i–v., April ; Chap. vi–xi., May ; Chap. xii–xiv., June ; Chap. xv–xviii., July ; Chap. xix–xxi, August ; Chap. xxii–xxvi., September ; Chap. xxvii–xxix., October ; Chap. xxx–xxxii., November ; Chap. xxxiii–xxxv., December.

1861. Gryll Grange. London.

1862. Memoirs of Percy Bysshe Shelley. Supplementary Notice. *Fraser's Magazine* (March), lxv. 343.

Gl'Ingannati. The Deceived : A Comedy performed at Siena in 1531 : and Aelia Laelia Crispis. London. [Reprinted in Furness' "New Variorum Twelfe Night" (Phil. 1901), pp. 341–59.]

1873. (?) Thomas Love Peacock. Biographical Notes. From 1785 to 1866. London. [This is merely a collection of notes, of which only ten copies were printed, never published, by (Sir) Henry Cole, for the use of Miss Nicolls in her Biographical Notice of her grandfather. It contains some letters and verses by Peacock.]

1875. The Works of Thomas Love Peacock, including his Novels, Poems, Fugitive Pieces, Criticisms, &c., with a Preface by the Right Hon. Lord Houghton, a Biographical Notice by his granddaughter, Edith Nicolls, and Portrait. Edited by Henry Cole, C.B., in three volumes. London.

1887. Headlong Hall and Nightmare Abbey. New York. [One of the volumes in Putnam's *Knickerbocker Nuggets.*]

Crotchet Castle. London, Paris, New York, and Melbourne. [In Cassell's *National Library.* Int. by Henry Morley.]

BIBLIOGRAPHY

The Last Day of Windsor Forest. *The National Review*
(September) x. 106–11, with note by Dr. Garnett.

1891. Headlong Hall, 1 vol., Melincourt, 2 vols., Nightmare
Abbey, 1 vol., Maid Marian, 1 vol., The Misfortunes
of Elphin, 1 vol., Crotchet Castle, 1 vol., Gryll
Grange, 2 vols., Calidore and Miscellanea, 1 vol.
London. J. M. Dent. [The collection was edited
by Dr. Garnett, who contributed a biographical
Introduction to the volume containing Headlong Hall.
Not all the Calidore fragment is included. A second
edition of Maid Marian was called for in 1892, and
a third in 1899.]

1895–7. Maid Marian and Crotchet Castle (1895); Headlong
Hall and Nightmare Abbey (1896); Gryll Grange
(1896); Melincourt (1896); The Misfortunes o
Elphin and Rhododaphne (1897). London and
New York. [Macmillan's *Standard Illustrated Novels*.
Edited by Professor Saintsbury, and illustrated by
H. R. Millar and F. H. Townsend.]

1895. Headlong Hall and Nightmare Abbey. New York.
[Putnam's *Stories of the Ages*.]

1902. Songs from the Novels of Thomas Love Peacock.
London. [Mr. R. B. Johnson's *York Library*.
Second edition in 1905.]

1903. The Novels of Thomas Love Peacock. London and
New York. [Newnes' thin paper *Caxton Series*.
1 vol.]

1905–6. The Works of Thomas Love Peacock. 2 vols.
London and New York. [Routledge's *New Universal Library*. The novels only.]

1906. The Poems of Thomas Love Peacock. London and
New York. [Routledge's *New Universal Library*.
Also in *The Muses' Library*.]

1908. Headlong Hall and Nightmare Abbey. London and
New York. [*Everyman's Library*.]

Unpublished Songs by T. L. Peacock. *Notes and
Queries*; from The Dilettanti and The Circle of Loda

BIBLIOGRAPHY

(December 5), Series X. x. 441 ; from The Three
Doctors (January 16, 1909), Series X. xi. 43-4.
[Edited by Dr. A. B. Young from the manuscript
in the British Museum.]

1909. Peacock's Memoirs of Shelley. London. [Edited by
Mr. H. B. F. Brett-Smith.]

Ahrimanes. Modern Language Review (January),
Vol. iv., No. ii. [Edited by Dr. A. B. Young from
the manuscript in the British Museum. Corrections
and an omitted stanza were supplied to this highly
inaccurate text by Mr. Brett-Smith in the same
journal for July.]

1910. The Plays of Thomas Love Peacock. London.
[Edited by Dr. Young from the manuscript in the
British Museum.]

Thomas Love Peacock's Essay on Fashionable Literature.
Notes and Queries (July 2 and 23). Series XI. ii. 5-6,
and 62-3. [Edited by Dr. Young from the manuscript in the British Museum.]

Thomas Love Peacock ; Letters to Edward Hookham
and Percy B. Shelley, with fragments of Unpublished
Mss. Boston. [Edited for the members of the
Bibliophile Society by Dr. Garnett. The volume
contains, besides the letters to Hookham and Shelley,
Ahrimanes, the complete existing fragment of Calidore, Boosabout Abbey, Julia Procula, The Lord of
the Hills, and Cotswold Chace.]

INDEX

291

INDEX

INDEX

INDEX

INDEX

INDEX

Stanley, Thomas, 132
Stanzas Written at Sea, 37
Statius, 132, 134, 136, 137
Stocqueller, J. H., 265
Strachey, Edward, 138, 140, 146, 150, 212, 213
Strachey, Sir Edward, 170, 197, 267
Strutt, 17
Sun-dial, The, 123
Swift, 80, 135
Swinburne, 268*n*.
Symons, Arthur, 264

TACITUS, 18, 19, 49
Taglioni, 202
Tasso, 20, 47
Taylor, Thomas, 102, 129–30
Tennyson, 17, 35, 267
Terence, 232
Thackeray, 18, 21, 122, 168, 249–50, 251, 255, 265, 268, 279
Thomson, James, "B.V.," 265
Three Doctors, The, 75, 76, 78, 88, 168
Tobin, John, 77

Tooke, Horne, 24, 56
Tree, Miss, 168
Trelawney, 235, 236

VILLIERS, Charles, 250
Virgil, 18, 19, 152
Volney, 28, 31
Voltaire, 18, 20, 80, 135, 205, 259

WADE, Hamlet, 11, 12
Waghorn, 214, 215
Walker, George, 78
Wallis, Henry, 262
Ward, T. H., 269
Watts, A. A., 267
White, Kirke, 14
White, Thomas W., 110
Wicks, J. H., 9
Wilkins, 185
Williams, Captain, 253
Wood, Robert, 28, 31
Wordsworth, 18, 20, 46, 63, 93, 101, 102, 116, 133, 135, 152, 199, 211

YOUNG, A. B., 31, 74, 155; 270